Journeys

An American Story

Journeys

An American Story

compiled by Andrew Tisch
and Mary Skafidas

RosettaBooks®

NEW YORK 2018

First edition published 2018 by RosettaBooks

Cover design by Alexia Garaventa
Interior design by Jay McNair

Library of Congress Control Number: 2017958682
ISBN-13 (print): 978-1-9481-2201-6
ISBN-13 (epub): 978-1-9481-2202-3

www.RosettaBooks.com
Printed in the United States of America

RosettaBooks®

To all the generations who came before...
...And to all who will follow.

Every immigrant has his or her own reasons for why they came to America. As we collected these stories, certain common themes began to emerge. Some immigrants came here primarily to be free from oppression, others to find opportunity; still others came as an act of love, and some by force or coercion.

We have grouped the various stories together according to the immigrants' rationales for coming to America.

We did so with the knowledge that this is an imperfect and subjective science, and that each story could have been told through many lenses. As you read these stories, know that it is only the totality of all of them, plus your own history or lore, that can properly convey the complete story of immigration and the role it has played in creating American greatness.

Contents

Our Journey   xi

The Changers

Cory Booker   4
Angela Warnick Buchdahl   9
A'Lelia Bundles   12
Gabrielle Giffords   18
Peter Gogolak   22
Linda Hills   28
Wes Moore   34
Morris Sarnoff   38
Marlo Thomas   42
John Zaccaro Jr.   46

The Lovers

Alan Alda   52
Arlene Alda   54
John Calvelli   58
Elaine L. Chao   61
Kevin Chavous   66
Mary Choi   72
Bradley Hirschfield   78
Deborah Norville   81

The Originals

Ray Halbritter   87

The Rescuers

Jon & Mary Kaye Huntsman   92
Zach Iscol   94
Ryan Platt   98
Debora Spar   100
Matt Tomasic   102

The Seekers

Karim Abouelnaga   108
Ahmed Ahmed   111
Ashok Amritraj   116
Barbara Boxer   121
Amanda Loyola   125
Carmen Osbahr-Vertiz   129
Dr. Mehmet Oz   131
Gina Raimondo   134
Mayo Stuntz Jr.   136

The Strivers

Michael R. Bloomberg	143
Joseph Bower	148
Andrew Cuomo	152
Ben Freeman	158
Peter Blair Henry	164
Declan Kelly	171
Jackie Koppell	174
Funa & Nonso Maduka	178
Mario Neiman	181
Tim Scott	186
Mary Skafidas	188
Jane Wang	191

The Survivors

Adem T. Bunkeddeko	196
Nataliya Demchenko	199
Misha Galperin	205
David Harris	209
Daniel Lubetzky	213
Stephanie Murphy	218
Jane Swift	223
Andrew Tisch	227
Jan Vilcek	233

The Trailblazers

Tony Bennett	240
Lisa Birnbach	244
Eugene Dattel	246
Mitchell Gold	254
Irshad Manji	259
"Mohammed"	262
Laura W. Murphy	266
Nancy Pelosi	271
Mao Ye	274

The Undocumented

Richard Uscher Levine	280
Erick Meza	286
Juliana Pérez-Calle	290
Helen Polychronopoulos	295
Nasser Yaghoobzadeh	298

The Institutions

American Ballet Theatre	304
Monticello	309
New-York Historical Society	314
UJAF / Catholic Charities	318

Write Your Own Story	321
American Renewal	329
Acknowledgments	331

The New Colossus

by Emma Lazarus

Not like the brazen giant of Greek fame,
With conquering limbs astride from land to land;
Here at our sea-washed, sunset gates shall stand
A mighty woman with a torch, whose flame
Is the imprisoned lightning, and her name
Mother of Exiles. From her beacon-hand
Glows world-wide welcome; her mild eyes command
The air-bridged harbor that twin cities frame.
"Keep, ancient lands, your storied pomp!" cries she
With silent lips. "Give me your tired, your poor,
Your huddled masses yearning to breathe free,
The wretched refuse of your teeming shore.
Send these, the homeless, tempest-tost to me,
I lift my lamp beside the golden door!"

"The New Colossus" was written in 1883 by Emma Lazarus. In 1903, the last lines of the poem were engraved on a plaque and placed on the pedestal of the Statue of Liberty, where they remain to this day.

Our Journey

Journeys: An American Story is a collection of personal accounts of the American immigrant experience. Each story brings to light a wave of American migration as immigrants came to our shores fleeing hate and oppression, seeking opportunity, escaping slavery or being brought here to become slaves, searching for love, or yearning for religious freedom. This book is intended to stand as a declaration and testament to America's distinctive culture and history.

Andrew Tisch came up with the idea for this collection after being invited by the New-York Historical Society to speak at a swearing-in ceremony for one hundred new citizens, from forty-one different countries. In preparing his comments, Andrew realized that an individual's or family's arrival in the United States is a monumental event in that family's history.

What began with the Jamestown settlement and the Pilgrims would eventually include immigrants of every ethnicity: Irish, Italian, Jewish, Chinese, Caribbean, Russian, Greek, Mexican, Ghanaian as well as many others. Each wanted a piece of the American dream—the opportunity to achieve more than they could in their land of birth.

Of course, every immigrant story is not of the Horatio Alger variety. West Africans were brought here against their will as slaves to build advantages for others. And Native Americans were here long before any other group arrived.

For many early immigrants who voluntarily came to America, we imagine their decision had to be momentous. They came knowing that they may never see their loved ones again. The journey was often perilous—weeks or months on a boat, often scrounging for food and water, fighting diseases, and evading those that wanted to take advantage of their vulnerability. Though these immigrants may not have had much in the old country, they often had even less when they arrived in the new one.

New arrivals weren't always welcomed. While America is a nation of immigrants, our citizens and our government haven't always necessarily acted with compassion. One hundred years ago, Congress passed the Immigration Act of 1917, an unprecedented federal law that greatly restricted immigration from the Asia-Pacific Zone, including people from countries such as China, Armenia, Malaysia, and Turkey. The act also created a literacy test specifically for immigrants and banned a broad group of "undesirables" including "epileptics," "idiots," "political radicals," "polygamists," "contract laborers," "persons being mentally or physically defective," and "vagrants."

It took four decades to overturn the Immigration Act of 1917 as legislators, businesses, and the public began to realize the social and economic value of immigration. While Americans have a long and ignominious history of barricading the doors, we have an even longer and more glorious history of tearing those barricades down. Despite today's contentious debate on immigration, 72 percent of Americans still think immigration is good for America.

We hope this book will remind people why.

Immigrants have always taken the jobs and pursued the opportunities available to them, usually starting at the bottom of the economic ladder. They recognize that implicit in those jobs was a beginning, a foot in the door, a first step toward success for themselves and their families. There is no other place in the world (with the possible exception of Israel, which also prides itself on being a country of immigrants) where one can come with an idea and find access to institutions which will help him or her prove the worth of that idea.

If the perceived negative impact of immigration on America has often been overstated, its positive impact has often been vastly understated.

A study in 2011 by the Partnership for a New American Economy showed that 40 percent of the Fortune 500 companies were founded by immigrants or their children. These companies directly employ more than ten million people worldwide and have revenues of $4.2 trillion. If this group of companies were a separate economy, their revenue would be larger than the GDP of any country in the world except the United States, China, and Japan.

According to the report, companies as American as AT&T, Procter & Gamble, US Steel, DuPont, Kraft, Goldman Sachs, International Paper, Capital One, and Nordstrom were founded by immigrants. Some of the newer additions include Google, Intel, eBay, Yahoo!, and Qualcomm. And seven of the ten most recognized brands in the world (Apple, AT&T, Google, GE, IBM, and McDonald's) were launched by immigrants or the children of immigrants.

Immigrants may also hold the key to securing America's social safety net. Programs like Medicare, Medicaid, and Social Security all rely on a steady and growing supply of workers paying into the system. These programs are funded on a current basis, not from historical deposits, and depend on today's workers paying into their coffers to support retirees. Under current trends, Social Security has only fifteen more years before it can no longer pay full benefits. Forecasters believe America is unlikely to produce the workers we need with only our homegrown population.

Where will these workers come from? Immigration is a big part of the answer, if we allow it to be.

The population of the United States is often referred to as a "melting pot"—a stew of many different ingredients combined and homogenized. We prefer to think of our country as a mosaic, tiles of many different colors and shapes which are indistinguishable from afar but quite distinctive the closer you get. A mosaic is only as strong as its grout, the sand and glue used to bind the stones together. After all, without the grout—our shared sense of ideology in democracy, opportunity, freedom of expression, and equality—the mosaic would only be a pile of stones.

Journeys: An American Story shows that the United States is greater than the sum of all its parts. Each individual brings something unique to the portrait of America to make this country the greatest hope on Earth. This book is about the people who built this country and kept it vibrant and forward thinking by becoming part of its mosaic. Some of the stories are written by famous people, others by citizens you may or may not know. Regardless of the author, every story brings to light a tale that helped make this country extraordinary.

In doing our research and writing for *Journeys: An American Story,* we began by asking a few friends about their families' experiences in coming to America. In virtually every case, the conversation became much more animated as our friends regaled us with the stories of their family history and lore. The telling of their story brought many smiles, and those smiles turned into gratitude as our friends thanked us for allowing them to revisit and relive their family's journey.

We expanded well beyond friends and family. We reached out to people we didn't know but who we thought had interesting family backgrounds. As word of our project spread, we even started to get unsolicited submissions.

We have sought variety in the stories told here. Not every story is a happy one, but each adds to the richness of the mosaic of the United States of America—a country that for all its shortcomings is still the most sought-after home for those searching to improve their fate.

We hope that in reading the stories you will, as we did, marvel at the diversity, perseverance, resilience, and courage of the American people and revisit your own family history. We've left some space at the end of the book for you to add your own story to the larger mosaic of America.

Journeys
An American Story

The Changers

/////

Cory Booker

Angela Warnick Buchdahl

A'Lelia Bundles

Gabrielle Giffords

Peter Gogolak

Linda Hills

Wes Moore

Morris Sarnoff

Marlo Thomas

John Zaccaro Jr.

It always seems impossible until it's done.

— Nelson Mandela, former president of South Africa

It's rare when a single person can create real and lasting change in how we think, how we live, and how we look at the world. In this chapter, you'll read about true change makers such as the immigrant from Lebanon, unable to afford medical care growing up, who changed children's health care forever; the boy from Hungary who revolutionized American football; the Scot who became one of the world's greatest industrialists and philanthropists; and the Russian telegraph operator who changed communications.

There are fascinating stories about political change makers including the daughter of an immigrant who went on to become a major party candidate for vice president of the United States; and a courageous Congresswoman who survived a horrific assassination attempt.

So many of us want to change the world. These amazing individuals did.

Cory Booker

The Honorable Cory Booker is a United States Senator from New Jersey. Previously he was Mayor of Newark, New Jersey.

> *My country 'tis of thee*
> *Sweet land of liberty*
> *Of thee I sing*
> *Land where our fathers died,*
> *Land of the Pilgrims' pride,*
> *From every mountainside.*
> *Let freedom ring!*

As a small child, I loved this song. It spoke to my idealism and hopeful notions of our nation, and singing it in chorus with other boys and girls made me feel a sense of belonging. I felt pride and a love of country that, reflecting now, I believe was embedded in me by my fiercely patriotic family.

Yet, in singing that song, I also felt like I was reaching a bit. As a boy I came to know that my family's journey to this land, now the United States, wasn't in any way similar to the Pilgrims'. Ellis Island, too, gave me pride (and even a sense of ownership, as it is in New Jersey). I loved the stories of the hopeful, triumphant entrances of the ancestors of my classmates whose Irish, Italian, and other European ancestors entered through that portal of promise. But these tales were different than the ones that filled my own family stories.

Even my family's entrance into the town I grew up in was different than those of my peers. In 1969, just to move in, my parents had to work with the Fair Housing Council—lawyers, activists, and tremendous leaders—to construct a sting operation to expose and overcome the housing discrimination that threatened to deny my parents entrance into the town.

My parents would show up to look at homes in white neighborhoods, and real estate agents would lie to them. They would be told the house had been sold or pulled off the market. The Fair Housing Council would send white test couples to the homes after my parents, and they would inevitably find that the house was still for sale. A white test couple eventually bid on a house my parents loved. The bid was accepted, and on the day of the closing, the white couple didn't show up: instead, my dad did, along with a volunteer lawyer. The real estate agent didn't capitulate when caught, and his illegal housing discrimination was exposed. He stood and punched the Fair Housing Council lawyer, and my dad had to wrestle with the agent's Doberman as the two men fought. Ultimately, after this fight and legal threats, my parents moved into my childhood home, and we became the first black family to live in the town.

In my family's stories, and the history from my elders, I knew of no courageous explorers, no Pilgrims seeking religious freedom, no escape from persecution or famine, no Lady Liberty opening her golden door beside Ellis Island. My American ancestry came up from slavery. Millions were killed—upwards of a fifth of the humans stolen from Western Africa died during the passage from that continent to this one. Those who made it faced inhuman brutality. Generations endured horrors in a system of chattel slavery marked by vicious beatings, rape, oppressive labor, and unimaginable anguish. African history, the cultural roots, the religious beliefs, the very memories linking families to their countries of origin were stolen along with the bodies of my ancestors. These historical possessions were robbed by a villainy that sought to eviscerate humanity, dignity, connection, and independence, an evil that sought to render human beings as property, obedient and enslaved.

My great-grandmother had memories of our family lasting back into slavery. My grandparents discussed these roots and remembered some circumstances, but going more than a generation into our past was difficult for my family. What followed the end of slavery was what

5

I knew better from family stories. Like so many families of all different backgrounds, there were humble stories of poverty and struggle. And because of my ancestors' race, these difficult paths were cruelly compounded with stories of discrimination, of citizenship rights violently denied, and too often of opportunities rendered unattainable. This reality resided in many family stories in one way or another. Simple stories of family trips would often involve mentions of the inability to use basic facilities like bathrooms, restaurants, or hotels. From accessing the ballot to going to a hospital to obtaining a job, the struggle against discrimination and for full citizenship, equality, and opportunity was a part of the culture in our American experience.

"America never was America to me, and yet I swear this oath—America will be!"

— Langston Hughes

As a child I learned the source of my parents' and grandparents' love of this country. Their faith and hope for America were intertwined with their larger view of the forward march of our American tradition. They saw connections between their struggles and aspirations and the heroic hopes of those early colonists in Jamestown, the religious freedom dreams of Pilgrims, the defiant demands of our original revolutionaries, the humble ambitions of refugees or immigrants, the equality struggles of the suffragettes, the freedom fights of the abolitionists, the justice dreams of the union organizers and so many others who brought America—marching, stumbling, striding, jumping—forward.

This was what my family heralded about this nation and our presence in it. In fact, our very survival, our very presence spoke to America's struggle for itself, the struggle to make a more perfect union, the ongoing mission to make this a land of liberty and justice for all. My childhood was filled with the elders in my family showing a devotion to this determined destiny: to have America achieve herself, not stories about how we got here, but what seemed paramount was the ongoing struggle to have America finally and fully arrive.

"We are caught in an inescapable network of mutuality, tied in a single garment of destiny."

— Martin Luther King Jr.

In 2012, Henry Louis Gates Jr. had me on his show, *Finding Your Roots*. A year before my father would die, he and the rest of my family got an incredible view into our history. Gates discovered astonishing facts. Not only was he able to enter a generation or two into slavery and reveal to me many of my before unknown black American ancestors and the circumstances of their lives, but he also was able to discover and illuminate many of my white ancestors as well, and, through DNA analysis, he revealed that I am also a descendant of Native Americans. From Gates's experience, he let me know that we in this country share far more DNA than we realize.

What had once been an inscrutable history now lay out before me in a host of documents and charts. I am the descendant of slaves and slave owners. I am the descendant of white Alabama militiamen who fought in the Creek Wars against Native Americans and I am descended from Native Americans who were forced from their land. I am the direct descendant of a Confederate soldier who was captured by Union officers and then escaped capture. And then Henry Louis Gates did something I'd never imagined. Along one branch of my family tree, starting with my grandfather, he marched backward and backward— thirteen generations into American history, to 1640, 136 years before the founding of our nation, thirty-four years after the Pilgrims came to Plymouth, and roughly two decades after Jamestown, when my direct forebears came to what is now Virginia to settle.

Settlers and slave ships; Native Americans and strangers in a strange land. It seems my ancestors got here and were here in a multitude of manners. But the lessons of my family still hold: we are all—from the latest new citizen in our nation to those, like me, who can trace their history to 1776 and beyond—bound together in this nation, bound by blood and spirit more than we know. We belong to each other; we need each other. I have some understanding of who my ancestors were, and I am appreciative. And even more so, I have great hopes for who my descendants will be. I honestly have no great desire that they know me or my name, or that they know how our family came to live in this country, but I do have abiding hope that this great nation that they inherit will have come fully to fruition and that they can join with their countrymen and women and sing with full-throated, prideful force these words:

> *My country 'tis of thee*
> *Sweet land of liberty*
> *Of thee I sing*
> *Land where my fathers died,*
> *Land of the Pilgrims' pride,*
> *From every mountainside.*
> *Let freedom ring!*

Angela Warnick Buchdahl

Rabbi Angela Warnick Buchdahl is the Senior Rabbi of Central Synagogue in New York City. She is the first Asian American to be ordained as a rabbi or cantor in the US.

My family's story is that of the stranger.

On my mother's side, my Korean great-grandparents and their children were forcibly removed from Korea during the Japanese occupation that began in 1910. Along with many other intellectuals and artisans, they were brought to Japan to serve and enhance Japanese culture. My grandmother Hwang Gae-Ran was five years old when she became an involuntary immigrant in a hostile new world. She grew up speaking Japanese and learned to adapt to her new home. But she always felt like a stranger in it.

As an adult, my grandmother fell in love with and married a renegade Korean nationalist who worked for the underground movement to free Korea from Japanese occupation. He ran messages back and forth between Korea and Japan, and each time he was in Japan, it seemed my grandmother would get pregnant. She bore six children in Japan; my mother was the fourth. Finally, at the end of World War II, Korea was freed from Japanese rule and my grandparents were able to move back to Korea with their family. My mother was five years old when her family returned as immigrants to their own homeland. She recalled how the women of her village would treat her mother like a stranger because she spoke Korean "with a Japanese accent."

My mother was a voracious reader and the first woman in her family to attend university, where she earned a master's in English literature. Her fascination with American stories led her to my Jewish American father, who was stationed in Korea as a civil engineer after the Korean War. My father fell in love not only with my mother, but also with Korea and its culture, and when my parents married, my father told my grandmother that they would stay.

But Korea was known as the Hermit Kingdom for its isolationist policies and culture, and it was not an easy place to live as a mixed-race family. Koreans judged the postwar influx of "half-breeds" that diluted their nationalist identity. My parents knew that America would be the only place where we would be fully accepted. I was five years old when we moved and I became an immigrant in my father's homeland, the United States. Just like my maternal grandmother and mother before me, at five years old I was an immigrant, a stranger in another land.

On my Jewish father's side, my roots as a stranger go back much farther, for we were strangers in the land of Egypt. This isn't just ancient history or biblical legend: Jews are obligated, in every generation, to see ourselves as if we *personally* went out of Egypt. Not only do we retell this story every year at our Passover Seders, among the most beloved of rituals, but our regular liturgy reminds us *every single day* that we were the stranger.

And it's not just that we Jews were strangers in Egypt; we were strangers even before we were Jews. The first Hebrews, Abraham and Sarah, were commanded by God, "*Lech L'cha*—go forth from your land, from your birthplace, to a place *you do not know*." God did not permit Abraham and Sarah to begin Judaism from the comfort of their hometown. They had to become immigrants! They had to be the Other in order to create a religion of the Other.

And, of course, the story of Jews as the Other continued for millennia. After we were cast out of our ancestral home in Israel, we were in exile, strangers in strange lands for the next two thousand years. Jews have lived as outsiders around the world. We have thrived as strangers everywhere from Babylon to Brooklyn, surviving the Crusades, the pogroms, and the concentration camps. It is the backdrop of everything we are.

Rabbi Angela Warnick Buchdahl.

So as a Korean, Jewish, American immigrant female rabbi, I know a thing or two about feeling like the Other! But what I find so surprising is how so many different Americans, in some way, feel like a stranger. In the last election, even many white Americans expressed their pain at feeling on the outside. We wrung our hands and lamented this state of Otherness that so many Americans experience.

But perhaps we should celebrate it instead; we should embrace what it means to be the Other, the immigrant, the outsider. Because if we personally know the soul of this stranger, then the force of that memory is an ever-present bulwark against bigotry, superiority, and apathy. If we can empathize with being a stranger, then we will never forget that person behind the barbed wire or the wall, that family forced to hide or run, that couple carrying all their belongings on their backs, those people of different colors, faiths, or philosophies. We can instead remember and protect and *love* the stranger—because we *are* that stranger.

A'Lelia Bundles

A'Lelia Bundles is the author of On Her Own Ground: The Life and Times of Madam C. J. Walker, *a biography of her great-great-grandmother. She is a vice-chairman of Columbia University's board of trustees, and immediate past chairman of the board of the National Archives Foundation.*

I was three years old when I first discovered the box of miniature Egyptian mummy charms in my grandmother's dresser. Nearby in the same drawer were mother-of-pearl opera glasses and a fan of ostrich plumes.

At the time, I was too young to understand these treasures and the opulence they implied. I now know they were the first clues of a quest to decipher my family's journey in America. More than sixty years later, I'm still learning about ancestors who have been here since the 1600s.

My family story is a very American story, but nothing like the version you learned in high school history class. There are no Pilgrims and there is no Ellis Island. Instead there are free people of color who served in George Washington's Continental Army and a baby girl born on a Louisiana plantation who became a millionaire. There is a grandfather who raised nine children on a laborer's wage during the Depression and a great-grandfather who was one of Newton Theological Seminary's first black graduates.

We represent the complexity and contradictions that shaped our nation's earliest decades. We blend DNA from three continents, but our story is defined more by migration across America than immigration to America.

Top row, left to right: Henderson B. Robinson (great-great-grandfather), Ida Robinson Perry (great-grandmother), Marion Rowland Perry Sr. (great-grandfather). Middle row, left to right: Marion Rowland Perry Jr. (grandfather), Madam C. J. Walker (great-great-grandmother), A'Lelia Walker (great-grandmother). Bottom row, left to right: S. Henry Bundles (my father), A'Lelia Mae Perry Bundles (my mother), Me (age 3).

Some of my ancestors came willingly. Many arrived against their will. Because of America's estranged and unsettled racial past, some branches of my family tree are severed. Roots remain buried and intentionally obscured. Ultimately, the ancestors who interest me most are the ones who made the best of difficult circumstances. With each generation they valued education, entrepreneurship, faith, and a strong work ethic.

13

On that day in 1955, as I touched soft ostrich feathers and colorful trinkets, I was too young to know that my maternal grandmother, Mae Bryant Walker Perry, had died a decade earlier. In the living room, I could see her gold harp and mahogany baby grand piano, but the aroma of my grandfather's pot roast and Lucky Strikes long ago had overwhelmed the scent of her Shalimar.

It was Marion R. Perry Jr.—my PaPa—whose booming voice and fierce family pride now filled the apartment. More than anyone, he introduced me to American history and to our family's place in that narrative, even when America would just as soon have erased our existence.

PaPa was in awe of his maternal grandfather, Henderson B. Robinson, a free black man who had moved from Ohio to Tennessee in the 1860s. After the Civil War, his ambitious spirit led him to Helena, Arkansas, a predominantly black Mississippi River town, where most residents were newly freed people who had been enslaved on nearby plantations. In the voting booth, their numbers translated into political power for the brief moment during Reconstruction when black men gained the right to vote after passage of the Thirteenth, Fourteenth, and Fifteenth Amendments to the US Constitution.

Henderson Robinson served as Phillips County tax assessor from 1868 to 1872, then as sheriff and superintendent of prisons. He owned a five-hundred-acre farm and one of the finest homes in Helena. But when the Ku Klux Klan terrorized black voters and reinstated former Confederates to political leadership during the 1876 presidential election, he was pushed from office.

Robinson moved his family to Oberlin, Ohio, and enrolled his children in Oberlin College's high school preparatory program. After graduation, they returned to Arkansas. In 1890, his eldest daughter, Ida Robinson, married Marion R. Perry Sr., who had made his way from a Mississippi cotton plantation to become valedictorian of his class at Lincoln University in Pennsylvania.

My PaPa followed his father to Lincoln, graduating in 1912. After serving as a first lieutenant in France during World War I, he completed a law degree at the University of Pittsburgh.

During the summer of 1927, while studying finance at Columbia University in New York, he met my grandmother, Mae, who had just extricated herself from a very unhappy first marriage.

Mae's earliest documented American ancestors were free people of color in North Carolina in the 1700s. Two great-great-great-grandfathers served at Valley Forge during the Revolutionary War. Despite their patriotism, their children and grandchildren felt compelled to flee North Carolina in the 1830s as the state legislature enacted laws limiting the rights of people of African descent after a series of slave revolts made whites feel threatened. They made their way to Indiana and established themselves as early residents of what now is known as the Roberts Settlement.

Mae's father died in 1909, when she was ten years old, leaving her mother—like her mother's mother and her mother's mother's mother—a widow in her thirties with eight young children to raise alone.

During visits to her grandmother's home in Indianapolis, Mae began to run errands for an entrepreneur named Madam C. J. Walker, whose factory was across the alley. Mae's very long braids made her the perfect model for Walker's best-selling product—Madam Walker's Wonderful Hair Grower—an ointment that was in much demand to heal a common scalp infection of the time. Soon she began to accompany Walker and her daughter, A'Lelia Walker, on sales trips throughout the United States. The Walker women persuaded Mae's mother, Sarah Etta Hammond Bryant, to allow A'Lelia Walker to legally adopt Mae with the promise that she would continue her education and be free to maintain contact with her mother and siblings.

With plot twists that resemble the fairy tales of Rapunzel and Cinderella, Mae attended Spelman College, traveled internationally, lived in the Walker mansions in New York, and eventually served as president of the Madam C. J. Walker Manufacturing Company.

Her daughter—my mother, A'Lelia Mae Perry—was born in July 1928 and grew up with the expectation that she would join the family business. To prepare, she majored in business and chemistry at Howard University. She was a Walker Company executive and active in Indianapolis political and civic affairs until her death in 1976.

My father, S. Henry Bundles, and my mother married in June 1950, three days before the start of the Korean War. My father was promptly drafted. In June 1952, almost nine months to the day after his return, I was born.

I know much less about my father's family history, though I witnessed his parents' strong work ethic. Both born in rural Horse Cave, Kentucky, they moved to Indiana at the turn of the last century ahead of the Great Migration that brought hundreds of thousands of African Americans out of the South. With little opportunity for formal education or decent jobs, they followed other relatives to Indianapolis's south side, near the Pennsylvania Railroad yard where many of the men in the family found work as laborers.

My father was the seventh of their nine children. With a degree in journalism from Indiana University and training in the Navy during World War II as a photographer, he hoped to become a reporter. When it became clear that the daily newspaper in Indianapolis had no intention of promoting a black employee to a position above circulation manager for paper delivery routes, he shifted his dreams to business, entrepreneurship, and community leadership. My father turned ninety-one in February, and he remains a keen observer of American politics and current events.

Before my PaPa died in 1983, he gave me a trunk full of letters, photographs, diplomas, newspaper clippings, journals, and legal records. He especially cherished the 1839 emancipation papers that granted freedom to Henderson B. Robinson's mother, Delphia Hendry Robinson, more than two decades before the end of the Civil War. When I posted an image of the document on Ancestry.com, I had no expectation that anyone else would notice. To my surprise, two people contacted me with information about Delphia's father, William Hendry, a white Tennessee farmer and surveyor, who had been born in Frederick, Virginia, in 1760. His great-grandfather, John Hendry, had emigrated from Scotland to Virginia in the 1660s. Other ancestors had begun arriving in Boston from England in the 1630s.

In addition to children with two of his four wives, Hendry fathered two children with Rose, an enslaved woman he owned. His will instructed that their daughter, Delphia, be freed upon his death.

Delphia Henry's emancipation certificate.

I grew up knowing nothing about this branch of my family tree, and yet I am deeply curious about how Rose negotiated her daughter's freedom and why William Hendry felt obligated to keep his promise to her.

I am as proud of Rose for insisting that her child be freed as I am of Madam Walker for becoming a millionaire and a funder of the NAACP's anti-lynching campaign. I am as thankful to the ancestors who embraced education as I am to my grandfathers who nurtured my love of gardening. I am grateful to both my parents for the gift of writing and leadership and for modeling a sense of style and a generosity of spirit.

We all are our ancestors' hopes and dreams. As Americans, we honor them by opening our hearts to those who bring new visions and aspirations across our borders and onto our shores.

Gabrielle Giffords

The Honorable Gabrielle Giffords is a former Congresswoman from Arizona who is the founder of Giffords, Courage to Fight Gun Violence.

As told to her husband, astronaut Mark Kelly.

Gabby's ancestry, like many Americans, has European roots.

Both sides of her immediate family are the products of immigrants coming to the US in the nineteenth century. There are no documents or letters relating how or when they arrived.

Gabby's maternal great-great-grandfather was an immigrant from Scotland. He fought in the Civil War as a cannoneer and was mustered out because he was deafened by the noise. He settled in Kansas and received a pension from the government for his service. His wife was Irish, a Jenkins from the Emerald Isle. They had a son, Alexander Washington Fraser, Gabby's great-grandfather, who was a cattle buyer and lived in Nebraska.

The other side of the family from Gabby's mom, Gloria, were the Hesses and Ackards and hailed from Coalmont, Pennsylvania. They (Gabby's great-grandparents) were immigrants from Leipzig, Germany, and the patriarch of the family was a tailor. Family lore said that Grandmother Hess sat on the family money to deter her husband, Thomas Ackard (born in 1865), from gambling it away while making the journey to the United States aboard the westbound ship. One of their sons was named Thomas, and he was convinced by his brother John to come to Kansas and join him as a homesteader. Their mother, Mary Hess Ackard, took out a homestead, too. Thomas had married another Mary,

18

and they had fourteen children (Lula Catharine, b. 1889, d. 1897; Ethel Florence, b. 1891; Ada Olive, b. 1893; John Baldwin, b. 1895; May Ruth, b. 1896; Thomas Carlton, b. 1898; Jessie Mable, b. 1900; Mary Edna, b. 1903; Protus Mycleta, b. 1905; Gladys Susie, b. 1908; Thora Elnora, b. 1910; twins Elta and Alta, b. 1912; and Robert Leon, b. 1915.)

One of the last three was Thora Elnora, better known as DoDee. This was Gabby's grandmother. And she adored her. DoDee married Lloyd Lewis Fraser. Ethel Florence, one of the eldest of the fourteen children, never married. In 1945, DoDee, her marriage to Lloyd Fraser dissolving, moved from Arizona to Kansas and settled in the town of Colby. DoDee's family were homesteaders, and Gabby's mom, Gloria, grew up in this small town of Colby in the heart of America on a farm like so many of our ancestors.

Gabby's father's parents were European Jews who emigrated to the United States through Ellis Island in the nineteenth century. Her dad's dad was born Akiba Horenstein, and he was the first non-rabbi in a line of rabbis that dated back to the eighteenth century (thirteen of them, perhaps). Akiba's dad, who may or may not have been one of these rabbis, had plans to move the entire family to Egypt and open a grain mill along the Nile. But the plans fell through, and like so many Europeans of the time, they got on a ship and crossed the Atlantic. When Akiba entered public school in New York City at five or six years old, his teacher decided that "Akiba" was too difficult to remember, or too ethnic, or maybe she just didn't like it, so she declared that he would be called Gif. Akiba didn't have much say in the matter, so from that point forward he became Gif Horenstein. As an adult he formed a home heating-oil company with his brother in New York and called it Giffords Oil, because they felt it would be better for business, given the anti-Semitism at that time. Customers would often call and ask for Mr. Giffords. Tiring of responding that he was Gif Horenstein, he eventually legally changed his name to Gifford Giffords. All three brothers followed suit. These four brothers are perhaps the origin of the last name Giffords. (Gifford is a common last name in the United States—Frank Gifford, the hall of fame NFL player, is probably the best-known Gifford. But anyone with the last name Giffords is probably related to Gabby's grandfather or one of his three brothers.)

Gif Giffords was a salesman who peddled harmonicas, even though he couldn't play a note. Later he sold hearing aids and real estate. And like so many on the East Coast, he was told to move west to deal with some health issues. He settled in Tucson, Arizona, in the 1930s and founded El Campo Tire and Automotive. Gif was a wonderful businessman and became a minor local celebrity through his television ads in which he would pitch tires, rotations, oil changes, and life advice to an expanding population in the desert. Gabby's dad, Spencer, grew up in Tucson, but at the age of sixteen he stuck a gun in his belt, got on his motorcycle, and moved to Mexico City, where, lying about his high school graduation, he enrolled in Mexico City College. By the time the administration discovered his non-high-school-graduate status, he was a sophomore, and because his grades were good, was allowed to remain and eventually graduated.

He married, had a child (Gabby's half brother, Alex), started a leather belt business, and embraced the Spanish language and Mexican culture, which he would later share with his second wife—Gabby's mom, Gloria—and their two kids, Gabby and Melissa. After divorcing Alex's mother, Spencer moved back to Tucson and later took over El Campo Tire from his dad. This is the same business that would lure Gabby back to Tucson after graduate school and help her settle back into the community where she was born. Like her grandfather, she pitched oil changes, new tires, and whatever your car might need—absent was the philosophy and life advice—Gabby just wanted to sell tires, and she became known throughout the area as the "tire girl."

Gabby's grandmother on her father's side of the family was Ruth Paltrow (originally Paltrovitch). Ruth and the film director Bruce Paltrow were siblings, which is how Gabby and the actress Gwyneth Paltrow are related. Ruth's father, Myer Paltrowitz (1877–1957), married a woman named Edith Ida Harriet Hyman.

In 2007, Gabby was elected to the United States Congress, where she represented Arizona's Eighth Congressional District. In January 2011, Gabby was the victim of an assassination attempt during a meeting with constituents near Tucson. She was seriously injured by a gunshot wound to the head. She resigned from Congress in January of 2012 in order to focus on her recovery.

Over the past six years, as Gabby has been continuing to recover, she and her husband, Mark Kelly, launched a nonprofit organization called Giffords, Courage to Fight Gun Violence, whose mission is to build a safer America by working with lawmakers and the constituents they represent to strengthen and improve gun laws. Gabby and Mark are some of the staunchest gun violence prevention advocates out there and have made a name for themselves nationally for their tireless work educating the public on the importance of enacting laws, policies, and programs proven to reduce gun violence and save lives.

Peter Gogolak

Peter Gogolak spent his business career with RR Donnelley. He is best known for being the first soccer-style placekicker in American football and was considered the catalyst for the negotiations that led to the merger of the NFL and the AFL in 1966.

I was twenty-four years old, standing on the sideline before a crowd of seventy thousand in Yankee Stadium. I had recently joined the New York Giants, and we were playing against the Dallas Cowboys. The national anthem started playing, and I remember holding my right hand over my heart, thinking, *how in the world did I get here?*

Ten years earlier, on the night of November 30, 1956, a car pulled up to my family's home in Budapest, Hungary. I was fourteen years old, and I'd never ridden in a car before. Carrying just a few small bags, my father, János, forty-six, my little brother, Charlie, ten, my mother, Sarolta, thirty-five and then seven months pregnant, and I drove toward the train station in the city center. It was five weeks after the revolution, and Hungarians were fleeing the country at the rate of thousands a day. What had started as a peaceful student demonstration became a bloody revolt against the Communist regime. Soviet tanks rolled into the streets of Budapest, and by November 11, the revolution was crushed. My parents were more desperate to flee than ever, and on November 29, my father sat us down for an announcement. We were leaving Hungary the next evening. "Don't tell anybody," he said.

As we passed bullet-ridden and bombed-out buildings, the fear inside my parents was palpable. It was the third time they were trying to flee Hungary—they had not made it past the border the last two times. They tried in 1944. And again in 1950. They knew we could be separated, or worse, at any point, but freedom was worth the risk.

Taken by Austrian police immediately after escaping
across the Hungarian border (January 1957).

The train station was filled with other refugees. Like us, they left everything behind and were rushing to get into Austria before it was too late. Hungary was no place to live. Life was dangerous; there was no freedom of speech; the government was increasingly repressive. Our house, along with my grandparents' properties, had been taken over by the state in 1950. My father, a medical doctor specializing in dentistry, worked for the state by day; by night he set up a private dentistry practice in the living room of what remained of our house, filling and pulling teeth for cash and bartered food.

For Charlie and me, our second home was on the soccer field. Some of my earliest memories are of walking with my buddies to the field across from our house, a sandwich my mother had fixed me in one hand and a soccer ball in the other.

By three o'clock on December 1, we made it to a safe house near the Austrian border to meet our guide. By six o'clock that evening, we set out on foot. Flares burst into the night sky, brighter than fireworks on the Fourth of July, illuminating the haystacks like a battlefield. We were exhausted; we were hungry. And we soon realized the guide hardly knew where he was going—he'd not smuggled anyone across yet, and we were walking in circles. My mother was so exhausted and stressed that she temporarily lost her sight. Her arms were swelling. My father helped her walk at first, and eventually we both carried her through the haystacks.

Meanwhile, along the way, we had another crisis: for almost ten minutes, we couldn't find Charlie. He was so tired that he'd stopped walking and sat down by a haystack. My parents rallied him to keep walking. That's all there was to do—keep walking. After ten hours, the flares were behind us. The sun rose, and we were in Austria. Finally, we had made it to freedom.

We slept in a barn that first night. We ate. We bathed. Then volunteers drove us to a refugee camp in Vienna. It was the first time I'd seen free, open life. When an opportunity to resettle in America arose, my father seized it: the country was the land of his dreams. In late December, we boarded a Red Cross plane carrying pregnant Hungarian women and their families, bound for Newark, New Jersey.

En route to America, there was one final hurdle: the winds were so strong that we had to make an emergency landing at a US army base in Newfoundland. My mother was carried off the plane on a stretcher; I thought that she was going to blow away. We slept in the barracks, and the next morning we had breakfast in the cafeteria—it was my first taste of America. Some officers gave me a tray. "Take whatever you want," they said. I couldn't believe it! Sausages. Eggs. Bacon. Potatoes. Oranges. I'd never seen a banana before! I'll never forget it. We stuffed ourselves, and then we got on the plane again, heading for Newark. The pilot passed over Manhattan. Talk about being in the new world, seeing the skyscrapers, thinking, *here we are, how did we get here?*

We lived for about three weeks at Camp Kilmer, a former army base in New Jersey, where some thirty thousand Hungarian refugees were given shelter as they prepared for resettlement. My brother and I spent hours and hours watching old Westerns—our first experience with television—as our father was arranging where he would be able to work again as a doctor, sorting out the pieces of our new life.

A classmate of my father's from medical school in Budapest, who had fled during World War II, was working in upstate New York. We spent the next four months in Saranac Lake, living with families who so generously opened their doors to refugees, as Americans had before and have since. I went with one family. My brother with another. My parents—and then my newborn brother, Johnny—with another. It was a big deal for the town, these refugees arriving. The local sports store gave us winter coats. It was an amazing way to welcome someone who needed it, but we were embarrassed to receive the help.

We moved when my father found work as a medical doctor in a state hospital two hours away, in Ogdensburg. I was heartbroken, because there was no soccer team at the high school. One night, I turned on the television and I saw an American football game for the very first time; I saw a player kicking a parabola-shaped ball, and I said to myself, "What a funny way to kick a ball," because he was kicking it straight on, with his toes. So I thought I'd try out football—at least there was kicking involved.

At my first high school game, I just kicked the ball soccer style, with the instep of my foot, and it went over everyone's head into the end zone. I was like some sort of freak. They all said, "Jesus, where did this kid come from? What is this?" It was then that the idea came to me that kicking was something I really could do in this country. That's when everything started. The rest, as they say, is history.

After kicking at Cornell University, the big professional teams weren't interested in me, which was a disappointment, because I had my heart set on starting a new trend in this traditional American game. I was even ready to get a bag of balls to go from pro camp to pro camp to prove myself. But then the Buffalo Bills gave me a contract just to try out at their training camp, as a novelty. To everyone's great surprise, in the first exhibition game in Tampa against the New York Jets, I kicked a fifty-seven-yard field goal, then the longest field goal in pro football history. Today every player in the game, from youngsters to college to the pros, kicks soccer style. Sometimes I joke that I should have patented it!

After two seasons with the Buffalo Bills, I kicked for nine seasons with the New York Giants, where I became the all-time leading scorer in the team's history, a record I still hold today. Upon retiring, I successfully dove into the financial printing business, with Donnelley Financial, where I work with some of America's greatest corporations. I met and married my wife, Kathy Sauer, in 1970, and our first son, David, was born in 1971. Our second son, Tom, was born in 1977.

Me in my element, as a placekicker for the New York Giants.

America is still a land of opportunities, even for someone who arrives here, like me, as a refugee. My parents taught me and my brothers: Try your hardest, try to be the best in whatever you do. If you work hard and succeed in this country, nobody cares where you came from.

The next generation of Gogolaks have built on the American dream. My sons are my greatest achievement. David followed in my footsteps at Cornell and became a successful restaurateur, owning nine restaurants in San Francisco by the time he was thirty-six. In his short life and before his tragic death in 2008, David accomplished more than most others do in a lifetime. My wife, Kathy, has a flourishing business building residential homes in Connecticut.

Our younger son, Tom, was born with hydrocephalus (fluid on the brain). Until he was sixteen, he suffered from severe seizures, and we did not know if he would survive. Then a miracle came our way: Dr. Orrin Devinsky, a doctor from NYU Langone, found the perfect combination of drug therapy, and Tom has been seizure-free ever since. He works at our local YMCA, lives in a group home that we built for handicapped young adults, and he just celebrated his fortieth birthday. I believe that Tom is alive today because we live in America.

Five decades after my parents decided to escape the old country in search of freedom, the Gogolak journey came full circle. We landed in New Jersey on a Red Cross plane in 1956, and in 2006 I flew back to Hungary on a White House plane, representing my new country—as a citizen envoy—with President George W. Bush's delegation to commemorate the fiftieth anniversary of the Hungarian revolution. Driving through Budapest, I remembered how the city looked through the fearful eyes of a fourteen-year-old refugee the night we fled. And I was reminded, more than ever, of the greatness of the American dream.

Linda Hills

Linda Hills is the great-granddaughter of Andrew Carnegie and a member of the board of the Carnegie Hero Fund Commission.

My great-grandfather, Andrew Carnegie, immigrated to America near-ly 170 years ago. He was one of 188,233 British immigrants who came to America that year alone.[1] In 1848 the most compelling reasons to immigrate to America were very similar to what they are today. In the Carnegies' hometown of Dunfermline, Scotland, his father, William, had been a master weaver, able to provide well for his family as a hand weaver of beautiful damasks, but as the wheels of industrialization have done in so many industries over the past two centuries, the arrival of industrialized weaving with steam looms rapidly stole his livelihood. With no way to earn a living in Scotland in his profession, William and his family, like so many others swallowed up in the hard economic times, left for opportunity in America. A favorite ditty William sang was popular at the time: "To the West, to the West, to the land of the free, Where the mighty Missouri rolls down to the sea; Where a man is a man even though he must toil, And the poorest may gather the fruits of the soil."

Different areas of young America's cities and farmlands attracted various nationalities of immigrants—Italians, Swedes, Czechs, Ger-mans, Irish, Scots, etc.—where the most recent immigrants joined their brethren seeking some attachment to the old ways of the homelands they had left. Pittsburgh, Pennsylvania, was a preferred destination of many Scots, who arrived from New York by making the three-week journey up the Erie Canal through Buffalo and then across Lake Erie to Cleveland, on to Beaver, and finally by canal boat up the Ohio River. For the Carnegie family of four, Scottish friends and family awaited them. An aunt offered them two rooms to live in for free. His mother cobbled shoes and his father unsuccessfully returned to weaving, never again able to support his family. At thirteen, Andrew needed to help his family make ends meet. Upon leaving Scotland his education "ended forever, except for one winter's night-schooling in America."[2] Andrew was quick, he was dedicated, he had a strong work ethic, he was filled with passion to do the best he could, and he keenly felt responsibility to his family—traits common to many immigrants, past and present, who leave their homelands under duress to seek a new life and new opportunities in America.

Andrew began his working career as a bobbin boy in a cotton factory owned by another Scottish immigrant. His subsequent hiring as an errand boy at the telegraph office presented him with a lucky opportunity—he began to network with smart, industrious people and had a chance to develop and demonstrate his skills. He was working in the heart of communication in the business world of the 1850s—an advantageous place to be, no matter the century—and he paid attention.

Andrew's road to success had many stages, and he passed into and out of numerous industries—from manufacturing Pullman railroad sleeper cars to building bridges to eventually founding the largest steel company in the world, whose profits made him extremely wealthy. Along with him, many of his Scottish boyhood friends, also fellow immigrants, benefited as his trusted partners. This one young Scottish immigrant's economic contributions to his new homeland, America, were priceless because of the jobs he created and the product he produced—steel upon which the country depended for transportation, building infrastructure, and construction of buildings that could never before have been contemplated.

At the pinnacle of his economic success, he made one of humankind's greatest contributions—one that to this day continues to enhance and enrich our lives here in America and throughout the world. What and why? Early in his career, at the age of thirty-five, while still actively building this business empire and enjoying immense success, he set higher goals. He challenged himself and others who, like him, were wildly successful to pursue his vision. He saw personal wealth as the means to put into motion undertakings that would help others benefit from the opportunities inherent in America. He felt that with his good fortune came a significant social responsibility. He was passionate about giving others who were less fortunate the opportunity to help themselves by providing education to others who, like he, had not had that chance. He believed it was far better to "teach a man to fish than to give him one to eat." His pledge to himself at age thirty-five was in his lifetime to give away all of his wealth. He preached his "gospel of wealth" to the other titans of his time, such as the Astors, the Vanderbilts, John D. Rockefeller, and J. P. Morgan. Some embraced pieces of this philosophy.

As this divestiture of wealth began, so began Carnegie's legacy of the greatest philanthropic effort ever undertaken. This effort produced twenty-four institutions. The fact that twenty-two of these are still in existence today (over one hundred years later), are more vibrant than ever, and continue to be actively engaged in significant work that profoundly benefits humankind and our planet is a testament to his vision and his determination to give back—especially to America, which took him in at age thirteen. We, as his family, and those who work in his broader family of institutions, think of him as the father of modern philanthropy. When there was no tax advantage or any other personal benefit, he gave his money to establish a plethora of institutions to aid his fellow man. He established the concept of the matching gift and bullied his contemporaries to follow his example.

Cognizant of the reality that a gift that is wholly given is often not as appreciated as one in which the recipient also bears ownership, Carnegie began with libraries, but he required the community to provide the land and raise the money to buy the books. In his lifetime, over twenty-five hundred libraries were built through his gifts. He was passionate about organ music and donated the money to construct more than seven thousand organs throughout America and Europe. When a tragedy took the lives of 179 coal miners in Harwick, Pennsylvania, and two heroic men lost their lives trying to save them, he was profoundly touched by their "selfless act of bravery and courage."[3] "Greater love hath no man than this, that a man lay down his life for his friends" — John 15:13. Thereby was born his concept of the Carnegie Hero Funds, which "celebrate the noblest, most unselfish behavior of which human beings may be capable." He established eleven of these funds—the Carnegie Hero Fund Commission in the USA and Canada, the Carnegie Hero Fund Trust in the UK, and nine Carnegie Hero Funds in Europe to recognize and reward those civilian heroes among us who are willing to risk their own lives, most often for a complete stranger.

Education and world peace stood as his two greatest passions. He sought to provide education for the families of Pittsburgh workers and founded the Carnegie Institute of Technology, which in 1967 merged with the Mellon Institute and became Carnegie Mellon University. The university has since become world renowned and respected as it educates students from all over the world at the highest levels of engineering, the sciences, and the arts. This dynamically diverse institution brings together young people who have and will continue to positively contribute their talents and energy to life in nearly every country on this globe.

Likewise, he was tireless in his effort to find a way to achieve world peace. He built the Peace Palace in The Hague in the Netherlands with the hope that the countries of the world could come there to work out their differences peacefully. The World Court now sits there. The Carnegie Council for Ethics in International Affairs is involved in substantial efforts to bring clear-thinking individuals together to find ways of "promoting *ethical* leadership on issues of war, peace, and global social justice."[4] He founded the Carnegie Endowment for International Peace, an international think tank for foreign policy that is "dedicated to advancing cooperation between nations and promoting active international engagement by the United States."[5]

There are numerous other institutions he founded—all of which deserve mention, but for which there is not space in this piece. However, the Carnegie Corporation of New York is the premier institution he founded with one single, immense gift (when he came to the realization that he would not live long enough to fulfill his promise of giving away all his wealth in his lifetime). He gave away nearly two-thirds of his fortune to this one entity and then entrusted the Carnegie Corporation with the responsibility of finding the best possible ways to use this, the majority of his wealth, for humankind. He relinquished control and trusted in future generations to know what would be best. This, in my opinion, is the key to the exemplary, ongoing, stellar influence that the endeavors of the Carnegie Corporation of New York continue to have on society.

Before drawing to a close, it is significant to speak of Andrew's personal story. He remained close to his homeland of Scotland throughout his life. He even got special permission from Britain's monarch to sew together the American and British flags, which he flew over his Scottish home in the highlands of Scotland. Devoted to his mother, it seemed he did not feel free to marry until her death. After her passing, he married the woman he had loved for more than a decade—Louise Whitfield, who was twenty-one years his junior. There was no question that they were very much in love and well suited. Louise wholeheartedly supported Andrew's goals of philanthropy and rejoiced when he retired from business in 1902, turning his attention to purposefully divesting himself of his wealth in the ways from which he felt the most benefit would be derived. They had one child, Margaret, and, after Andrew's death, four grandchildren.

Andrew was way ahead of his time in his respect for and recognition of the contributions of women, and of individuals of all races, religions, and skin colors. He supported the Austrian Baroness Bertha von Suttner, the first woman to win the Nobel Peace Prize. He entertained the likes of Booker T. Washington, Mark Twain, and Rudyard Kipling, as well as presidents and heads of state, at his home in New York City and in Scotland. He gave generous grants to Tuskegee University so that "our

African brethren have not been overlooked." He worked tirelessly for the good of America and the world, even going to Kaiser Wilhelm II of Germany in June 1913 trying to promote peace and underscore national ties and cooperation to prevent war.

Except for those Americans who can trace their ancestry to the great tribes of the Native Americans who occupied this vast continent before the arrival of the first immigrants from abroad, every single other American is either an immigrant or can trace their roots to family who immigrated to America in the past three to four centuries. The beautiful blending of all these peoples is what makes America so unique, and the opportunities she has provided for generations of immigrants make her golden. But America would not be great had it not been for the talents, energy, and strength brought to her from every other corner of the globe. We are an open and welcoming people, and I hope that will never change. Andrew Carnegie brought his best to America, and she gave him her best back. Let's be sure we provide that opportunity to today's generations who endure hardship elsewhere and need to start a new life. The vast majority of these people will enrich us immeasurably, as they have for generations. The next Andrew Carnegie may come from Africa, the Middle East, Asia, Europe, Australia, South America, or an island somewhere else. However, he or she will not come if we close our doors, and we will be the poorer for it, and truly neither we, nor the world, will be safer.

Finally, I would be remiss if I did not mention that today many of our highly successful business entrepreneurs have embraced the example of philanthropy Andrew Carnegie set, and like him, they have bequeathed their fortunes to the ongoing benefit of humanity. I do believe Andrew Carnegie would be prouder of this than nearly anything else he achieved in his eighty-four years on this earth.

1. Wall, Joseph Frazier, *Andrew Carnegie*, 73.

2. Carnegie, Andrew, *Autobiography of Andrew Carnegie*, 12.

3. Carnegie Hero Fund Commission, *A Century of Heroes*.

4. The *Carnegie Council for Ethics in International Affairs* website.

5. *Wikipedia*; "Carnegie Endowment for International Peace".

Wes Moore

Wes Moore is an author and founder of BridgeEdu, a college support program for at-risk students. He was recently named Chief Executive Officer of the Robin Hood Foundation.

My grandfather: the immigrant, the American.

My grandfather's American story began with fleeing persecution—not to America, but from it. My great-grandparents had moved from Lowe River, Jamaica, to South Carolina in search of that elusive American dream. My grandfather, James Thomas, the son of a minister, was born there—a natural-born citizen of the United States.

South Carolina, my grandfather's birthplace, has a long and tortured history. Once the place that held the highest number of slaves per capita, and the first state to secede in the Civil War, it also has an incredibly rich African American history, including in the ministry, where the first African Methodist Episcopal church in the South was founded in 1816. During reconstruction, many of our nation's first African American political leaders came from South Carolina, bolstered by the network and history of the black church in the state.

South Carolina should have been a welcoming place for a family of Jamaican immigrants involved in the ministry, but unfortunately, South Carolina in the early 1900s did not represent the America my grandfather and his parents sought. Before long, my great-grandparents gave up on their American dream and moved back to Jamaica, chased away by an emergent Ku Klux Klan.

My great-grandparents were done with their American experiment and completely uninterested in giving the racism they experienced a second chance. For my grandfather, though, something was different.

His taste of America never went away, and as he grew into a young man, he vowed to make it back. Like many immigrant stories, my grandfather's relation to America was one of inexplicable magnetism. He longed to be here.

My grandfather grew up in Mount Horeb Church in St. James Parish in Jamaica. He dreamed of following his father into the ministry, dreamed of one day leading his own congregation. The church meant everything to my grandfather, and it was there that he met my grandmother, whose family had just immigrated to Jamaica from Cuba for work.

But still, my grandfather felt the pull of the United States, and shortly after he married my grandmother he returned to America for his studies. He enrolled at Lincoln University, a historically black institution in Pennsylvania, and arrived for his studies in the middle of November. Now, bear in mind, this is a yardie from Jamaica. Of course he arrives in Pennsylvania in the winter wearing shorts and open-toed sandals.

The first person he met on campus called him over and took him under his wing.

"Where are you from?" the man asked him.

When my grandfather answered, the man said, "I knew you were not from here. We need to get you some appropriate clothes. Don't worry. When I first came here, I did the same thing."

The man came to be a mentor, friend, and teacher to my grandfather. His name was Kwame Nkrumah, and he would go on to become president of his home country, Ghana, one of the first black presidents of an independent African nation.

This was a very different United States than the one my grandfather had fled as a young boy. This was a place where people from around the world came to pursue their dreams, and where their dreams were collaborated upon and shared.

My grandfather resisted his mentor's calls to get into politics and chased his dream to be a minister. By 1952, he was an ordained Presbyterian minister, just like his father.

With my grandmother joining him, they settled in the Bronx. My grandmother was a public-school teacher, and my grandfather made history by becoming the first black minister ordained in the Dutch Reformed Church. Their first priority was to save enough money to buy a small three-bedroom house on Paulding Avenue in the Bronx. The house was modest, but to my family, it would prove to be a castle. At various points, it was home to between five and nine people. It always seemed to be as big as it needed to be to keep my family safe and warm. When my mother moved me and my sisters there from Baltimore in 1984 after my father died, it was a life-changing safe space for us to learn, grow, and be loved.

Over the span of a half century in the Bronx, my grandparents watched their neighborhood transform from a Jewish community to one home to African Americans and Latino immigrants. Their community was as complex as their immigration story. My grandparents saw their neighborhood shift from a tightly knit community to one that was chronically neglected, where poverty and crime levels sought to define a diverse and proud community in the 1980s and '90s. But my grandfather, the Reverend Dr. James Thomas, a leader in his community, a man of the cloth, a pioneer, never gave up on his community, his home.

So much of my grandfather's life, from his very presence in the United States to his groundbreaking career in the ministry, has an element of fate and determination to it that is so uniquely American. From his birth to his death, he saw the best and the worst of what this country has to offer.

No more than five feet, six inches, my grandfather was a giant to me. He had a presence that commanded every room he ever entered and was a sight to see at the lectern. He was my family's patriarch, my father figure when I needed one the most. When my father died and my family had to move in with my grandparents in the Bronx, they were both recently retired. They had spoken of returning to Jamaica, but ultimately the Bronx, and America, were home. They couldn't give it up.

My grandfather passed away while I was in Afghanistan. Despite a herculean effort from my command to get me home in time to say goodbye, I didn't make it in time. I know today he'd be proud of the man I've become—the husband, the father, and the American.

Morris Sarnoff

Jeffrey and Richard Sarnoff, on behalf of their grandfather Morris Sarnoff 1894–1973. Richard Sarnoff is Chairman of Media and Communications for KKR. Jeffrey Sarnoff is principal at Diadem Special Projects.

It was shortly after my birth that my father left Uzlian, a shtetl—village— in Belarus, for America to avoid conscription into the Czarist army. To be Jewish in the Russian Army at that time meant serving at the front of the front lines. Few survived the assignment. It took him nearly five years—working as a day-job painter in New York City and spending nearly nothing on himself—to save the $144 necessary to secure passage for Mother, my brothers, David and Lew, and me (ages nine, eight, and six). We rode on a cart to Minsk and then took a train to Lithuania. From there we boarded a ship bound for London, where we changed to a ship to Montreal. From Montreal we took the final legs of the journey by train and steamer to arrive at the dawn of a new century.

Travel by ship was difficult for us, as it was for so many refugees and immigrants. We were booked in steerage, a large, open space overfull with other families. Mother had carefully packed kosher food for the voyage in a large bundle. An uncaring bosun's mate took our bundle and threw it into the deep, dark hold, which would be sealed before disembarking. A moment of wordless panic—then David boldly jumped in after it, and they had to haul him out. Of course, he had scrambled around down there and was clutching our precious bundle when they did. I did not speak English at the time, but I am told one of the deckhands said to David, "Boy, you'll do okay in America." Never was a truer prediction made.

David, Leah, Lew, and Morris Sarnoff in Belarus before their voyage to America.

So we were able to eat on the ship, but each day more people in steerage got sick, and the smells got worse. It was both insufferably hot and terribly cold on that voyage. My clothes stayed damp a long time after washing them in the big basin. I wondered if the place we were going was worth this hardship, but the "Land of Opportunity" had a special ring to it for those, like our family, who felt oppressed in their own country.

When we finally arrived, it was not exactly the shining city of my dreams. My whole family was living in one small place on Monroe Street in Brooklyn, America. The building had five separate tiny apartments, each home to large families, and two hallway bathrooms. Our apartment was distinguished in that it included a separate bedroom with its own door. Sadly, that soon became a sickroom for my father, who already suffered from the tuberculosis to which he would succumb a few years later, after the birth of my brother Irving and sister Edie.

David, Lew, and I lived just inside the big door that opened into the apartment. For sleeping, we would unroll the night mat and lie down next to one another. The kitchen had a stove, so it was always the warmest room. We had someone paying us to sleep there: my father could not work as a painter anymore due to his health issues, so that money helped pay for our food. Buying food from the neighborhood stalls took both a strong disposition and a head for negotiating. My mother had both. I would walk with her every day to help carry our food home. Sun, rain, cold, it did not matter; I liked that walk very much. We earned a meager living from working a newsstand for its owner. Father and David would take turns minding the stand and selling papers.

One terrible day, Father was watching the newsstand and someone came up and coldcocked him and stole the newspaper money. In poor health to start, he was now severely injured. I asked everyone I knew who had done it until I found out. There was no anonymity in those days. I took a bat with me and waited for him. He was older; that did not matter. I returned the favor. Afterward, I disappeared for days, sleeping in basements and eating handouts and what I could find on the street. When I came back home, the police had lost interest.

My eldest brother, David, then had to become the primary breadwinner for the family. Despite being only fifteen, without even a high school education, he talked his way into a good-paying job as an office boy with Commercial Cable Company, and then another one with Marconi Wireless. Possessed of an extraordinarily keen mind, David rose up quickly, and the whole family rose up around him.

Epilogue

In a way, the whole country rose up with David as well. Marconi Wireless would become Radio Corporation of America (RCA), and David, known after World War II as General Sarnoff, would lead the company for nearly fifty years. His work helped to transform communications in the twentieth century and make the world into the more understandable, transparent, and entertaining place we know today.

My brothers and I all enjoyed successful careers in diverse businesses. That said, our own early career traction can undoubtedly be traced back to David's trailblazing accomplishments and his efforts on our behalf. My own sons and even grandsons have derived some advantages just from the halo of the last name. Radio, television, and all the communications technologies that followed owe a huge debt to David, but the debt that I and the rest of my family owe him is far greater.

Marlo Thomas

*Marlo Thomas is an actor, producer, and social activist. She is
Outreach Director for St. Jude Children's Research Hospital in
Memphis, Tennessee, which was founded by her father, entertainer
Danny Thomas.*

As my Lebanese grandfather lay in his bed during his final days, he took
my father's hand.

"Never forget your heritage," he whispered into Dad's ear. "He who
denies his heritage has no heritage."

Those words have resonated in our family for all of our lives. When
I was growing up in the '40s and '50s, Lebanon was not much in the
news. So, when I told the kids at school that I was Lebanese, they asked,
"Is that like Chinese?"

I reported this to my grandfather. "You go back and tell them that
your people gave the world navigation as we know it today," he said
sternly. I did as he commanded, saying those very words into the quiz-
zical faces of a group of third graders. Still, I felt proud of my little-
known heritage, because my grandpa had taught me to be.

His name was Charles Yakhoob, but as he came through Ellis Island,
the registrar recorded his surname as Jacob. With him was his sixteen-
year-old bride of an arranged marriage, Margaret Taouk, who would
also now have this new name of Jacob.

Like millions of immigrants who passed through Ellis Island, Charles
and Margaret carried all of their possessions in cloth bags. They had
fled a land of poverty and hunger to come to America, a place of dreams
and abundance, to begin a new life.

My grandparents, Charles and Margaret, with five of their ten children—including my father on his father's lap.

My grandfather settled his family in the farmlands of northern Ohio, where he sold dry goods on consignment from a horse-drawn wagon. He and my grandmother had ten children, nine boys and a girl. My dad was number five. They all proudly spoke the language of their heritage, Arabic, as well as the language of their new country. They were very poor, but at Sunday Mass they always left something in the collection basket for the less fortunate.

They loved America. And they believed in its promise. But one thing fell short of their hopes: health care. They couldn't receive any. After food, clothing, and a roof over their many heads, there simply wasn't any money left over for doctors. My grandmother had all ten of her babies with just the help of her sister and a lot of hot water. Kids of other immigrant families in their neighborhood died of influenza and appendicitis.

Thankfully, the Jacob family survived, and each of the children embarked on their own lives. My father came a long way from those farms in Ohio to creating a career in show business and raising his family in Beverly Hills, always carrying with him the richness of the Lebanese culture. Indeed, among my most vivid memories of my childhood were the annual Lebanese festivals we'd go to as a family—*mahrajans*, they were called. Men, women, and children from Lebanese communities all across Los Angeles would gather for a day of celebration.

It was like a grand picnic. Music and cigar smoke would fill the air, and the women and girls would serve plate after plate of traditional Lebanese cuisine—tabbouleh, hummus, and my favorites, kibbe and fatayer. There was always lots of singing and laughter and especially storytelling. My grandmother was a wonderful storyteller—her timing was impeccable. My father always said it was Grandma who taught him the art of holding an audience.

But along with these colorful touchstones of his heritage, my father also held fast to indelible memories of his family never having the care of a doctor, no matter how sick they got—and the faces of the boys and girls in his neighborhood who died because of it. And he never forgot his promise to his father to remember his heritage.

So, after many years of success, he founded St. Jude Children's Research Hospital, a place of hope for the world's sickest children, where no family would ever have to pay a doctor for their child's treatment—or for travel or housing or food. And in 1958, when Dad broke ground for the hospital, he did so in the name of the Lebanese and Syrian people, with gratitude to America for opening her arms and embracing them in this great land.

When I think of how I got here, this is how: with pride in my heritage, with a deep love of this country, and with the understanding that we bear a responsibility to ease the suffering of those less fortunate.

In 2014, I was awarded the Presidential Medal of Freedom, an honor that was profoundly humbling. As President Barack Obama clasped the medal around my neck and the honor guard read aloud the proclamation, I thought about my immigrant grandparents, Charles and Margaret Yakhoob, carrying their cloth bags and taking their first step onto this new land of hope. How would they feel today, seeing their granddaughter, just two generations later, at the White House receiving this honor from the president of the United States? What would they think?

I know what I thought. I thought of my heritage. And I thought of the promise of America for people of all heritages. And, like my grandfather, I was very proud.

John Zaccaro Jr.

John A. Zaccaro Jr. is a principle of P. Zaccaro Company Inc., a third-generation privately held real estate firm, an attorney, and the managing partner of Zaccaro Associates LLC., a real estate Development Company.

My mother, Geraldine Anne Ferraro, was a first-generation Italian American, and my father, John Anthony Zaccaro, was a second-generation Italian American. Their family history is a somewhat typical one of Italians, Italian Americans, and Americans. If you go back two generations you'll find many similar circumstances involving those who immigrated in search of a better life.

My great-grandfather on my mother's side was John Vacca, born on May 29, 1890. He came to the United States from Naples, Italy, in 1894. At the time, crossing the Atlantic by boat was an ordeal that took over a month. After arriving in this country, he worked as a wholesale fruit dealer. John married Josephine Guerra, and they had five children. The second eldest of their brood was my grandmother Rose Vacca. Mema, as we called her, was born February 29, 1906.

Rose's future husband and my grandfather, Philip Zaccaro, was born on November 5, 1895. Philip was the second of seven children of Francis and Anna Zaccaro, both of whom had been born in this country. In 1912, at the age of seventeen, Philip entered the real estate business in lower Manhattan. He formed P. Zaccaro Co. Inc. five years later in 1917, and became the exclusive representative for the real estate departments of the Bowery Savings Bank, Dry Dock Savings Bank, Central Hanover Bank and Trust Company, Central Savings Bank, East River Savings Bank, and Emigrant Industrial Savings Bank, as well as other entities. P. Zaccaro Co. Inc. also was the appointed agent for the City of New York assembling and managing properties that became Stuyvesant Town, Peter Cooper Village, Knickerbocker Village, and the Water Street widening.

My father, John Anthony Zaccaro, joined P. Zaccaro Co. Inc., by that time a privately held real estate investment, development, and management firm, in 1956 after graduating from Iona College. He had a career of more than sixty years in real estate and was a principal of P. Zaccaro Co. Inc. My father was a member of the NYC Housing Council, trustee of the bankruptcy court, and served on many private and public boards.

My maternal great-grandmother, Maria Guissepe Caputo, left her one-room home on a cobblestone street in Terranova, Italy, at the age of sixteen. Generations of her family worked in the fields tending grapes in the mountain region. She also came in steerage on the SS *Italian* in 1890, and made the trip with her aunt Maria Antonia Caputo.

Maria Antonia was forty-seven at the time of their crossing, and was part of an era of women who arrived in the new world to put their skills to work in textile mills, agriculture and the domestic industries. At that time only 10 percent of the immigrants from Italy were women. The aunt and niece arrived in New York Harbor on June 27, 1890, and settled at 250 Mott Street in Little Italy. Tragically, nine months after her arrival in America, Maria Antonia died of malaria, leaving her niece, my great-grandmother, Maria Guissepe, alone to fend for herself in her new homeland. As a result, at a very young age, my great-grandmother married Domenico Corrieri of 250 Elizabeth Street, who worked as a New York City street cleaner. He was also an Italian immigrant, and a widower whose wife had died during childbirth. He had arrived on the SS *Rhynland* on Christmas Eve 1881. The couple was married at Old St. Patrick's Cathedral on Mulberry Street in May 1891. Eventually they moved uptown to an area known as Italian Harlem, on East Ninety-Seventh Street.

My grandmother Antoinetta—Nana, as we called her—was born in 1905 and was one of ten children. The family lived in a three-room apartment with a bathroom located in the hallway. Nana attended public school until she was twelve years old, at which time she was forced to leave school to help support her family because her father had suffered a stroke. She worked as a crochet beader in a factory, what would now be called a sweatshop, on New York's Lower East Side. At the age of twenty-two, Antoinetta married Dominic Ferraro, who had emigrated from Italy in 1920. Dominic's father was an engineer, and his family were landowners in Italy.

The promise of America.

My mother, Geraldine, was born on August 26, 1935. She was the fourth child of Antoinetta and Dominic. Two of their children passed away earlier in life, one shortly after birth and the second in a car accident at the age of three. The family lived in a three-story house on Dubois Street in Newburgh, New York. Dominic owned and ran a bar and restaurant called the Roxy. Antoinetta ran the five and dime store that they also owned. At age forty-four, Dominic died of a heart attack; my mother was eight years old. Nana lost the family businesses and was forced to move to a small apartment in the South Bronx, where she resumed working as a crochet beader.

My great-grandmothers and grandmothers were raised in an era when education and independence were not considered necessary or even important for women. Yet they sacrificed so their children could have more. My grandmother Maria Guissepe never learned to write her name, and Nana, although not able to pursue her own education, understood its value. She would say, "If you educate a boy, you educate a boy alone. If you educate a girl, you educate a family." Nana's understanding of the importance of education led to her insistence that my mother attend not just college, but also law school, where she was one of only three women in her class. It was Nana and the nuns of Marymount whom my mother always credited with instilling in her a sense of responsibility to others and the importance of giving back to her community.

My mother began her career as a public-school teacher in Astoria, Queens, while attending law school at night. She practiced family law and then was an assistant district attorney. In that position, she created and ran the first special victims' bureau set up to prosecute crimes committed against seniors and children. She first ran for and was elected to Congress in 1978; she served three terms. In 1984, she was nominated to be the Democratic vice presidential candidate, thereby making history as the first woman on a major party ticket. Subsequently, she served as ambassador to the United Nations for Human Rights and was an author, columnist, and a political commentator. She believed she had a duty to make the world she lived in a better place for her friends, family, and fellow citizens. She understood that the promise of America was about opening the doors of opportunity for everyone.

My mother also put a premium on her children's education, as her mother had done. The first in her family to go to college, my mother is survived by her three children, all of whom have graduate degrees and are successful in their respective fields as a doctor, a lawyer, and a documentary filmmaker. Each of us also have our own families now, teaching our children the lessons and values of the generations that preceded them and made America their home.

The Lovers

///

Alan Alda

Arlene Alda

John Calvelli

Elaine L. Chao

Kevin Chavous

Mary Choi

Bradley Hirschfield

Deborah Norville

The love of one's country is a splendid thing.
But why should love stop at the border?

— Pablo Casals

Perhaps this section should more aptly be titled "Love," because there may be no greater motivator for change than love.

These are real American love stories—about how people's love for their parents, spouse, or children, and their love of country and humanity shaped their American experience.

One couple found love with each other based on a shared Korean heritage discovered halfway around the world. Another found love in Taiwan after fleeing from Shanghai and the rise of communism in China.

Whatever the circumstance which now finds all of these families in the United States, their profound love for this country shines through.

Alan Alda

Alan Alda has focused his recent life on teaching scientists and doctors to be better communicators. He was the star of M*A*S*H, arguably one of the most successful television programs in history.

According to *National Geographic*, where I recently sent a swab chock-full of DNA, I come from a long line of immigrants.

My ancestors seemed to have traveled all over the place.

We started out in Africa, and as we got more sapient, we started traveling north. We got to Europe, eventually, and couldn't resist the charms of the neighborhood Neanderthals at the occasional social mixer down by the river. *National Geographic* tells me I'm about 2 percent Neanderthal, so they seemed not to mind having us around.

Some of us went farther north and wound up in Ireland. That group must have mostly stayed there for a long time. I seem to be about 60 percent Irish and English.

Others of us must have wound up in what became Spain, because my Italian grandfather told me the family left Spain at one point and went to Italy. He wasn't exact about the date they left, but it would have been about 1492, which is when Ferdinand and Isabella expelled all the Jews (first making sure to take possession of their houses and family silver).

My family probably settled in Naples for a while, but Spain controlled that region in those days, and about two years after Ferdie and Izzy had kicked out the Jews, Naples did the same. It was then, I think, that my crew moved north again, this time to the Abruzzo region of Italy. Some time later, when things calmed down, they must have moved back to Naples, where their name indicated the region they had escaped

52

to: D'Abruzzo ("from Abruzzo"). This was also my name at birth—Alphonso D'Abruzzo.

I'm guessing this is the route my Italian family took, because I have relatives named D'Abruzzo who now live about thirty kilometers east of Naples.

So, after all of that, it seems everyone stayed put, living where they had settled for generations—until famine in Ireland and hard times in Italy started getting them moving again.

This time they went not north, but rather off to the west.

America.

As they entered New York Harbor, they passed the statue with the welcome sign that read, "Give me your tired, your poor, your huddled masses yearning to breathe free." They must have been cheered, because they qualified on all counts.

But not long after they got off the boat, my Irish ancestors were asked to ignore ads for employment, the Italians were asked to take a bath, and all of them were asked to stop having so many children.

Eventually, two of those children met one another—a pretty Irish girl and a handsome Italian boy who had a nice singing voice and found, in the middle of the Depression, that he could earn a few dollars a week singing at amateur nights in movie theaters.

They married and had a son. And that's how I got here.

And I'm staying. I'm not going north, east, south, or west.

I'm here.

And I'm not closing the door behind me.

Arlene Alda

Arlene Alda is an author and photographer. Her most recent book is Just Kids From the Bronx: An Oral History.

The studio photo on my desk shows a teenage girl with a turtleneck wool sweater and a Persian lamb hat worn toward the back of her head. She's looking down at the camera, smiling from above. She's young. She's beautiful. She exudes a gentle confidence along with her sense of style.

There's a hypothetical question that I've heard asked: If you could meet or have dinner with any person from the past, who would that be? The name of Einstein comes to mind, however, what would we talk about? But when I think of the young girl in the photograph—Chernya from Poland, who later became my mother, Jean—my mind races with excitement.

I only knew her many years later as my mother of nondescript age, an overworked immigrant housewife with a love of singing, who wanted her children to have a good future in her adopted country, America.

I was her third child. The baby. The spoiled one. In other words, I took so much for granted. As an inquisitive adult, I realized I knew just the bare outlines of my parents' lives. The Kalmanovskys, my mother's family, came from Lida, Poland, which had a dizzying history of conquests and rulers. Was it part of Russia? Or Lithuania? Or Prussia? I never understood how borders could change and people's lives could be torn apart. Now that Lida, since the breakup of the Soviet Union, is part of Belarus, I have a better understanding of how that can be.

My mother, before she came to America.

In her native country, which became Poland again after WWI, my mother and her family lived through pogroms, economic hardships, and war.

When my maternal grandfather, Avram Kalmanovsky, left Poland and immigrated to New Haven, Connecticut, in 1921, he already had relatives living there. After he was settled as a grocer, he sent for his wife, Chaya, his daughters, Chernya (aka Jeannette, and later on, Jean) and Evelyn, and his son, Louis. Jean was twenty-one years old. Left behind was the oldest sister, Sonia, who was already married. During WWII, and with no news to the contrary, it was presumed that Sonia and her family were murdered in the Holocaust.

Years later, when I was a young girl in our Bronx apartment, my mother, on the one or two times she talked about Sonia while looking at a family portrait, would get tears in her eyes. I had no understanding of what a terrible sense of loss that was. I looked dumbly on while she silently mourned.

A year after Jean (Chernya) Kalmanovsky arrived in New Haven, Shimon Warshvasky, a twenty-four-year-old commercial lithographer from Kovno, Lithuania, left to join four of his six living brothers in America. His parents were both deceased, and the brothers, except for the oldest, Moshe, who stayed behind in Europe, had settled in Connecticut, New York, and New Jersey. During WWII, Moshe and his family suffered the same fate as my mother's oldest sibling, Sonia.

I always thought that my parents met through one of their relatives, but more recently I learned that Jean met my father, his name Americanized to Simon Weiss, at Yale University, in New Haven, sometime in 1922. They bonded, not in Psychology 101 or at a football game, but at night school, where they both were learning to read, write, and speak English.

In less than a year, Jean and Simon married.

After living in New Haven for a few years, they moved to New York City with their two children, a boy, Harold, and a girl, Shirley. I was the first family member born in the Bronx, into a new apartment building known as the Mayflower.

The Mayflower was a beehive of working-class and middle-class Jews, in the middle of a mostly Jewish neighborhood. I'm guessing that for my parents, that voluntary ghetto was a comfort and a bridge between the old world and the new. The melting pot was the prevailing philosophy of the time, which meant if you put all the immigrants into a big pot and kept stirring... voilà, the stew would yield Americans. In other words, leave behind the old ways, the old customs and languages. Adapt to the new, and you'll get assimilated.

The local schools were expected to do a good job of leveling the playing field for all the children in the neighborhoods. I was educated throughout in a public system, which included PS 76, Evander Childs High School, Queens College (for a year), and then Hunter College. My entire college education at Hunter cost my family twelve dollars in accumulated bursar's fees, plus the cost of subway tokens from the Bronx to Manhattan. The books for each class were free, borrowed for the semester, to be returned at the end of the term.

It was suggested by my mother that, although I was training to be a professional classical clarinetist, I get my teacher's credentials, too. We knew that gender discrimination was a reality and that women generally weren't hired for male-designated jobs. I did get my teacher's license, but first I auditioned for Leopold Stokowski, who defied the norm by hiring many women for the Houston Symphony, which he conducted in the 1950s. I got in. At the end of that concert season, Alan and I married, having met in New York City the year before. Several years after our three daughters were born, I became involved with photography, took lessons, and eventually started to write. The clarinet took a back seat.

My sister, Shirley, has noted that our parents' direct lineage includes three children, six grandchildren, sixteen great-grandchildren, three great-great-grandchildren, and one great-great–legal ward.

These offspring encompass the fields of engineering, home making, music, photography, writing, law, medicine, social work, chaplaincy, teaching, acting, documentary filmmaking, web design, psychology, art, journalism, urban planning, and business. Three of the youngest are still in high school, off to college in 2018 and 2019.

Could any of this have happened if Chernya and Shimon hadn't emigrated and then met one another in New Haven, Connecticut? I would say the answer would be a resounding, "No."

John Calvelli

John Calvelli is Executive Vice President for public affairs at the Wildlife Conservation Society. He spent much of his earlier career in various staff positions on Capitol Hill.

I have always considered myself an immigrant born in the Bronx. You see, when I was a young boy, my parents decided to move back to Europe and we left the place that I considered home—Arthur Avenue, the real Little Italy of New York. So at the tender age of four, I spent an evening at the newly opened Bronx Park Motel with my family, awaiting our boat that would take us to Naples and a new life in the old country. Well, less than eighteen months later, Mom, my brother, Louis, and I were back on the *Michelangelo*, the pride of the Italian Line, steaming into New York Harbor. Dad, having left Italy earlier, awaited us at the pier on the west side of Manhattan. Our Italian adventure had been just that, an adventure. Dad and Mom realized that the future was in America—in an area of New York City that has been welcoming immigrants from the day a Swede named Jonas Bronck arrived more than three hundred years ago and bequeathed his name to what would become the borough of the Bronx.

And yet my family might be rather blue blood if the first Calvelli who came to America had decided to stay. You see, my great-great-grandfather Luigi had come seeking opportunity in the late 1800s. In those days it was not uncommon for Italian immigrants to attempt several Atlantic crossings in order to make some money, with the full understanding that they would return to their small town and make a better life for their families. They were called birds of passage, and just

58

as a bird migrates seasonally, Great-Great-Nonno would come back to Vico, Aprigliano, a small hamlet in the province of Cosenza in southern Italy. Unfortunately, his son, Great-Grandfather Francesco, was not as fortunate. On his first passage to the new world, family history tells us, Francesco died, leaving behind a son he never met: my grandfather. Therefore my nonno was rather adamant that his children would remain in Italy. That is, of course, until my dad fell in love with his childhood sweetheart (aka, my mom).

Mom's family story likewise has the makings of a novel. Her father, Grandpa Rocco, had come to America after World War I to make his fortune with his brothers, Pete and Francesco. Their desire to improve their lot in life took them to a homestead in Alberta, Canada; the Model-A factory line in Detroit; the mines of West Virginia; a restaurant in Riverhead, New York; and—my personal favorite—a dairy farm in upstate New York. Grandpa Rocco was also a bird of passage and had returned several times to wed Nonna Annina and then conceive two children, my aunt Mary and Mom. Unfortunately, World War II intervened, and Grandpa could not bring his family to America until the war ended. Mom met Grandpa as a young child of twelve when she landed on that same Italian Line pier where I greeted Dad upon returning from Naples those many years later.

Mom then moved to Accord, New York, where she started her American journey living on a dairy farm and attending a one-room schoolhouse. There were three children in the school who did not speak English: Mom and two young Jewish girls who had lived through the Holocaust. She shared with me her greatest achievement that first year in America. Her teacher, Miss Josephine Lawrence, had made a pilgrim dress for her and asked that she recite "The Landing of the Pilgrim Fathers" by Felicia Dorothea Hemans. She had only arrived three months earlier, but Mom dutifully memorized the poem for the Thanksgiving service that was to be held that year in the local Jewish synagogue. Mom can still recall the last stanza.

Ay, call it holy ground,
The soil where first they trod;
They have left unstained what there they found—
Freedom to worship God.

I often think about those refugee girls who had lived through unspeakable horrors and the young Italian girl who had suffered through the privations of war. Yet there they were, believing in the power of the American dream in a small town in rural America in a Jewish house of worship.

Mom's saga did not end there. She made it to the "big city" of Brooklyn, eventually returned to Italy, and met up with her childhood sweetheart once again. Thankfully for me, they wed! The pier Mom and I arrived on from Naples is now gone, but when I drive down the west side of Manhattan with the Statue of Liberty in the distance, my mind wanders to that fateful decision made by my parents to come back to America and the lives they chose to build together in this great country. So even though I was born on 180th Street and Hughes Avenue, I still consider myself that immigrant kid who realized early in life that this nation has truly been a noble experiment, welcoming millions of people from all corners of our planet, assisting them as they learned to become Americans, yet never mandating that they walk away from their traditions. We are all better off because of that rich cultural stew that is America... but in Italian we like to call it *minestra*.

Elaine L. Chao

Elaine L. Chao is the current US Secretary of Transportation. She has also served as the US Secretary of Labor, Director of the Peace Corps, and President and CEO of United Way of America. She is the first Asian Pacific American woman appointed to the President's Cabinet in American history.

The story of my family is one of enduring love—love between my parents Dr. James S.C. Chao and Mrs. Ruth Mulan Chu Chao, and their love for their family. Without their courage, sacrifices, and hard work, our family would not have been able to come to this country, overcome so many obstacles, and ultimately find our place in America.

My father, Dr. James S. C. Chao, and mother, Mrs. Ruth Mulan Chu Chao, grew up in twentieth-century China, which was buffeted by domestic turmoil, natural disasters, foreign invasions, and civil war. My mother came from a distinguished and prominent family in Anhui Province. Her parents were ahead of their time in believing in education for girls, so my mother attended the well-known Ming Teh Girls High School in Nanjing. But the Sino–Japanese War, World War II, and China's civil war intervened, driving her family from their ancestral home in search of safety and security. During their relocation to Shanghai, she met her future husband while she was attending his alma mater, No. 1 Jiading County High School, in a suburb of Shanghai. Their acquaintance was brief because the civil war soon climaxed and her family relocated to Taiwan, but that meeting was to change both their lives.

My father was born in a small farming village in Shanghai, China. His father was a respected schoolteacher, so his parents always emphasized the importance of education. My father won scholarships that enabled him to attend college in pursuit of a maritime career. In 1949, my father boarded a ship to finish his last requirement for graduation—a seagoing apprenticeship. His father came all the way from the village to send his only child off for what was meant to be a short voyage. Several days later, however, the government changed and all the ports were blockaded. James Chao never saw his father again.

Unable to return to its port of origin, my father's ship then set sail for Taiwan. There my father searched for my mother, hoping to see her again. By chance, he happened to read the newspaper listing my mother's graduating class and tracked her down. Eventually my father was able to convince my mother's parents that he was a worthy suitor. My parents were married on November 12, 1951, and started a family.

Even at a young age, my father was already a man of achievement. He became one of the youngest sea captains of his day at the age of twenty-nine. But seafaring life was difficult, as he was away from home for months at a time. Hoping to build a better life for his family, he took the national examination. Not only did he score number one in the national examination, he broke all the previous records and earned a chance to study abroad. This turned out to be the key factor that changed his and my mother's lives forever.

Despite the fact that my mother was three months pregnant with their third child at the time, she encouraged my father to go to America to pursue greater opportunities for our family. My mother, my sister, and I stayed behind in Taiwan.

It took my father three long years before he was able to bring us to America. Even so, he could only afford passage on a cargo ship. It was a sea journey of over eleven thousand nautical miles that took thirty-seven days, and we were the only females on the ship. My mother was so brave. During that voyage, one of my sisters, May, became very ill. There was no doctor onboard, so my mother stayed up for three days and nights, soaking her in cold water to bring down her temperature.

When we finally landed in New York, it was the first time that my father saw his third daughter, now three years old.

Dr. James S. C. Chao reunited with his wife, Ruth, and daughters Jeanette, Elaine, and May after a three-year separation during which he was in America forging a new future.

Our initial years in America were difficult. We couldn't speak English and couldn't eat the food. We didn't understand the culture or the traditions. There were no family members or friends to offer support.

At first, our little family of five lived in a small one-bedroom apartment in Queens, New York. My father held three jobs to support the family. At that time, it was difficult to get Chinese ingredients and vegetables, as most supermarkets did not sell them. Yet somehow, my mother was able to prepare healthy, delicious Chinese meals for our family every night. She managed our household budget so skillfully that we never felt deprived. Growing up, we had profound trust in our parents. She and my father created a loving, secure home for us. Despite much hardship, they never lost their optimism, determination, and hope in America. They held our family, which grew to six daughters, together and we were confident that a bright future awaited us.

I entered the third grade not understanding a word of English. Every day, I would sit in the classroom and copy whatever was on the blackboard into my notebook. Every night, my father would come home after a hard day's work and go over my notebook with me, translating the day's lessons. Often, my father had a difficult time deciphering my childish scrawls. That's how I learned English.

Cultural differences were a challenge. On my first day of school in the third grade, my father took time off from work to accompany me. Upon meeting my teacher, like any well-behaved Chinese child, I bowed deeply from the waist. The other children all laughed, because they did not understand the Asian custom of bowing to show respect. Another time, in late October, we were home doing our homework when we heard knocking on our apartment door. We opened the door to find children dressed in strange costumes, thrusting bags in our faces, while chanting an indecipherable chant. We didn't understand what was happening, so we gave them the only things we had in our meager cupboard—slices of bread. Later, we learned we had just experienced our first Halloween!

While adapting to our new country, my parents always made sure we appreciated our Chinese heritage and celebrated all the Chinese holidays. On Saturdays, to give my mother a break, my father would lead the daughters to clean the house and weed the backyard. Being a diligent, energetic person, my father enjoyed fixing things around the house. While doing this, he would always have one daughter with him, helping to carry the toolbox and hold the flashlight. While he worked, he shared with us his philosophical thinking, as well as stories about his childhood in China and his parents. To build teamwork, even though we could afford to contract out the jobs, he devised summer-long projects for the family. One of the most memorable summer projects was blacktopping the driveway of our house, which was 120 yards! Another summer project was painting the entire house.

My parents taught by example. We learned to work hard, to be willing to make sacrifices, and to be disciplined. They encouraged us to always work for something bigger than ourselves, contribute to society, and bring honor to our family and community. My mother returned home to the Lord on August 2, 2007, but her memory continues to inspire us today. My father has an indomitable spirit, overcoming many obstacles in his career that would have crushed a weaker spirit. His strong character and moral center are the keys to his success in building one of the most respected shipping companies in the world.

Because of their own life experiences, my parents started many philanthropic initiatives to help build greater understanding between Asia and America. One of their earliest foundations has funded thousands of scholarships to help cultivate a new generation of leaders who will help build a more peaceful and harmonious world. Recently, Harvard dedicated the Ruth Mulan Chu Chao Center, the first building named after a woman and the first building named after an Asian American in Harvard's 380-year history. A scholarship fund, the Ruth Mulan Chu and Dr. James Si-Cheng Chao Family Fellowship Fund, was also established to help outstanding students access education and cultivate better leaders for our world. We've come a long way.

Kevin Chavous

Kevin Chavous is the President of academics, policy, and schools for K-12 Inc.

In the winter of 1953, Lieutenant Harold P. Chavous, better known as HP to family and friends, went with a couple of army buddies to an Indianapolis jazz club for a blind date. HP was temporarily stationed in Indianapolis, waiting to be deployed to Korea. Raised on a farm in rural Aiken, South Carolina, HP eschewed city life, but he liked jazz. At the time, Indianapolis was known as a jazz town, so while there, he soaked in as much of the music as he could.

HP's buddies had also done a good job of talking up his blind date. Bettie Jane Lowery was a doctor's daughter, born and raised in Indianapolis. Her father, Dr. Gerald S. Lowery, was one of the first African Americans licensed to practice medicine in the state of Indiana. Indeed, her adolescence was quite different from HP's. While HP grew up poor amid virulent racism, had a single mother, and walked seven miles each way to a one-room schoolhouse, young Bettie Jane had two loving parents, attended integrated Catholic schools, and would regularly wake up to see the likes of Duke Ellington or Billie Holiday sitting in her kitchen having breakfast. As was the case at the time, traveling African American entertainers would stay in the homes of prominent local African Americans in each city where they performed, because they were not allowed to stay in most hotels.

Against this backdrop, HP and Bettie met on a cold, wintry night in Indianapolis. While it wasn't love at first sight—at least from her vantage point—when HP saw her, he instantly liked her. "She had these big brown eyes, a beautiful smile, and walked with class," he often said. "She was the woman of my dreams."

She, on the other hand, thought he was a little arrogant. "I could tell he was educated and super smart, even for a country boy. But he knew it!" she recounted.

It didn't help when he first visited her house and swiped a finger over a coffee table. "I am just checking for dust," he said with a devilish grin. Still, Bettie Jane admitted years later that HP's outward confidence and self-assurance were attractive traits.

Love intervened, and six months later, HP and Bettie married. While he was deployed to Korea, Bettie continued with her classes at Butler University. HP happened to be one of the first African Americans to command white troops following President Harry Truman's order desegregating the armed services. Those white troops under his command came to respect him so much that they held a party in his honor as the war was winding down. During combat, HP suffered a serious eye infection from the smoke from mortar shells. While recuperating at Fitzsimmons Army Hospital in Denver, he ended up playing poker with President Dwight Eisenhower, who was at the hospital recovering from a heart attack. HP was told that old Ike only played with officers, so the hospital staff and military brass scoured the hospital to find patients who could play poker. Only in America could a poor black boy from rural South Carolina who grew up during the height of segregation end up playing cards as an equal with the president of the United States.

Bettie, fraught with worry over HP losing his eyesight, came to Denver and stayed there for several weeks as HP recovered. Apparently, I was conceived during that time. As the oldest of Harold and Bettie's four children, I grew up with an acute understanding and appreciation for both of my parents' ancestry and the journey that brought them together.

In the mid-1700s, several French brothers with the last name Chavous migrated to the Carolina coast in the Americas. In no time, those brothers mingled with the cultures in the new land called America.

Among them, they chose African American, white, and Native American spouses. Even today, the uniqueness of the name broadcasts our ancestry. Every Chavous in America—black, white, brown—is related and can trace their roots to those French brothers.

In South Carolina, the African American Chavouses were known for their independent streaks and their fighting spirit. In the 1800s, Chavous families began purchasing land in and around Aiken County. The families worked with friendly and sympathetic white compatriots to help get their deeds filed and certified. Today, various members of our family still own thousands of acres in the state. True to that heritage, my father left us nearly two hundred acres near Aiken.

One of the more legendary figures in my father's family tree is his grandfather Willie Chavous. Willie lived until he was eighty-four, and had seven wives and twenty children. Willie also essentially adopted several children from some of his wives' previous marriages. He outlived all but one of his wives. My grandmother Emma was one of Willie's children. Emma was named after her mother, who, like some of Willie's other wives, died giving birth. To say that Willie Chavous was a character is an understatement. Like his relatives, however, he was a strong believer in family supporting each other. That commitment to family was passed on to his grandson HP, who, despite his somewhat impoverished background, and being Emma's only child, always yearned for a big, loving family to grow and nurture.

Interestingly, while her childhood was much more privileged, Bettie Jane Lowery did not have the same sense of family knowledge or history that HP possessed. On her father's side, Bettie Jane only knew about her grandmother Cordelia, and had heard bits and pieces about Cordelia's husband, Edward, but knew nothing about anyone else. Bettie Jane knew that Cordelia worked in the fields and sacrificed to get her son through school. To that end, Bettie Jane's father, Cordelia's son Gerald Lowery, exceeded all reasonable expectations for a boy of color in the early 1900s. Born in Lynnville, Tennessee, like his father, he graduated with honors from Fisk University in Nashville and then graduated from Nashville's Meharry Medical School, one of the few medical schools for African American students at that time. Gerald set up his general medical practice in Indianapolis, where he met Estella Powers, who hailed from Kentucky.

Estella Powers was one of the children born to Alexander and Nannie Belle Powers. Alexander and Nannie Belle had a love story for the ages. He was born near Vicksburg, Mississippi, as Alexander Powell. He was a mulatto with striking good looks much like Harlem politician Adam Clayton Powell. Still, since everyone in his Mississippi community knew he was African American, he was treated as a second-class citizen just like other blacks. As a young man, he traveled between Mississippi and Kentucky as a domestic worker. As fate would have it, Alexander met a pretty young girl with a shock of red hair, unlike any he had ever seen, and was instantly smitten.

Nannie Belle Dale's family was originally from Ireland, and they also lived in Kentucky. Apparently, the attraction between the two was more than mutual, leading to a clandestine months-long relationship that soon became hard to hide. Nannie Belle's father was furious, as were the other white fathers in the town. Alexander's family became fearful for his safety, for good reason. Lynchings and public castrations were commonplace for African American men who engaged in any romantic relationship with white women, consent notwithstanding. As the rumor mill regarding violence against Alexander grew, he and Nannie Belle decided they needed to live in another part of the state. The couple got married, changed the family name from Powell to Powers, and settled in Owingsville, Kentucky. Over the next several years, Alexander and Nannie Belle had nine children, including my grandmother, Estella. As their children entered adulthood, one son, John, got a job in Indianapolis. John, a family patriarch in the making, began to bring his siblings, one by one, to Indianapolis. He helped them all find jobs and a place to stay. Indianapolis became the family hub for the descendants of Alexander and Nannie Belle Powell, today numbering nearly four hundred people.

While in her early twenties, Estella Powers met the successful Indianapolis physician Gerald Lowery. Like all her siblings, Estella had an extremely fair complexion and often was mistaken for being white. Plump and bubbly by nature, she had a pleasant, warm, and welcoming face. Gerald, on the other hand, was a slightly built, dark-skinned, quiet, and serious-looking man. He was also eighteen years older than Estella. The two of them presented as an oddly matched couple, but they loved each other deeply. Gerald absolutely adored Estella. Both parents showered their only child, Bettie Jane, with literally anything she wanted, even a brand-new car when she turned sixteen years old—something unheard of for teens at that time.

Building on their histories that brought them together, HP and Bettie Jane raised me and my siblings to believe in God, the blessings of family, the power of education, and the beauty of America. My father taught us that our destinies were ours to create, that education, hard work, and determination could overcome nearly anything. His example was one for all of us to follow. After his military service, HP graduated from Butler University's highly regarded pharmacy school and became one of the first African Americans licensed to practice pharmacy in Indiana. For several years, we all worked in Chavous Drugs, the family business that my father started. And while racism was rampant in Indiana during the '60s and '70s, my father always preached self-reliance and personal responsibility, traits he believed could help one excel. Both parents, however, impressed upon us to take righteous stands against injustice and intolerance. My mother was active with the NAACP and the League of Women Voters, so she regularly took us to marches throughout the state. In fact, while my father was working at the drugstore, my mom, my siblings, and I stood in the rain on that misty night in April 1968, when Bobby Kennedy announced to the crowd that Martin Luther King Jr. had just been shot and killed in Memphis.

Through it all, HP and Bettie Jane instilled in us an inner strength and confidence that has steeled us through our own life journey. Both have now passed on, but their legacy lives on in their children, grandchildren, and great-grandchildren. As their oldest son, I am so thankful for that legacy and infinitely proud of how I got here.

Mary Choi

Mary Choi, MD, is a nephrologist at Weill-Cornell Medicine in New York. She is married to Dr. Augustine Choi, a lung research specialist and dean of Weill-Cornell.

In 2017, we celebrated our thirtieth wedding anniversary, as well as fifty years since our families had left Korea. When we first met in the United States as doctors in training, we were struck by how similar our stories were and felt as if we had been living completely parallel lives. Maybe our friends were right—maybe meeting each other was meant to be.

***

Both of our families were part of the large migration of people from the north of Korea to the south in the years following World War II and leading up to the Korean War. Mary's grandfather was a lawyer and a landlord who also owned a factory in the south, and her parents grew up in Pyongyang, now the capital of North Korea. As trouble started brewing, the family decided to pack up and move. Mary's father was smuggled out in the middle of the night in a wagon as the border was closing and hid in the mountains. Fortunately, he and everyone in the family made it through to the south. Augustine's family was not so lucky. His grandfather was a trader who had gone north in search of work and settled near the border with Manchuria. When the family later fled south, the younger brother of Augustine's father became separated from them in the chaos, and they never discovered what happened to him.

Traditional Korean wedding ceremony known as Pyebaek, symbolizing the joining of the two families, rather than just two individuals: Bride, groom, and parents wearing the hanbok—traditional Korean attire for the wedding ceremony. Left to right: Philip and Connie Choi (parents of the bride), Mary Choi, Augustine Choi, Jung Hee and Young Soo Choi (parents of the groom).

In 1950, North Korea—backed by the Soviet Union and China—invaded South Korea. The Communists started rounding up young men and killing people, including academics and medical students, sparing only the senior students capable of sewing sutures—a useful skill during wartime. Augustine's father, Benedict Young Soo Choi, was a medical student at Seoul National University and was made to face a firing squad, blindfolded, seven times. He managed to survive due to misfires, a false claim that he was a senior, a bribe from his mother, and sheer luck. He said that after those experiences, he was never frightened by anything else again.

Mary's father, Philip Sang Koom Choi, also made a narrow escape. After hearing that the Communist Army was coming, he hid in the attic, and Mary's mother, Connie Chungyul Lee, told the soldiers that she was alone in the house. When she noticed that a stack of books had been left directly beneath the attic door, she frantically began distracting the soldiers with story after story so they wouldn't see the books and look up.

Both Choi families were able to start over from scratch in Seoul, the capital of South Korea. Our fathers went to Seoul National University College of Medicine at the same time, although Augustine's was a couple of years younger and the two men didn't know each other. Augustine's father became a cardiothoracic surgeon and went to the United States in the early 1960s to train in heart bypass surgery. He was the first person in Korea—and is believed to be the first in Asia—to perform a successful bypass on a patient. Mary's father became famous for having the crispest white doctor's coat, which always hung perfectly straight. He was a pediatrician and family practitioner, and the family lived upstairs from his clinic in the middle of the old city in Seoul. Augustine's mother, Cecilia Jung Hee Lee, was a ballerina, and Mary's mother stayed at home to take care of the kids.

Both families were also unusual in being Catholic at a time when most Koreans were Protestant or Buddhist. Mary's grandfather had been quite active in promoting Catholicism in the north and became very good friends with a priest who lived with the family for many years. Augustine's father converted to Catholicism as a young man, then asked his fiancée to convert with him and attend catechism classes before getting married. All of our parents and siblings have Catholic names in addition to Korean names. We are both third children, and Mary's brothers are Charles, Thomas, and Joseph. Augustine's siblings are Francisco, Lucia, and Anna.

Coincidentally, our fathers came up with similar plans to leave Korea in 1966 and 1967. Although Augustine's father was doing well as a general surgeon, he felt that the government was corrupt and couldn't see South Korea becoming a first-world country with a good future for his children. He got a government contract to work in Malaysia, as a stepping-stone to moving to the United States, and Augustine left Korea at the age of six. His father was the only physician in a city of seventy-five thousand people and soon learned how to practice all different kinds of medicine. The family lived behind a six-bed infirmary, and Augustine helped the nursing staff and ran chores when he wasn't at school.

Mary's father decided to leave Korea to expand the family's horizons—so his children could experience different cultures and learn English. He also got a government contract, on the island of Jamaica, and took his wife, daughter Mary, and youngest son to live for five years in Kingston. At the age of eight, Mary didn't speak a word of English and learned her ABCs from a multicolored children's dictionary in a Catholic girls' school, eventually skipping a couple of grades when the nuns realized how advanced she was in other areas. Mary's two older brothers stayed in Korea with their grandparents to finish high school. When his contract was up, her father thought it was the right time to move to the United States so the boys could attend colleges.

Most Koreans who immigrate to the US end up going where other Koreans are. They generally move to California, New York, or maybe Chicago. Our parents looked around and didn't want to move to the big cities. Augustine's family ended up settling in Kentucky. Mary's landed, like Dorothy, in the middle of nowhere, Kansas. We both grew up as part of the only Korean families in our communities.

Although our fathers had been licensed and practicing physicians for more than fifteen years when they arrived in the US, they were considered foreign medical graduates and couldn't treat a single patient until they had completely retrained. Both had to pass an exam for certification in the US, using the English they had just learned, even though medicine in Korea was then taught using German texts. Then they had to go through internship and residency training again in their mid-forties, with young doctors telling them what to do. Augustine's father decided to specialize in geriatrics, and Mary's became an internist.

Our fathers were the first physicians in our families, and both of us decided early on that we wanted to follow in their footsteps. In many ways, we were living the somewhat typical lives of Korean immigrants in the US. But everything changed for us based on a single night, when our fathers decided to attend a gala dinner in Los Angeles for alumni of their medical school. They met for the first time there in LA, discovered that they both had children in medicine, and thought that maybe we should meet and at least become friends. They were also pretty traditional and, since they hoped their children would marry someone Korean, had been trying to do some matchmaking. We wanted to be good kids and agreed to meet.

Left to right: Justin Choi (older son), Augustine M. K. Choi,
Mary Choi, and Alex Choi (younger son).

The only problem was that we were on opposite ends of the country: Mary was in California doing her residency, and Augustine was in North Carolina doing his. Augustine insisted we meet on neutral ground in the middle of the country, no strings attached. So we both came up with a weekend date when we would be off duty, flew to Chicago, and met at the Marriott Hotel—with our parents along for the ride. We were all curious to meet each other. After we had checked into the hotel, Augustine called to let everyone know he was in the hotel lobby. After hearing his deep, low, projecting voice on the phone, Mary's father remarked, "This is it, Mary."

Mary met Augustine for lunch and thought there could be some potential there. We were both very nervous and a little awkward. But as they say, the rest is history.

Today we have two sons, Justin and Alex, who are the third generation in medicine—a physician and a medical student. We've lived in the US much longer than we ever lived in Korea, and our close relatives have all since immigrated. Our children were born here and don't speak Korean but still identify with their Korean heritage. We consider ourselves to be Korean at times, American at times, and Korean American. We both feel a strong responsibility to do what we can to help Korean Americans and Americans in the US through charitable and professional organizations. We are also very proud whenever we meet students who want to go into medicine. Perhaps we sense a little bit more of a connection with them, and maybe they see us as role models, an example of what is possible in the US when people from all ethnic backgrounds are able to pursue their dreams, which is the quintessential American dream.

Bradley Hirschfield

Rabbi Bradley Hirschfield is an author and an Orthodox rabbi who is President of the National Jewish Center for Learning and Leadership, a think tank for Jewish leaders, rabbis, and scholars.

How does an Orthodox rabbi descend from great-grandparents who had a general ambivalence about all organized religion, and no love for rabbis in particular, to say the least? It's a story of faith, actually—faith in themselves, in each other, in the future, and in the promise those great-grandparents saw in the United States of America.

My maternal grandmother's parents, Sam Plotkin and Sarah Plotnikoff, both came from the district of Minsk, in the country today known as Belarus. Sam was born to a reasonably prosperous family of coach- and cabinetmakers, and even though he worshipped Sarah and Sarah loved him back, Sarah's father and stepmother couldn't stand Sam. He had three strikes against him, even if that was not how they would have described it, either in Russian or in Yiddish.

For starters, Sam was two years younger than Sarah, which was a minor scandal in their world. Next, he was a largely secular Jew, while her parents were strictly religious. And finally, Sam had every intention of going to America, where he believed he could make more of his life than the Russian imperial authorities would allow, having denied him permission to expand an already thriving family business from the Jewish towns around Minsk to the city center itself. They didn't want Jews "stealing" business from "real Russians."

Once he heard that, Sam knew it was time to go. He just hoped to marry Sarah and take her with him after he did so. Her parents determined to stop that, even if it meant sending their daughter far away to live with her brother in Glasgow, Scotland. Off on a boat Sarah was sent, but a fiercely determined Sam soon followed. Almost comically, her father, stepmother, and two half sisters soon followed in what became a global game of "follow that girl." They were, however, too late—at least from their perspective.

By the time the Plotnikoff parents got to Scotland, Sam and Sarah had married, and she was already pregnant. Sam had wasted no time, knowing that the only thing worse in his father-in-law's eyes than having him for a son-in-law would be having his precious Sarah become a single mother. Sarah's parents then accepted their new son-in-law.

With his family life reasonably settled, Sam set out for America, Sarah's parents returned to Russia, and Sarah lived with her brother, who divided his time between being a professional wrestler—Plotnikoff the Wrestling Jew—and building what became prospering businesses in both lumber and wool.

It took until 1902, more than three years after his departure from Glasgow, for Sam to be financially secure enough to send for his family and care for them as he hoped to. Sarah and Sam were reunited at a port in Detroit, where he not only reconnected with the long-not-seen love of his life but met two-and-a-half-year-old Lottie, the eldest of what would be the six children that he and Sarah ultimately had. My grandmother, Sophia, was the fourth among them.

Sophie, as she was called, was raised along with her siblings in suburban Detroit, and that too is part of my great-grandparents' great American story. Not only did Sam build a thriving business, constructing and operating small hotels and rooming houses and even being included—to his family's great pride—in a volume entitled *Men Who Made Michigan*, Sam and Sarah raised their family in a grand home in Birmingham, located about midway between downtown Detroit and Pontiac. It turns out, that was a very big deal.

Birmingham, in those years anyway, maintained covenants that did not allow Jews to purchase homes. So how did they pull it off? When I was a child, I asked my great-grandmother that very question. "Easy," she said, in her thick Yiddish accent, which she kept as she aged, along with her perfectly coiffed hair, brightly colored silk dressing gowns, and more gold jewelry than Mr. T. "Money. We paid for the house twice—once to the owner and the same amount to our neighbors." That day in the living room of her Palm Springs, California, home, Sarah told the story not with shame about what they had had to do, but with a deep sense of pride about having been able to do so. And the pride she felt was about much more than money.

To settle in Birmingham was to prove that what was true in Russia—that there was no room for all people to rise to their own full potential—was not true in the United States. Settling in Birmingham, even with all the shenanigans it required, was light-years ahead of the world that Sam and Sarah had left behind. And even though there was plenty of anti-Semitism in America then, especially among the very elite ranks to which Sam and Sarah wanted to belong, they believed it could be otherwise, and they were able to make it so. Like I said, it was a story of faith.

Sam and Sarah Plotkin might not have believed in God or the Bible, but they certainly believed in the Bible's first story—the story in which all people, regardless of race, religion, or ethnicity, are endowed with infinite worth and dignity, and are meant to live up to the fullness of their creative capacities and abilities, whether in good times or in bad. They not only believed that story, they bet their lives on it, and on the faith that thousands of miles from the lives they knew, in a country where they couldn't speak the language, they could build their own path to greater dignity, worth, and freedom. If that isn't faith, I don't know what is.

I love Sam and Sarah's story, both because it is uniquely mine—or, at least, my family's—and because it is so typical of millions of other stories. I love that their story includes personal idiosyncrasies and Jewish particularities, even as it also reflects the universal striving that has built, and continues to build, the country Sam and Sarah made theirs, and that made them who they were. I love it, not because it is a story with a clear happy ending, but because it is the story of a great new beginning, and that is what I mean by faith, and among the things I love best about this country.

Deborah Norville

Deborah Norville is a journalist and businesswoman. She is host of the television show Inside Edition.

Chicken thieves. Growing up, I had been led to believe that I was descended from a bunch of chicken thieves. On my Southern-born daddy's side, that is.

On my Midwestern mother's side of the genealogical divide, it was different. There was the Swedish pastor who'd written a book and the great-uncle who'd been a cop. We still had the nightstick he once carried on his rounds.

My mom's family tree was a tidy, espaliered specimen whose branches were easy to read with relations that could be traced back centuries. My mother was second-generation Swedish American. Her grandparents came through Ellis Island during the great migration of the late 1880s. Back in the old country, thanks to Sweden's famed neutrality, there had been no wars to destroy birth and death records—so the Olsons and Axelsons and Dahlsons from which I come can be easily traced.

My dad's family tree seemed more like an overgrown bush. It appeared to have so many branches and tiny shoots, you figured pretty much everyone in the county where Daddy grew up was a cousin. So you greeted someone as a cousin even if you couldn't quite prove it.

I never knew how the chicken-thieves story got started, but I think it always irked Daddy to imagine there were unsavory folk among his kin. In his later years, it gnawed at him so much he just had to know the truth. That's when Daddy—and anybody he could drag along with him—started haunting graveyards and visiting county courthouses.

81

Ground zero on his search was all those cousins in Oconee County, Georgia. Armed with his lined yellow legal pads, he wrote down everything anybody could remember about their relatives, and what they couldn't remember was generally written inside the family Bible. Then Daddy visited innumerable probate offices, where he no doubt sweet-talked a clerk or two into helping him find birth and death certificates. That, of course, was just the beginning. It wasn't enough for Daddy to see the piece of paper confirming a forebear's departure from this mortal earth—he had to then find the cemetery where their bones moldered in the grave. My younger sisters were often along for this grim task—which always included making chalk rubbings of the headstones.

The weeks and months of Daddy's quest grew into years—and the picture of who he was in terms of where he came from grew clearer. And there were no chicken thieves anywhere to be found!

There was the relative who fought at Gettysburg in what was sometimes referred to where I grew up as the War of Northern Aggression. The apocryphal tale that Daddy told about him was that he was shot in the chest and left in the mud, which somehow stanched the bleeding and saved his life. There was the forebear who was enough of an elder statesman in Colonial Williamsburg that a church pew bears his name. Daddy found relatives who fought for our nation's independence during the Revolutionary War and in the French and Indian War before that. But the capstone in Daddy's quest had to be when he made the provable link to Peter Brown—one of the passengers on the Mayflower. Mayflower—not chicken thieves!

While Daddy was on his quest, I took a genealogical journey of my own, traveling to Sweden to see where my great-grandparents on my mom's side had come from. I felt guilty for laughing at Daddy's graveyard jaunts, because here I was doing the same thing.

On Sweden's west coast, I found the grave of Great-Aunt Bertha. She had immigrated to the United States but then returned home to Sweden, disappointed the streets of America were not paved in gold as she'd been led to believe. In a tiny church in central Sweden, I found a baptismal stool with the name Axel Anderson—Grampa Axelson's father had been christened here!

But the real magic of that trip to my Swedish roots came on Midsummer Eve. An old Swedish wives' tale holds that if, on Midsummer's Eve, a single girl picks seven different wildflowers and sleeps with them under her pillow, she will dream that night of her future husband. Wildflowers indeed were picked, and we danced around the Midsummer pole, as all Swedes do on that day of round-the-clock sun. Truth be told, there was no pillow and no one slept. We stayed up all night and delighted in the perpetual light.

There must be something to that wives' tale.

The following day, a couple I had met at the party ran into an old friend back home in Sweden from New York. They mentioned me to him—and whatever they said must have sparked some interest. Karl Wellner called me for a date. Two years later, we were married—intertwining his modern immigrant story of a man who came to America and created businesses and opportunities for others—with mine, which extends centuries before.

When I was a child, the words *Remember where you come from* would often be the last thing I'd hear as the screen door slammed behind me. Back then, I took it as a threat: "Whatever trouble you get into, I'll find out about."

Today I see *Remember where you come from* as a bumper sticker for a richer life. Knowing more about the roads traveled by those from whom I am descended has made history come alive for my children and me. It is also a source of quiet comfort. What I might see as challenges are mere inconveniences compared to my ancestors' struggles. Accomplishments shine less brightly, too. I am after all, only one patch in my family's immigration story, which is in turn only one square in this giant quilt we call America.

A quilt square on its own is of little use. Joined together with others, it is part of something extraordinary. Like America.

The Originals

/////

Ray Halbritter

"You don't stumble upon your heritage. It's there, just waiting to be explored and shared."

— Robbie Robertson

Every American is an immigrant, with the exception of the Native Americans, who are the indigenous people of the Americas. They formed the first of many confederacies that would govern this land.

This chapter brings to life the story from one of the leaders of the Oneida Indian Nation, an indigenous nation of Native American people whose sacred and sovereign homelands are located in Central New York. The Nation was a key ally of the United States during the Revolutionary War, and it has been a cultural and economic anchor for the region. Through its diversified business enterprises, the Oneida Nation has become one of the largest employers in Upstate New York.

Ray Halbritter

Ray Halbritter is National Representative of the Oneida Indian Nation Inc. and CEO of Oneida Nation Enterprises.

My people and I did not come to America; we were on American shores welcoming immigrants to our country. We have been here since before there ever was a thing called America. We have been here since before there was even a word for history. We have been here since time immemorial. But even with our heritage that spans the eons of time, our story in many ways has a similar arc as immigrants' stories—it is the tale of the other being treated as an invisible stranger in a seemingly strange land.

I am the grandson of an Oneida leader and the son of a nurse. I was part of a community barely subsisting in broken-down trailers on a remote cornfield. We were a forgotten people, neglected in a country that so often lauds itself for its devotion to community. In those difficult years, we were not just forgotten—some of us did not survive. Members of my family burned to death when local officials quite literally refused to respond to a fire.

Even before that tragic blaze, I remember that feeling of otherness in our isolation as an Indian tribal nation surviving on thirty-two muddy acres, the remainder of a homeland originally spanning six million acres. Like most of my fellow Oneidas, we grew up without material wealth. Not poor. Early in life, my mother would walk three miles each way to catch the bus downtown to work cleaning houses, and remarkably, she was able to teach herself how to read by listening to hymns at church and following the words in the songs.

In my twenties, I was working as an ironworker in Washington, DC, to try to make a living. It was grueling physical work, but it was the kind of work that Native Americans gravitated to because it was challenging and one of the few viable opportunities for us. Even though we were the first Americans, and even though my people had literally fought alongside George Washington in the Revolutionary War, we were, in those years, all but forgotten allies.

Working in the nation's capital was a fortuitous turn of events for me. In the early 1970s, when I was twenty-one, there was an event there that I was fortunate to be a part of known as the Trail of Broken Treaties. It was a Native American protest against the federal government, which culminated in a long standoff in the offices of the Bureau of Indian Affairs in Washington, DC.

I distinctly remember it being one of those awakening events that tend to happen in your early life. I began to consider our people, our plight, and how we might alter our destiny, and so I came back to central New York with a renewed sense of purpose and mission.

That sense of purpose, though, still faced a great test. I was living in my trailer on the small patch of Oneida Indian Nation land we still had. Just across the road an inferno broke out, and that is when that haunting feeling of otherness kicked in.

That night, we frantically called the local fire department for help. Despite the sounds of desperate cries, the local authorities ignored us, leaving members of my family to die in the blaze. To this day, I have never been able to forget the smell of their bodies lying there smoldering in the carnage. I felt incredibly deep resentment for a long while after that, and I struggled against letting it consume me. I experienced all of the typical feelings of alienation and loss: depression, anxiety, and anger. Those powerful emotions could have consumed me and my tribal nation, but we did not allow that. We would not allow the otherness to be a cultural death sentence, and instead, we made it our strength—a rallying motivation.

Yes, just like immigrants, we are different and we are unique. Yes, like immigrants, we have our own history and our own culture. Yes, like immigrants, we still face the ugly trifecta of xenophobia, racism, and bigotry. And yes, like immigrants, we do not retreat or cower—we create our own place in this country and in this world, and we feel enigmatic pride in the greatness of our distinct heritage.

After the blaze, I had a life mission—one focused on working to make sure our people are truly self-sufficient and never have to rely on others for our most basic necessities. That mission focused me on education, and I got a great one at Syracuse University and then at Harvard Law School. That education provided to me the tools to give back to my community by strengthening our sovereign rights and beginning to plan new enterprises that could begin a renaissance for our people.

It has been a long and difficult path, but we have been successful. Nothing succeeds like success. Our journey has made us more determined and stronger, and it has constantly reminded us of why we must stand in solidarity with all those who face otherization. Whether Native Americans or immigrants, we will always face hostility from those who seek to denigrate our heritage and our community. But we will always know that we are all brothers on this Earth, and that the coming together of the diversity of this country's culture is its biggest strength.

The Rescuers

///////

Jon and Mary Kaye Huntsman

Zach Iscol

Ryan Platt

Debora Spar

Matt Tomasic

Ask Me What I Was
I'll reply with what I've done.
Those things others would not do, I did,
Those rivers others would not swim, I swam,
Those hills others would not climb, I conquered,
Those bridges others would not cross, I crossed;
I have celebrated. I have mourned.
I have smiled and I have frowned.
I have seen death and felt its warm breath.
It did not faze me, for I was different.
I was a warrior.
You ask me what I was?
It was my destiny. Until my last breath.
To be a United States Marine.
And my spirit shall live forever.

— US Marine poem

It takes a special kind of compassion and courage to risk your own life in order to save another's. As you'll see in this chapter, saviors and rescuers can come in many shapes and sizes. They are adoptive parents who opened their homes and their hearts to children from other countries, established immigrants who help families that have recently arrived in the US, or an Iraqi interpreter who risked his life and the lives of his family to help Marines stationed in Iraq.

The Rescuers keep others from harm and remind us of our common humanity.

Jon and Mary Kaye Huntsman

The Honorable Jon and Mary Kaye Huntsman are in Moscow, where he serves as the United States Ambassador to Russia. Previously he served as Governor of Utah and Ambassador to China and to Singapore.

We have seven children total, including two adopted daughters, one from China and one from India. It all started when we were living in Taiwan in 1987 and I was pregnant with our third child. There was a Catholic orphanage down the street from where we lived, and every time I passed it I wanted to go through those doors.

One day I just knocked on the door, and a nun answered. She couldn't speak English and I couldn't speak Chinese, so I just motioned that I wanted to come inside. I saw children lying on a mat, and it made me terribly sad that many of them would never be adopted. After I saw those children, I went home and told Jon that we had to adopt one day. He said maybe someday, but not today, as we already had two children and a third on the way. Twelve years went by, and we had two more children. On May 19, 1999, Jon came to me suddenly and said he wanted to adopt, and that he wanted to adopt from China. "What if we called her Gracie Mei?" he said. I couldn't believe that after twelve years he was finally ready.

We went through the adoption process and got a call that there was a six-month-old girl in Yangzhou, China, who had been left in a vegetable market. I asked when her birthday was, and they told me it was May 19, 1999. It's just one of those things in life, that the night Jon decided we should adopt was the night she was born. We've been back to Yang-zhou several times since, and Gracie Mei has a real connection to the city. They made a postal stamp in her honor, and many people looked to her as the bridge between the US and China when Jon was the US ambassador to China. We have visited the orphanage where she lived and the market where she was left, and it has had quite an impact on her. Gracie considers herself very lucky, because she still has friends in the orphanage who remember her from when she was there, the older kids who never left. She feels that she has a great responsibility because she was given a great opportunity. She's very mindful, always, that she wants to give back to others.

When Asha arrived, Jon had just become the governor of Utah. It was 2005, and we decided that it was just so amazing with Gracie that we had to do it one more time. We wanted to go to India, because Jon had spent a lot of time there, but also it was just another one of those things. People always ask why did you go here or there to adopt, and my answer is because that's where my baby was. You're just kind of drawn somewhere.

We got a picture of Asha when she was two months old, but we didn't get to hold her until she was fourteen months old. She was left in an abandoned field filled with wild animals in Gujarat, and a farmer happened to hear her cry. She was a brand-new baby, hadn't been cleaned or anything, and she wouldn't have made it through the night. The farmer brought her to the police, who brought her to the orphanage, where she stayed for fourteen months.

Our greatest gift to our biological children was the gift of our adopted girls. Our older kids have been able to watch their sisters grow up and have opportunities that they wouldn't have had otherwise. There are many ways that people come to America. For us, we felt strongly about giving Gracie Mei and Asha a better life. It's interesting to talk about immigration and why people come here. Everyone has a story. And every story is important to tell.

Zach Iscol

Zach Iscol is a combat-decorated former Marine Corps officer. Zach served two tours in Iraq and on other assignments throughout Africa, the Middle East, and Central Asia in the infantry and special operations.

In the far-off distance, bombs and artillery lit up the night sky from just beneath the horizon. Every so often, a large flash would illuminate the buildings on Fallujah's northern edge that faced the desert like a fortress wall.

"It looks like the walls of Troy," Abood remarked as he shifted his seat and lay back down on the bench in our Humvee facing the open sky.

Weeks earlier, during a mission on the city's southern edge, Abood and I had walked down the bank of the Euphrates River. Abood loved history, and he would tell me and any other marine who would listen about ancient Mesopotamia, the birthplace of civilization, right here in Iraq. How far back did we have to go to find a shared relative who farmed along the banks of this river?

On other nights he would point to the constellations and ask what we called them in English.

"That one is Dub Al Akbar, the great bear."

"That's the Big Dipper," I'd reply.

"And that, that is Al Jaffar, the giant."

"We call that Orion, the hunter."

When US forces first entered Iraq in the spring of 2003, Abood Al Khafajee was one of thousands of Iraqis who greeted them as liberators. He had grown up with American movies and pop culture.

America meant something to him, and he made his way to greet the first American unit that entered his town south of Baghdad. When an officer from that unit asked him if he could help them find a translator, he promptly ran back to town and brought back a carpenter. That began his five-year career as an interpreter for US and coalition forces in Iraq. Two of his daughters would also go on to serve as interpreters.

I met Abood on July 4, 2004. I had assumed command of a combined action platoon of 250 Iraqi National Guard soldiers and thirty US Marines. Abood was assigned as one of my translators.

That summer was one of Iraq's most violent. Al Qaeda in Iraq held the city of Fallujah and was using it as a base to launch suicide attacks and kidnapping attempts. For four months, we operated twenty kilometers east of Fallujah in a small town called Nasr Wa Salaam.

At first, I was concerned how this small, slight man who looked like Geppetto from *Pinocchio* would ever be able to keep up with marines half his age on long patrols in 120-degree heat. I soon realized how wrong I was. I also realized that he was our unit's most important asset.

Abood guided me through the intricacies of meetings with tribal leaders, city council members, my Iraqi officers, and the local citizens. He made sure I was a gracious host who followed local customs. He did far more than translate words—he interpreted subtleties in conversation and actions. One sheikh's refusal to eat and break bread with us was a threat. Another's inquiry into a never-completed construction project was a hint about corruption in the coalition-appointed city council. I'm convinced that our unit was never attacked in the city where we lived because of the relationships Abood helped us build.

In November, we were ordered to retake Fallujah in what became the biggest battle of the Iraq War and the largest one fought by US Marines since the battle for Hue City in Vietnam in 1968.

Throughout it all, Abood was as fearless as he was compassionate. There was the time my platoon was hit by a roadside bomb. Abood was headed home to see his family, and when he heard the news, he turned around his car and drove out to meet us where we'd been hit. Having his personal car seen in that situation put him in grave danger, but he was more worried about his young marines.

And then there was the time during the battle of Fallujah when we needed to evacuate a dozen civilians. We'd encountered a suicide bomber the day before and were worried that there might be another hidden among the group of older men, women, and children. This was made more complicated by the fact that it wasn't culturally acceptable to have a marine search Iraqi women. Instead, Abood stepped forward, walked into the small crowd, and started patting people down, comforting kids and ushering them through our lines. As an older Iraqi man, this was a far better option than having an eighteen-year-old marine in body armor, Oakley sunglasses, and armed to the teeth do the job.

Like thousands of other interpreters in Iraq and Afghanistan, Abood wore the Marine Corps uniform in combat. And he did so at great risk to himself and to his family.

Two years later, insurgents left a severed dog's head on his doorstep. A note warned that he and his family would be next if they didn't flee Iraq.

Abood emailed me that he was headed to Jordan with his wife and daughters. And that's when another fight began—to get them to the United States.

As Iraq succumbed to greater sectarian violence, interpreters and other Iraqis who worked with US and coalition forces became easy and valuable targets. Insurgents and terrorist organizations knew how valuable they were. Unfortunately, the US government had no programs in place to provide them safe passage to America. Instead, many fled to Syria, Jordan, and Kurdistan.

With little recourse, I put on my uniform and traveled to Capitol Hill and began knocking on doors of senators and representatives, hoping and praying that someone in the halls of Congress would do the right thing and establish a special immigrant program to provide asylum to those who put their lives in danger in service of our country.

Senators Arlen Specter and Ted Kennedy answered my prayers. A few months later, they held hearings on the issue, and Abood and his family received refugee status and referral to the United States for resettlement. Eventually, Congress established a special visa program for other interpreters and Iraqi and Afghan allies.

The day Abood arrived in New York, we settled his family in a small apartment in Bay Ridge, not far from where my own family settled a hundred years ago on their journey to escape the Russian pogroms targeting Jews in Eastern Europe. We then walked through the city.

Abood was awestruck.

Four years later, Abood passed away from lung cancer, but his daughters continue to follow in his footsteps. One is an NYPD officer and another is applying to join the force. Though their family has already given so much to our country, like so many other immigrants, they feel a deep sense of gratitude reflected in their continued service.

Ryan Platt

Ryan Platt is an undergraduate at Cornell University.

To be honest, I've never thought of myself as an immigrant.

Although I was born 江福兵 in Guangzhou, China, a sixteen-hour plane ride is where my story really begins. At only eight months old, I was taken from the Social Welfare Institute of Yangjiang City and brought by my adoptive mother to the United States of America. I have no information on where I was born, who birthed me, or why I was rejected. I can theorize as much as I like, but I will never know the truth and I will never hear an explanation. Was my abandonment the result of China's one-child policy? Was I the only girl in a family of boys? What was it exactly that brought me to the doorstep of that orphanage?

Surprisingly, or maybe not so surprisingly, not knowing my origins has never been a big concern for me. When I started kindergarten, kids would often pepper me with questions: Why don't you look like your mommy? Have you ever met your real parents? Do you know who they are? While I shrugged most of them off, there was no denying my adoption. It only took one look at my Caucasian mother to know that we do not share the same DNA.

Unlike other immigrants, adapting to life in the United States was not really an issue for me. It's all I've ever known. In my mind, I was just another New York City kid whose days were filled with school, playdates, ballet practice, and banging on the piano in my attempt to make music.

It was only a couple of years ago, after watching a documentary about a little girl returning to the country where she was born, that I became curious enough to do the same. Thus, in 2015, my mom and I hopped on a plane heading to China, toward the place where I had been an orphan fifteen years prior.

After traveling as tourists along the eastern coast of China, we journeyed to a run-down town called Yangjiang. There, I came face-to-face with my past.

We entered a square surrounded by concrete buildings with barred windows and faded colors. What I saw did not resemble a space made for children. Upon our arrival, the orphanage director led us up a flight of stairs to a group of at least twenty orphans: little girls of all ages with short-cropped hair, dressed in hand-me-down clothes and many sadly disfigured. A low gate separated us from them as I tried to speak to these children, hoping to be more than just another person passing through. The reality that I was once on the other side of the barrier was overshadowed by my pangs of sorrow. I imagined all the times these deserted kids had to watch people come, just to see them go.

The visit did not feel personal; it was more upsetting than anything else. My brain was occupied with finding ways to help the orphans but realizing that I couldn't. I failed to even once think that that small, impoverished town was where I was born.

Looking back, I see the life I could have lived. No family. No support. I would have been in a place devoid of opportunity. My future would be drastically different had I been raised in China and had I not been given a second chance.

Not that I wasn't grateful before, but this visit made me a thousand times more appreciative of having been brought up in this country I call my home. On top of that, seeing my history in person confirmed what I already knew to be true: my mom is my *real* mom, family is stronger than blood, and I am a New Yorker and an American through and through.

My story may be a bit unlike other immigrants'. There is nothing I know or can say about what came before me. I arrived in the United States on a green card and with a Chinese passport in hand. And being so young, I never had to study to become a national. As the child of an American, I was automatically eligible for citizenship under a law passed during the Clinton administration in 2000. So no, I wasn't born here. No, I can't become president. But I am nonetheless an American.

Debora Spar

Debora Spar is the former President and Chief Executive Officer of Lincoln Center for the Performing Arts. Until recently she was president of Barnard College.

My family aren't generally into genealogy. Maybe it's because, as my mother is fond of saying, we are so very small. Or because our most immediate forebears were scattered across both time and place, some trooping over from the French-German borders of Alsace, others from the even vaguer regions that have slithered, historically, between Russia, Poland, and Belarus. There are no family tartans or regal bloodlines, just snippets of family lore that no one's ever really bothered to investigate.

I know they all came from Europe around the turn of the twentieth century, before the Nazis decimated whoever had been left behind, and once railways and regular ocean passage began to pave a possible escape to the purported riches and liberty of the United States. They came, like hundreds of thousands of European Jews, through the entry point at Ellis Island and into the streets and tenements of the Lower East Side. My paternal great-grandfather was reportedly one of thirteen sons who emigrated from somewhere around Minsk, each sequentially earning his way in New York and then sending cash back for his next brother's passage. They—we—didn't stray too far from New York over successive generations, or even from the rag trade that had supported these initial journeys. My paternal grandfather owned a ladies' lingerie shop in Yonkers. My maternal grandfather sold small woven goods around the mid-Atlantic region. He died when I was still young, but two tangible memories remain: the big cars he so proudly drove, reeking, always, of cigars, and the knit toilet paper covers he sold, a tiny doll's head attached to a voluminous knit skirt, stretched ever so modestly to cloak the offending roll.

We are five generations removed now from my birth family's migration. My built family, by contrast, is newer and more diverse. A husband who emigrated twice himself, from Greece and then Canada, and a daughter whom we adopted, at age six, from Russia. My eldest son moved to Brooklyn a few years ago, recapturing the newly hip neighborhood from which his great-grandparents so eagerly fled three generations ago. The restaurant along the Brooklyn waterfront that was mother's favorite place to celebrate as a child is now a Russian grocery store where I take my daughter to stock up on the candies she remembers from home. And, after I moved back to New York in 2008, a cousin I didn't know I had told me of our mutual great-great-grandfather, who was apparently a carpenter to the last Russian tsars living in Ekaterinburg. If that's true, then my birth roots stretch back to the exact town from which I would eventually adopt my daughter, over a century later.

Meanwhile, my children—like most of their friends, and colleagues, and classmates—are happy mutts, mixed from generations of those who searched for a better life and began to marry across what once were impenetrable, inconceivable boundaries. My own brood are French and Russian and German and Polish and Greek. They are adopted and not. Jewish and Greek Orthodox. Rootless, but not. They are American.

Matt Tomasic

Matt Tomasic is a retired police officer who served with the Kansas City, Missouri police force.

My grandpa Nicolas Tomasic was the best. He was a kind man, and I wish you could have known him. He was my friend and I loved him very much. I can't imagine growing up without him. He was also an immigrant. If his life was judged by material possessions, he would not rank near the top, or the middle, for that matter.

By the time I was born, he was well into his seventies and retired, living on Social Security, from over fifty years of work in the Kansas City meatpacking houses. He and my grandma lived in a nine-hundred-square-foot house one block away from us. He never owned a car or had a driver's license and never spoke English well.

Growing up, I lived with my parents and five brothers and sisters, down the street from my grandparents. There are eleven years between my oldest sister and youngest brother. Most days I would go and visit my grandpa. This worked out for my poor mother, because she had her hands full with all of us kids.

Many mornings, before I was in grade school, I would go to his house and have coffee and canned peaches with him. My coffee was 95 percent milk and sugar. We would sit at the table and talk. Weather permitting, we would go on walks around the neighborhood. As I grew, we would often talk about the Kansas City Royals baseball team and their chances of success. He was a huge baseball fan. He always had or made time for his grandchildren, seldom missing one of their games.

My grandpa was born in Croatia, in extreme poverty, where there was often not enough food to eat. His parents knew that there was not a chance of a future for him in Croatia. When he was twelve years old, they had saved enough money to purchase a third-class ticket on a ship bound for America. When he boarded the ship, he knew nothing of America, the culture, or the English language. He had almost no education and even less money. What he did know was that he was alone and terrified and that he would probably never see or speak with his mother and father again. This is something his parents also knew before putting him on that ship.

My grandpa arrived at Ellis Island after several days at sea. He had contracted smallpox while on the voyage and was placed in observation. If his condition did not improve, he would be returned to Croatia. After several weeks at Ellis Island, he was cleared for further travel into America.

After train rides and more time, my grandpa arrived near Kansas City, where he lived with a cousin he had never met. He got his first job at a meatpacking house. He worked six days a week, opening the doors to the kill floor and holding them to let the cattle pass. He made nine cents per hour.

Nine years after he arrived in Kansas City, he married and then had four children. The first two were girls. Both girls died of pneumonia before their second birthdays.

Penicillin had not yet been invented. His next two children were boys, Tom and Nick Anthony, my father. They lived and grew up in the mostly Croatian community, known as Strawberry Hill, in Kansas City, Kansas.

Like many immigrants, my grandpa struggled with the English language and spoke with a very thick accent. He lived in a neighborhood, attended a church, worked with and had friends who spoke his native language. When you go to a church service, you want to pray and understand it in your own language. My grandpa knew that if he could learn the English language, life here would be simpler and he would have greater economic prospects. With no formal education to speak of and the demands of work and trying to survive, it seemed an impossible task.

The meatpacking houses of today are full of immigrants—the difference being the country of origin of the employees. They live in much the same way as those Eastern Europeans who were seeking their future did 120 years before them. They live in neighborhoods with people from their own country, as it is often the most affordable housing available. They struggle with the language and culture. Not because they do not want to assimilate, or choose their culture over American ways. It is for protection and comfort.

My grandpa worked in the meatpacking houses of Kansas City until the age of sixty-eight. His job was one that placed him at the very bottom of the economic ladder. He endured physical labor and dangerous conditions that are now almost unthinkable. I remember his hands, scarred and arthritic from old knife wounds, the product of years of butchering livestock. I remember the burn scar on his back and how it seemed to be the size of a manhole cover. He almost died the day scalding water, used to loosen the hair on hog hide, was accidentally dumped on him while at work. He would talk about the discrimination he faced, having to change his last name from Tomasic to Thomas on an application to get a job. It was because that particular plant would not hire "Hunkies," which is a derogatory term for Croatians. I never heard him complain, it was just the way it was, another challenge he overcame.

He loved this country. Just like his mother and father before him, his sacrifices were made intentionally, to provide a better life for his children. He knew that in America, his hard work could mean a better life for his kids, and his plan worked. His eldest son Tom retired as a decorated captain of the Kansas City, Kansas, fire department. My father, Nick, was the district attorney in Wyandotte County, Kansas, for thirty-eight years. Both of Nicolas's children chose a life of service and never had to work in the packinghouses.

After many years of living in this country, my grandpa became a US citizen. He was then able to participate in an election. He cast his first vote for his son, who was running for district attorney. That was his dream come true.

The Seekers

///

Karim Abouelnaga

Ahmed Ahmed

Ashok Amritraj

Barbara Boxer

Amanda Loyola

Carmen Osbahr-Vertiz

Dr. Mehmet Oz

Gina Raimondo

Mayo Stuntz Jr.

Ask and it will be given to you, seek and you will find, knock and the door will be opened to you.

— Matthew 7:7

Here are the people with indomitable spirit, fearlessness, and more often than not, a bit of luck!

Whether it's a Somali refugee who grew up to become a Rhodes Scholar, an elected official, or a famous doctor, all of these individuals sought and achieved the American dream. The promise of America to all immigrants is opportunity. Hopefully by reading these stories we can all be inspired to help protect that promise.

Karim Abouelnaga

*Karim Abouelnaga is the founder and CEO of Practice Makes Perfect,
a benefit corporation that partners with K-12 schools to deliver high-
quality academic summer programs.*

My father, Adel Abdou Abouelnaga, was the first of our family members to make his way to the United States. He was the oldest of the four
kids my grandfather Abdou Abouelnaga had. My grandfather on my
father's side worked in a shipyard in Egypt in the small city of Port Said.
My father never enjoyed school. He would always share stories of the
adventures he would have jumping off rooftops and catching pigeons
that he would later sell to other people. As he got older, my grandfather
had fallen into some financial hardship and borrowed some money
from one of his siblings. Apparently, he never let my grandfather live
it down.

To pay his uncle back and clear my grandfather's debt, my father left
Egypt and went to France. With no money in his pockets or family in
France, my father slept in the streets and found work as a dishwasher in
a restaurant. He worked as much as he could, taking every opportunity
he could to send money back to his family. Within a couple of years, he
left France on a tourist visa to come to the United States. After a couple
of months, he fell in love and got married. I don't know the full story,
but my father would tell my brothers and me that his marriage to his
first wife, who ultimately helped him get his citizenship, did not work
out because she could not have children.

My father went back to Egypt in the late 1980s to marry my mother,
Mahassen Elkattan. He went to school with one of her siblings when they

were children, and their families knew each other. My mother was one of the youngest in her family of at least ten children. Her father was a successful entrepreneur. For most of my mother's life, her father was building out a furniture business that was later inherited by her older siblings. My father helped my mother get to the United States and get her citizenship.

In 1990, my parents had their first son, my older brother, Moez. I was born second, in 1991, and my parents went on to have three more boys. Though rather strange in the United States, my father had two wives and had two additional kids, who were our half siblings that we grew up with. In the early 1990s, my father drove a yellow cab while my mom stayed home to raise us. At some point in the mid-'90s, my father got into a car accident and won a lawsuit that provided him with what turned out to be seed capital to launch our family business.

Little Egypt Corporation was a dream come true for my father. He imported Egyptian arts and crafts from back home, and we'd sell them at a premium during street fairs in NYC and eventually at a store that he leased on Fifty-Seventh Street and Seventh Avenue. Since the age of five, I would shadow my father. He taught me how to sell, how to negotiate, how to build relationships with customers, and how to manage people.

In the mid-2000s, my father was diagnosed with terminal lymphoma. He passed away in 2007. Neither my mom nor my older brother could continue the family business. Because of my father's lack of life insurance, we sold the merchandise in the store to help cover the funeral costs. Without any income, we gave up the house we lived in and moved into a two-bedroom apartment. Given my parents' inconsistent income, that was the sixth time we'd moved.

My siblings and I all attended public schools. Given our early ambitions of taking over the family business, we had spurts where we wouldn't go to school or care what was happening there. I had sixty absences in seventh grade. I attended my local high school, which at the time had forty-four hundred kids and a 55 percent graduation rate.

I was fortunate enough to escape a dead-end life because of a series of nonprofits and mentors who took an interest in me and invested in my success.

I graduated high school the same year as my older brother, and we were both college-bound the same year. My older brother dropped out two years later. I was the first one in my family to graduate from college. I graduated in the top 10 percent of my class from the School of Hotel Administration at Cornell University. I held internships on Wall Street at Goldman Sachs and at BlackRock. When I was eighteen, I'd learned about the inequalities in public education and rallied a group of friends to start an education organization to address some of them.

Upon graduation, I turned down my full-time job offers to continue building out my education organization, Practice Makes Perfect (PMP). Our company partners with public schools to create high-quality summer learning programs. Today, PMP is a multimillion-dollar education company. After this summer, my team at PMP will have supported over five thousand low-income children, trained almost four hundred aspiring teachers, and created over fifteen hundred seasonal jobs across NYC.

My family's journey to America is still nascent. However, I'm excited by the possibilities that exist for my siblings and me as we continue to grow and learn about all our great country has to offer. We're grateful for the opportunities and the support we've been given during the good times and the challenging times. We stand on the shoulders of giants—the immigrants who came before us and paved the way for the opportunities afforded to us. I'm excited to continue playing a small role in helping level the educational playing field so more immigrants can enjoy the fruits of America's labor.

Ahmed Ahmed

Ahmed Ahmed is a Somali-American who was born in a refugee camp in Kenya and immigrated to the US as a child. He was recently selected to be a Rhodes Scholar and is studying at the University of Oxford.

"Ahmed, what I've come to find in this world is that money does not matter. It comes and goes like the winds." These subtle words from my mom—in the dark confines of our overdue electricity bill—captured the roller coaster of our family's journey. Things weren't always this way for us. In fact, in the context of Somalia, some would say we were living the good life.

My parents met under unusual circumstances. My mom was from a wealthy and well-educated family, while my dad was the son of hard-working blue-collar parents. Their lives crossed paths in a ubiquitous yellow vehicle: my dad was the driver, and my mom was his passenger. My dad was extroverted and eager to converse, which my mom kindly welcomed. They had resonating discussions about faith and family during their trip. "He was very charming," my mom still tells me. They kept in contact, not knowing that they would forge a love that would traverse cultural bounds, shift generational expectations, and challenge societal norms.

After months of dating, my dad eventually proposed to my mom—despite the disapproval of my mom's family. Arranged marriages were commonplace, and my grandparents had an educated wealthy bachelor prepared to marry her. Rebellious and daring however, my parents chose to run away and start their own family.

My parents, like many other couples in Somalia, were eager to have children. Even without a steady source of income, they opted to have three kids, one of whom had to be raised by my grandparents because our circumstances were so challenging. Having little hope for the future of his taxi-driving business, my father began to shift his attention toward entrepreneurial ventures. He would go on to own a small stand in the marketplace selling cigarettes and basic goods. This allowed us to live more comfortably, but my father was always striving for more. It was around the birth of my sister Alwiya, the fifth child in our family, that my father entered a lucrative business as a travel agent. He became one of few people who could book flights out of Somalia, a venture that very quickly raised our socioeconomic status. By the birth of my brother Abdi, the sixth child in our family, we had upgraded our home to a twelve-bedroom mansion with gates and butlers. Our home was not only home to our family, it also housed a few of my father's siblings, as they still faced financial struggles. We were fortunate—we lived comfortably and were able to give back to our local community. These were luxuries we took for granted.

Soon after the birth of my brother, a darkness began to hang over Mogadishu. Resistance from rebel groups would leave the country in turmoil, and eventually those groups overthrew President Siad Barre's regime. With limited law enforcement or protection for Somali citizens, criminals began to decimate the country from within. These were men, not of peace and liberty, but rather machine hearts and machine minds. As one of the more wealthy families in Mogadishu, our home became one of their top targets. Deeply concerned about our well-being, my mom desperately tried to relocate our family, but my father always refused. "This is our country, and these are our people," he would say to her, believing in the generous Somalia that he once knew.

But we soon realized that place my father thought of no longer existed for Somali citizens. In the next three years, our home would be violently robbed multiple times—the last robbery was the tipping point for my family. With violence continuing to increase across our nation, my mom made the executive decision that she would leave Somalia with the kids, and my father could choose to stay if he pleased. After much resistance, he decided to leave with us.

Like many other Somalis fleeing the war-torn country, we followed a "beaten path" and relocated to a small refugee camp in Mombasa, Kenya, called Barawan—a reference to the region of Somalia that most of the refugees had relocated from. Our refugee camp was bare; our home was constructed from primitive materials, including sticks and cloth, and a hole in the ground served as our bathroom. This was a far cry from our life in Mogadishu. But, we made do with what we had. We still considered ourselves fortunate, because even these circumstances were better than life in war-torn Somalia.

It was here, in our refugee camp, that my mother gave birth to me—their eighth and final child. They called me "the lucky baby," because soon after my birth, we were sponsored and granted asylum by the United States—a privilege that my mom still considers to be the greatest of her life.

Surprisingly, when I recently asked her, "Did you have any fears about embarking on a journey to America? Were you scared because you did not know English, or what the country would be like?" my mom responded by saying, "Son, in that moment it was pure joy, no fear whatsoever. There was nothing that we were afraid of because we knew we were free, that we were getting a new chance at life." That hope. That light. That beacon of freedom that our country has served to immigrants from all over the world was what my family saw.

Certainly, they understood that it would not be easy transitioning to a new country without any savings or higher skills, but they did not let that deter their bold visions for our lives in the US. They believed in the American idea and promise that all people were created equal, and that we are all endowed with certain unalienable rights, among these being life, liberty, and the pursuit of happiness. They believed in the land of opportunity—the country that welcomed all people from different walks of life. But, above all, my parents believed in the American people.

We, as citizens of this revolutionary country, sew the fabrics of the American covenants. The premises that our nation was founded on are nothing more than sketches on paper if we do not uphold them with our actions. My parents understood this. Our founding fathers understood this as well. We shape and create America every day.

Me and my mom.

I write this today as a testament to my parents' vision and the American dream that I was afforded. As an undergraduate at Cornell University, I had the opportunity to learn and grow with some of the brightest thought leaders in the world. The Ivy League doors that existed only in the pixels of my computer screen became my reality. I have also been honored to be one of the few who were awarded a Rhodes Scholarship to study at the University of Oxford.

These incredible privileges and opportunities are markedly different from where my journey began. And upon reflection, I recognize that it would not be possible for me and my family to pursue such a life, today. Somalia, our native home, has been placed on a travel ban, limiting the ability of any family from the country to immigrate to the United States. This policy, which is rooted in fear, is at odds with the America that we know and love. The beauty of our nation is that we open our doors—not close them—when we hear the cries of humanity. We welcome those of all backgrounds because each person adds to the beauty of the American mosaic. That is something we cannot lose in the midst of our own fears.

"Give me your tired, your poor, your huddled masses yearning to breathe free, the wretched refuse of your teeming shore. Send these, the homeless, tempest-tost to me, I lift my lamp beside the golden door!" These words, etched on the base plaque of the Statue of Liberty, represent who we are as a country—a generous, kind, free, and welcoming nation of immigrants.

Ashok Amritraj

Ashok Amritraj is an award-winning filmmaker and producer in California. He is a United Nations India Goodwill Ambassador and played tennis professionally for many years.

My father was born in a small town called Erode in southern India in the Salem District of the Madras Presidency, as it was called during the British raj. He was an English honors graduate and an excellent athlete. My father applied to the Administrative Service, did extremely well on the test, and opted to work as an administrator in the Indian Railways.

My mother was one of six children. Her father, Dr. Dhairyam, was a distinguished psychiatrist, which was quite unusual for the time. He was also a huge tennis fan and besides getting his daughter, my mother, into tennis, he always wanted someone in the family to play at Wimbledon. My mother went to Presidency College in Madras and was the first woman chair of the student union as well as the captain of the tennis team at this prestigious institution, an extremely unusual accomplishment and position for a lady in India at that time.

My father moved from the railway offices in Perambor to Sterling Road, where the railways provided living accommodations for their officers, and at the same time, my mother's family moved from a place called Kilpauk to their property on Sterling Road. This seemed to be a geographical assertion by fate.

My father was duly presented to the good doctor and clearly remembers the first time he saw the girl who would be his future bride, perched on a stepladder hanging a painting that had arrived from their old house. The families met to talk and agreed that their children were the perfect match. My parents' wedding took place on December 29, 1949.

When my parents were married, India had recently won its independence from the British, which resulted in the partition that would yield India and Pakistan. The promise that great opportunities were opening up for once-colonized people was clouded by the turmoil that accompanied this forced displacement of citizens from their country and their homes. It was in these difficult times that my parents were married and settled into the Dhairyam household. Soon their first child, Anand, was born, followed by Vijay, and in 1956, I came into the world, as Groucho Marx said, "at an incredibly early age."

The British left us several legacies of their raj and presence, not the least of which was that we all spoke English at school and most of the time at home as well. My mother was a brilliant and pioneering businesswoman who started a business manufacturing corrugated cardboard boxes in our garage. Packaging was new to India. When you bought vegetables or street food, these products were given to you wrapped in an old newspaper. But the country was progressing, and packaging became imperative. My mother spotted this opportunity and potential for future growth. She used the money she made from the factory to buy each of us our first tennis rackets.

Tennis was a very big part of our lives as children, and I thank my mother with all my heart for pushing us to play. We were each chosen by the Indian Junior Davis Cup team to travel abroad to London and Europe to play in the European tennis tournaments with the chance to go pro if we performed well enough. This was my first step toward coming to America, which I had always dreamed about.

English and American movies were quite popular in India, and from a young age I acquired a strong appreciation for them. In between tennis and schoolwork, I would go to the cinema and view some of the classics—*Ben-Hur*, *Guess Who's Coming to Dinner*, *The Graduate*, and of course *The Sound of Music*. Little did I know then that I would meet the stars of these films, the people who stirred these childhood obsessions of mine, and that our paths would cross as friends, colleagues, and partners many years later.

In 1974, I reached the finals of the Wimbledon Junior tournament and very soon thereafter was invited by Dr. Jerry Buss to come to Los Angeles to play for the Los Angeles Strings, one of the teams on the newly created world team tennis tour—the brainchild of Jerry Buss and Billie Jean King. It was the opportunity of a lifetime.

When I first set foot in Los Angeles, I dropped off my bags and visited the great movie studios I had grown up hearing about. I was full of awe and amazement. It was, to me, magical. I knew that this was the place where I wanted to live and this was the industry I wanted to be a part of. This was the industry I wanted to be successful in. But tennis was the family business, and I had to figure out how to make the transition at the right time.

All through the '70s, my brothers and I played at Wimbledon and in the US Open. This was the first time, to the best of my knowledge, that three brothers had played in Wimbledon in the same year. My parents were in the stands, and I hope my grandfather was watching from above and was proud that his grandkids made history at Wimbledon.

In 1978, playing with Ilie Nastase, Chris Evert, and my brother Vijay, I won the World Team Tennis Championships with the Los Angeles Strings and was voted MVP. I got to meet many of my childhood heroes who enjoyed tennis: Sidney Poitier, Charlton Heston, Dustin Hoffman, Frank Sinatra, and many, many more.

Life is a medley of moods and choices; there are ups and downs, triumphs and failures. The most interesting moments are not the highs and lows, but the turning points, the trembling moments of decision, of choosing one direction over another.

While the decision to come to America was not difficult, the decision to leave tennis, a game I loved and that was a great part of my life since a very young age, to enter a profession I knew nothing about, was daunting. I decided to take the plunge, and for the first ten years, it was slow going—learning my craft, persevering even when it seemed pointless, but remembering the lessons I was taught from my previous career. Today, some thirty-five years later, I've had the good fortune to have partnered with every major studio, worked with great movie stars and talented filmmakers, and produced over one hundred films with revenues in excess of $2 billion.

The second major decision I made in my life was an even more personal one. I decided I was ready to get married. It was to be done in the age-old tradition of Indian arranged marriages, with certain concessions to modernity. My parents traveled around the world, and the search yielded three hundred families and girls. The inquiries were discreet, the meetings taking place between the adult relatives of the prospective partners.

Ironically, the young lady who I could not stop thinking about lived ten minutes from our family house in Chennai (formerly Madras) and, luckily, she could not stop thinking about me, either. Both families strongly supported the union, and we were married in 1991 at the same cathedral as my parents. We have been happily married for many years with two wonderful children, born and raised in America.

While I have always worked hard to combine the philosophies of East and West, the opportunities granted to me in America, both in tennis as well as in my career in the entertainment industry, would not have been possible anywhere else in the world. In the early days in the '70s, when my brothers and I stayed with American families while playing on the tennis tour across the United States, we got a very personal glimpse of the extraordinary kindness of families in cities like Columbus, Ohio, Louisville, Kentucky, and South Orange, New Jersey, many of whom still remain our friends. We also learned about the great sense of generosity and the welcoming nature of the American people.

The sense of hard work, discipline, and focus that was forged throughout my tennis career stayed with me when I entered the entertainment industry and has kept me in good stead through the last thirty years in Hollywood. While my parents always instilled in us the importance of taking care of others, it was in America where I realized the true value of philanthropy, and I focused much more on the importance of being a part of and contributing to your community.

As a first-generation Indian immigrant to this country, I could not speak more highly of the extraordinary generosity and courage of the people we've met, the lessons we've learned from families across America, the successful people who have shown us the importance of duty and the responsibility we have to help our fellow citizens, and the encouragement that I have received from my peers, both in tennis and in the entertainment industry. To the young men and women across the world who are ready to persevere, embrace hard work, take chances, follow your dreams, and fulfill your passions, I would say come to America, where it does not matter where you are from or what the color of your skin or chosen religion is—the doors will be open to you. I should know. I have lived it.

Barbara Boxer

The Honorable Barbara Boxer served as a United States Senator from California from 1993 to 2017. A member of the Democratic Party, she previously served in the US House of Representatives from 1983 to 1993.

When I was born on November 11, 1940, my American name was Barbara Sue, while my Jewish name was Brucha Shalomit, meaning "Blessing of Peace."

Yes, I was born on Armistice Day, as it was then called, celebrating the end of World War I, "the war to end all wars." If only that had been true. But on the day of my birth, the world was already in turmoil, with Europe on a war footing for more than a year.

Yet, to my parents, "Blessing of Peace" had another meaning, because to them and to their families, being in America meant peace, and being in America meant freedom.

My mother was brought to New York in 1911 wrapped in the hopes and dreams of her mother's arms. Her family, which included her mom, dad, and five siblings, escaped from the anti-Semitism that had reared its ugly head in Austria many years earlier. They saw the ugly writing on the wall and left. Mom never had the chance to graduate from high school. She was the youngest of six children and the only one living with her parents in New York when her father fell ill and died and she had to work to support her mother. So her plans for her daughters could be described in three words: education, education, education. My dad added a fourth word: education.

Dad was the youngest of nine children and the only one born in America, in 1908. His mom, dad, and eight siblings came over at the turn of the century seeking that peace, security, and prosperity in a new land.

As the boat carrying them entered New York Harbor, my uncle Isaac, the eldest at about twenty years old, determined that the family needed a new name. Blauvasser, a German name—even though they were from Russia—was just too foreign. Of course he could have gone with Blue or Waters or Bluewater, but no. He wanted a truly American name. So he looked at the glory of the New York Harbor and spotted a large retail store that sold men's clothes. It was called Levy's. It looked beautiful, it looked prosperous, and most of all it looked American. So that became our family name. A true American name, said my uncle—not Smith or Jones but Levy.

Uncle Isaac became a very successful businessperson who manufactured lighting fixtures in upstate New York. The other brothers did all kinds of things, from clothing manufacturer to lightweight boxer! My dad was the true American in their eyes and they showered all kinds of things on him, like a brand-new piano, which he often played... American showtunes, of course.

I grew up in a tiny apartment in Brooklyn six blocks from Ebbets Field. Baseball was my family's way into America. We were fanatic about the Brooklyn Dodgers and I cheered my head off for Jackie Robinson and learned my first lessons of equality and civil rights as I saw his courage and bravery in the face of hatred.

My parents loved America so much that I can hardly describe their discussions with me about how lucky I was. I quickly learned that if I had been born in 1940 in Western Europe, my chances of survival would not have been good. Through the many conversations about the Holocaust and Anne Frank, I learned of evil and hatred and tyrants.

All these lessons were to serve me well as I went into politics—a completely accidental happening.

Every time I tried to encourage my mom and dad to take a trip to Europe with me for a summer vacation, they begged off. They truly had not one desire to visit a place that held such pain for them. And when I complained to my dad that I didn't understand why I had to pay taxes to the government when I was a student and had a lowly job at minimum wage, he said, "Kiss the ground of America every time you pay your taxes and count your blessings, honey." (Once I told that story at a community meeting and several people rolled their eyes, as they couldn't rationalize their tax rate, patriotism aside.)

My parents, Sophie and Ira Levy. Taken at my wedding to Stewart Boxer—held in our Brooklyn apartment (January 1962).

My dad went to City College at night, and when he was forty continued to Brooklyn Law School. We were all so proud of him, our renaissance man.

Dad and Mom lived long enough to see me get elected to my first office in California, Marin County supervisor. Mom saw me get to the House of Representatives, where she got to meet one of her heroes, Tip O'Neill.

I have few regrets in my life, but a big one is that neither of my parents lived to see their first-generation daughter on her mother's side get to the greatest legislative body on earth, the United States Senate. I regret it most of all because I never got to tell them that the lessons I learned from them enabled me to be tough and strong and win. They gave me my deep patriotism; they gave me confidence; they said I could be anything I wanted to be if I worked hard; they told me to always do the right thing and not act out of anger but out of clarity. They told me, "In America anything is possible," so I was never afraid to go for the gold.

America welcomed my father's side from Russia and my mother's side from Austria. Nothing was handed to them. They made their way. They played by the rules. They always knew that as immigrants who were tired, who were poor, who were yearning to be free, that they would have a chance... a real chance to become Americans. And they never lost the idea of America. They never doubted for one moment that their offspring could move easily in a place where opportunity and optimism were the guiding lights, and America would always be the shining light for immigrants headed to liberty.

Amanda Loyola

Amanda Loyola is entering her first year at Harvard Business School.

Standing with their heads held high and their hands on their chests, my parents recited the words they had recently memorized to the Pledge of Allegiance. They were in a courthouse in Brooklyn on March 24, 2000, and they were only two out of hundreds of people, all with beaming smiles across their bright, cheery faces. They had finally made it—they had finally received the golden ticket. After years of working hard, paying taxes, sending their children to school, and helping the economy grow, they were given the ultimate stamp of approval and belonging. I was only seven years old when my parents were finally sworn in as the newly minted citizens of the United States of America.

My parents met when they were in high school in Rio de Janeiro, Brazil, in 1978. Even though they grew up in the same city, they came from two very different worlds. My mother grew up in an upper-middle-class neighborhood in Rio, where her mother supported the family with a stable, high-earning job as a nurse at one of the best hospitals in the country. My father grew up in Rocinha, one of the largest favelas (mountaintop slums) in Rio, where the land was free and running water was a work in progress. My paternal grandparents moved to Rio from the northern, more rural region of Brazil, looking to realize their own dreams, but were instead met with subpar living conditions and low wages in the hospitality industry.

What both families did have in common was how much they valued education. My paternal grandfather enrolled my father from a young age at a school that was a thirty-minute walk from home, instead of at the local school in the favela. He scoured the newspapers for scholarships to English classes his children could take beyond their regular schoolwork. And my mother's family was no different. After my parents married, my grandmother continued to pay for my mother's college tuition when, as a young married couple, my mother and father could not afford it. At the time, my father was working part-time as a pharmaceuticals salesperson to pay for his own tuition and cover their rent. When they were halfway through college, the political and economic environment in Brazil worsened, and job opportunities on the other side of graduation became even more scarce.

From 1964 through 1985, the dictatorship ruled Brazil with an iron fist. The government tortured and banished dissidents, brainwashed the general public through the use of propaganda, and censored most Brazilian creative pursuits, which were typically avenues used by artists to speak poorly of the government. Because of this, Brazilians at the time were heavily influenced by American culture through movies, television, literature, and music. My mother loved all Hollywood classics, including *Gone With the Wind*, and my father became obsessed with everything related to rock and roll and the California surfer lifestyle. Disenchanted with pursuing a career in Brazil given the hyperinflation, high cost of living, and limited job opportunities, my parents were looking for a solution that somehow emulated their favorite celebrities and idols in the American media.

In January 1985, my parents put their college degrees on hold, sold all their wedding gifts, and bought a one-way ticket to New York, with only a couple hundred dollars in savings and a few friends they could crash with.

When my parents first landed in New York City more than thirty years ago, there were many firsts: seeing snow come down from the sky, having to use English every day with real-life Americans, and working at a fast-food chain—my mom as cashier and my dad as cook. Their original thought was that the move to the US would be a temporary solution. They would spend a few years saving up and eventually go back to their lives as they knew them. However, as they stayed longer, they saw just how much more opportunity they had in this country and, eventually, began putting down roots to stay for good. Having never lost sight of the importance of education, within fifteen years of arriving, both my parents decided to go back to school and finish their college degrees.

My mother was accepted to the State University of New York's Fashion Institute of Technology, where she studied textile arts and received her associate's degree. My father earned a bachelor's degree in hospitality management from the New York City College of Technology. We often did our homework together on weekends and weeknights—my mother chipping away at her latest piece of fabric on the loom in our living room, my father testing his latest éclair recipe in the kitchen, and me, practicing my multiplication tables on the living room floor.

My parents, like many immigrants in the US, are the ultimate examples of perseverance, hope, courage, and integrity. And like their parents, they understood that hard work, combined with education, was the key to success. When I was three, they negotiated with the New York public school system to help me gain acceptance to a public lower school outside our designated "catchment area" rather than the school in our neighborhood. When I was nine, they sought out Prep for Prep, a leadership development program that offers promising students of color access to a private school education that helped me gain full-scholarship acceptance to Horace Mann, one of the best private schools in the country. Alongside Prep for Prep and Horace Mann, my parents urged me to attend the best undergraduate university I could find. Today, they are the proud parents of a Stanford University graduate.

Without my parents' example, support, and encouragement, I would never have made it to where I am today. My parents came in search of the American dream, and in some ways, they found it the second they landed. They landed in a country with better than average public education for all, a thriving not-for-profit sector filled with organizations happy to help them get their feet on the ground, and a booming economy with opportunity across all sectors. Like no other country in the world, the US gives the world's hungry, tired, injured, frustrated, and oppressed the opportunity to dream like they never have before. What you set your sights on, you can accomplish through hard work, perseverance, patience, and a positive attitude. Even though they came in search of just a few years of savings, my parents found so much more than they were looking for; they found a future for themselves, one better than their ancestors could have imagined. Although they have looked back, they never for a single day regret it.

Carmen Osbahr-Vertiz

Carmen Osbahr-Vertiz is an immigrant from Mexico who is the performer of Rosita on Sesame Street.

My name is Carmen Osbahr-Vertiz. I was born in Mexico City. My father was Emilio Osbahr, and my mother was Carmen Vertiz. I had an older brother, and his name was Emilio Osbahr. My family was a loving and caring one, and I was surrounded by family, friends, and people who loved me. I never thought that one day I was going to be a US citizen. My family's roots were in Mexico. My life was happy and comfortable. I didn't think of the United States as a place of refuge, nor was it a home for me. Home is where the heart is, and Mexico was still my home.

My career path took me to work on television, performing with puppets on children's shows and game shows. After working for a few years, I went to audition for the children's show called *Plaza Sésamo*, which is the coproduction of *Sesame Street* in Mexico. The thing is, that audition didn't get me the job, because they didn't have female characters at the time. However, it gave me the opportunity to visit the US to see the set of *Sesame Street*. I had the opportunity to see Jerry Nelson, Frank Oz, Kevin Clash, Richard Hunt, and, of course, Jim Henson at work. I was really excited to bring all the things I learned from them to my shows in Mexico. As my time of observing and learning went by, I realized how much I wanted to be part of that group. These people were talented, generous, caring, and willing to share their love of puppetry with the world. My life changed completely, and I wanted to work hard, to one day be as good as them.

That was in 1988. In 1989, while I was in Mexico, I got an invitation from Jim Henson to participate in a workshop (kind of an audition), because he was looking for new puppeteers. I was extremely excited and honored, because at that point in my life, I really wanted to be a part of *Sesame Street*. After a very long and arduous time of work and auditioning, Jim Henson asked me in person if I wanted to be a part of his "Muppet family." It was amazing that Jim Henson described his group of puppeteers as a family, and that he so willingly let me into this family.

I officially started working for *Sesame Street* in 1990. I spent a year studying and shadowing puppeteers, learning English, and realizing how important the mission of Sesame Workshop was, making kids smarter, stronger, and kinder, no matter their background, color, or race. Every child has the right to be a kid, and to receive an education. At the beginning, I worked in the US for a few months and would go back to Mexico when we finished the season. But after a few years, I started working more and I became more involved in the show and performing Rosita. Because of this I decided to live in New York City. Sadly, during that time I lost my mother, father, and brother. *Sesame Street* became my family.

Sesame Street produces different outreach projects. These are my favorite, because I'm able to use both English and Spanish. One that is very important to me is the community work they do with military families. For six years, I was able to meet incredible military families, traveling around the world to military bases and seeing how strong, selfless, loving, and kind these families are. They are always willing to help, even if they're in the worst circumstances. That made me want to become an American citizen. Since I've been part of this country, I've been adopted by an incredible Muppet family, an incredible military family, and an incredible country. Now I'm proud to say that my son, who was born in New York City, is a first-generation American. He is representing the US at an international school, the UWC in India, and I hope that with my parents' love and example, along with Jim Henson's trust and generosity I can give back the same to more people.

I'm so proud to be an American.

Dr. Mehmet Oz

Mehmet Oz, MD, is a cardiothoracic surgeon affiliated with Columbia University. He also has his own television talk show on the Oprah Winfrey Network and has written or coauthored six books.

My mother had just arrived in Cleveland when I was born. She had met my father under unusual circumstances, but their desire to migrate to the US was a very usual route for educated Turks trying to improve their lots in the 1960s. But let's not rush the story.

My father grew up in a poor village in central Anatolia, the son of a farmer in a worldwide depression that hit Turkey harder than the US. He was educated completely on scholarships, starting in middle and high school in Konya, which is the Nashville of Turkey. The whirling dervishes dance in their mosques in a very conservative community. He won a competition to enter medical school that was granted to a precious few and spent the Second World War learning medicine from brilliant Jewish physicians who were fleeing Europe.

He graduated first in his medical school class and won a funded position at Western Reserve Hospital, located seemingly a galaxy away in Ohio. His family took him to the airport, and his mother, who had never seen an airplane, insisted on meeting the captain. He kindly obliged and was handed a bagged lunch to serve my father and told to keep his flying mechanical bird low to the ground and avoid high speeds. Ironically, immigrants instinctively know that this is bad advice. To leave their homelands and thrive in our land of opportunity, they learn to take risks as they soar to the heavens.

My mother comes from a wealthy family and would have her dresses hand made. Their trusted seamstress was my aunt Ayse, who let slip (knowing her, on purpose) that her brother was in the States making his name as a young surgical resident. But he was coming home for the holidays and perhaps a meeting could be arranged. Despite their reservations, my mother's parents permitted the meeting, because, as I have been reminded throughout my life, my mother is stubborn, tenacious, determined, and dogged. This part of the story is always vague in my parents' usually sharp minds, but they appear to have met and married faster than Amazon Prime delivers my socks. I was born a year later and witnessed their absorption in the American melting pot.

Me with my parents while my father was training in Atlanta (1961).

They started with little and often remind me that they would collect cans on the shoreline for the deposit money. Despite these modest beginnings, my father rapidly progressed through a training facilitated by other recent immigrants who felt expatriate camaraderie. Their names sounded like a UN roll call, and their customs merged into ours for social events. Pig roasts with Philippine physicians at picnics with Turkish baklava, elevated by US music. But the real recipe for success was the kindness of Americans who respected the bravery needed to leave one's homeland and respected this nation's need to attract the brightest minds on the planet. Mr. Slobody, who ran the local car dealership, held a welcome-back party when my father returned with his new bride. Mrs. Slobody advised my mother on caring for her first child, since she was five thousand miles away from her mother. I grew up hearing these names uttered with great reverence and even called their children a few years ago to personally thank them for creating a new family for my parents upon their arrival.

At Harvard with Mom. She seems relieved that I was finally out of the house (1980).

Many speak of the melting pot of America. I think we are even better than that metaphor. Our nation has always reinvented itself by making immigrants part of the family. You don't always like your family. In fact, many joke that we fight so much with our families because if we were not related, we would not be friends. But family ties are thick and weave us into a quilt of community. They force us to deal with uncomfortable realities, while comforting us that tomorrow brings hope, because family members never abandon each other. My parents appreciated this tug to join the American family and shared these values with all the kids they raised, students they mentored, and other immigrants they met. These ideals are in our DNA, which, as the blueprint of life, is supposed to be passed along and is my defense for frequently regaling my kids with the stories above.

Gina Raimondo

The Honorable Gina Raimondo is the Governor of Rhode Island.

My grandfather Pietro came to live with my family after my grand-mother died, when I was a child. Pop was from a small volcanic island called Ischia, off the coast of Naples. His father died when he was a baby, and he said goodbye to his mother and came to America, alone, at fourteen years old. Pop spent most of the weeks-long trip across the Atlantic Ocean in the ship's galley, where, presumably, some of the cooks were Italian. He arrived, penniless, in Boston and somehow made his way to his sister's apartment in Providence, Rhode Island, where he announced a plan to parlay the culinary skills he'd picked up on the journey into a career as a chef.

Pop was very proud to be an American. He often told the story of how he learned English by reading newspapers at the Providence Public Library after a long, hard day working on his feet in the Italian restaurants on Federal Hill. He became a US citizen as soon as he was able and quickly enlisted in the army when the United States entered World War I.

Like so many immigrants, Pop paired an indomitable work ethic with a deeply held conviction that America was a land of opportunity. He did in fact forge a long and successful career as a master chef. He got married, raised a family, and became a pillar of his community. I still recall his disapproval when he returned from tending his two gardens and caught me sitting on the sofa on a Saturday afternoon, watching cartoons. "Gina," he said, "get up. Bring these tomatoes to your friend next door." He was ever on the lookout for someone who might need a hand. Not everyone on our street owned a car, and Pop was always offering someone a ride. Once, when word came that a newborn in the neighborhood was ill, he insisted on driving the family to the parish priest to have the baby baptized.

If Pop had opinions on politics, I wasn't aware of them. But he was a voracious consumer of local and national news; he loved *Time* magazine and read the evening edition of the *Providence Journal & Bulletin* front to back. He was a relentless advocate of the value of a formal education, of which he had received very little. At Pop's insistence, my mother earned a college degree before getting married and starting her own family. He was just as focused on my sister and me getting the same education as the boys. That was unusual in those days.

Pop also taught us, by example, to take pride in our heritage and hold fast to our traditions. Prejudice against Italians was still a real thing when I was a girl. I never felt prouder than when walking to church every Sunday with my olive-skinned, Italian-accented grandfather—trim and dapper in his waistcoat, fedora, and gleaming shoes, his head held high. After church, Pop would spend the afternoon in the kitchen cooking for his family, sipping wine and listening to Italian-language radio.

He never raised his voice. He was respectful of women. I never saw him brag or wag his finger. He showed us kids what it looked like to be modest and bighearted. Every so often, my family would take a long car ride to share Sunday dinner with our cousins in Lawrence, Massachusetts. It was a more economical meal, with less of the deliciously prepared steaks and fresh fish that Pop served us on Sundays. He was unfailingly appreciative and generous in his praise of the food.

Pop died in 1983, when I was in the sixth grade. All these years later, I find myself thinking about him often in my work as governor. I believe that Pop's resourcefulness, patriotism, and willingness to lend a neighbor a helping hand are reflected in our successful efforts in Rhode Island to create economic opportunity for every family, provide every child access to quality, affordable health care, make record investments in public education, and make college affordable for everyone. Our steadfast commitment to inclusion, tolerance, and diversity is what makes us American.

Mayo Stuntz Jr.

Mayo Stuntz Jr. is cofounder and principal of Pilot Group LLC. Prior
to that he held senior management positions at Time-Warner and
America Online.

My family has been in the US for a long time, but as with most of us, it began with the stories of two immigrants.

On my father's side, it all started with Conrad Stuntz. Born in Wurttemberg, Germany in 1738, Conrad was training to be a weaver, his father's trade. But Germany was at war, so he was drafted and fought for King Fredrick of Prussia in the Seven Years' War. He briefly returned to civilian life, but was then conscripted by the Prince of Hesse Hanau to join a mercenary force to be sent to America to fight for the British.

Conrad arrived in Staten Island with his Hessian unit in 1776. But very quickly, he realized that the Americans were fighting for independence and freedom. All his life, he had been subject to the dictates of others, but the American dream called out to him. Some family members tell the story that Conrad needed shelter on Staten Island, so he "borrowed" an officer's coat. He was subsequently caught and accused of theft, which may have given him extra incentive to defect to the Americans.

He immediately got his chance. In the battle for Long Island, he managed to escape the British and join Washington's army. As an experienced soldier, he was immediately put into service training the American recruits before the Battle of White Plains. He went on to fight with Washington through 1776 and 1777, before being wounded at Monmouth Courthouse in 1778. He received an honorable discharge, and was given a grant of land in what is now West Virginia.

In Germany, his neighbors had a young daughter, Anna Margaret Briefling, who was just a girl when Conrad left. With his army service, he lost touch with her. But after her parents died, she indentured herself to a Quaker family and moved to Philadelphia in 1773. Sometime after that, Conrad and Anna reconnected, and in 1778 they were married in Lancaster, Pennsylvania.

The couple moved to his land grant in Martinsburg, where they built a log cabin and lived off the land. They had seven children, and six survived. Years later, the family moved to Crawford County where they purchased a large farm. Conrad died in 1810, and Anna died in 1830.

Their children went on to have large families, and George, their youngest son, was my great-great-grandfather. He lived his life in Crawford County, and his son Albert Conrad Stuntz moved to Wisconsin, where my grandfather Stephen Conrad Stuntz was born in 1875.

My grandfather graduated from the University of Wisconsin in 1899, conducted historical research for the State Library in Madison, and became a classifier for the US Library of Congress in Washington. Grandfather later served as a botanist for the US Department of Agriculture, introducing plants from around the world to the US. He was also a novelist, writing three books, and spoke many languages. Married to Lena Grayson Fitzhugh in 1907, he died in the 1918 flu epidemic.

Stephen had five children, one son who was a journalist for the Associated Press, one who died flying a mission in WWII, two daughters, and my father, Mayo Stuntz. Mayo had a long career in the CIA and was a local historian in Northern Virginia, publishing several books with my mother, Constance Pendleton Stuntz.

On my mother's side, the history goes back even farther.

Eleven generations ago, my ancestor Brian Pendleton was born in England in 1599. Not much is known about his early history, but it is thought that he was well educated and was a man of means. He arrived in America in the early 1600s, and the first record of him here is as one of the founders of Watertown, Massachusetts. He was a Puritan and a strong supporter of the Bay Colony of Massachusetts. He moved on to help found Sudbury, Massachusetts. He was an officer in the militia artillery company of Massachusetts.

In 1651, Brian moved his family to Portsmouth (now New Hampshire), to take advantage of the undeveloped land north of Massachusetts. He acquired land and became active in politics, always arguing for extending the Massachusetts Bay Colony influence northward into what is now New Hampshire and Maine. He led the militia and was responsible for the town's defense.

By 1665, Brian had acquired a great deal of property in Saco, Maine, and he moved his family there that year. After several years of quiet, the town of Saco was attacked by Native Americans during King Philip's War. The townspeople sought refuge on Brian's farm, and all were saved.

Brian died in 1681, leaving three children. His son James, my ten-times-great-grandfather, was born in 1628 and grew up in Portsmouth, but in 1674 moved with his family to Rhode Island, where he eventually settled in Westerly. With his second wife, Hannah Goodenow, he had eight children, the second of which, born in 1661, was Joseph, my nine-times-great-grandfather. Joseph spent his life in Westerly involved in business and politics. He died in 1706. Joseph's second son, William, was born in 1704 and also lived his life in Westerly, Rhode Island. He was a colonel in the militia, fought in the French and Indian War in the 1750s, and died in 1786.

Colonel William's eldest son, William, was born in 1726. He owned a schooner and traded to the coast of Maine from Westerly. In 1769, he came across an island in the Penobscot Bay, now called Islesboro, and bought six hundred acres at the southern tip. He relocated his family there over the next few years. During the Revolutionary War, he led a regiment of the Massachusetts militia but did not see action. William died in 1820.

William's move to Islesboro proved to be permanent for the family, as four successive generations of Pendletons lived on the island and worked as sea captains: Jonathan (b. 1751), Robert (b. 1796), Charles Agustus (b. 1824), and Charles Robert (b. 1857).

My grandfather Charles Arthur was born on Islesboro in 1892. He left the island to fight in WWI and came back to work for the Veterans Administration in Washington, DC, where my mother grew up.

My mother, Constance Pendleton Stuntz, and my father, Mayo Stuntz, met in Virginia after WWII and were married in Falls Church in February 1947. They had four children, three of whom lived to adulthood and became a media executive, a congressional aide, and an investment banker and historian. My parents have eight grandchildren and four great-grandchildren.

The stories of Brian Pendleton and Conrad Stuntz demonstrate the amazing opportunities that were available to those able to take advantage of the American experiment. The dreams and hopes of Conrad and Brian have come true throughout the eleven generations that have lived in America. The family is widely scattered, all pursuing their own destinies and working to ensure that America will always be the land of opportunity that our immigrant ancestors risked so much to help build.

The Strivers

/////

Michael Bloomberg

Joseph Bower

Andrew Cuomo

Ben Freeman

Peter Blair Henry

Declan Kelly

Jackie Koppell

Funa Maduka and Nonso Maduka

Mario Neiman

Tim Scott

Mary Skafidas

Jane Wang

*A man's [or woman's] homeland is wherever
he [or she] prospers.*

— Aristophanes

People come to America so that they and their families can flourish. They learn the customs and traditions of their new country, they become active, engaged citizens, and they put extraordinary effort into ensuring that their children are well educated.

The Strivers are individuals who arrived in the US with very few possessions aside from an abundance of drive and determination to do great things. These attributes proved to be more than enough to propel each one of them to exceptional achievement.

Michael R. Bloomberg

Michael R. Bloomberg is an entrepreneur and philanthropist who served as Mayor of New York City for three terms. Since leaving city hall in 2014, he has resumed leadership of Bloomberg LP and become a UN Special Envoy for Climate Action, and the World Health Organization's Global Ambassador for Noncommunicable Diseases.

One reason I ran for mayor of New York was to improve the city's failing public school system. When I visited classrooms, I saw bright, eager students—many of them immigrants and children of immigrants—whose ambitions and aspirations personified the American dream. Yet for too long, the city's public schools did not give them the tools and skills they needed to fulfill their potential. I was determined to change that, and my own family's history gave me a sense of just how important the work was.*

Three of my grandparents and six of my great-grandparents were immigrants. All placed education and reverence for the United States at the core of our family values. Their stories are quintessentially American, and they made my story possible.

My maternal grandparents were Ettie and Max Rubens. Ettie was born on Mott Street in 1881. She grew up on the Lower East Side, a haven for immigrants. Ettie's parents, Louis and Ida Cohen, had come from the Kovno region of present-day Lithuania. Louis Cohen arrived in New York City in 1869. He was so proud to become an American

---

* I would like to thank my sister, Marjorie Bloomberg Tiven, whose archival research and commitment to our family history made it possible to write this piece.

citizen that he hung his naturalization certificate on the wall. Great-Grandmother Ida lived in New York City until she died in 1917 at 64 East 105th Street, between Madison and Park in East Harlem, a house her son Henry owned. Her death notice listed her membership in more than a dozen Jewish and community organizations.

Ettie was educated in a Lower East Side public school, where students wrote on slates because paper was too precious. I don't know the school's name or how long she attended; I do know that throughout her life she was a voracious reader, and she completed the daily and Sunday *New York Times* crossword puzzles until she was ninety!

In 1903, she married my grandfather, Max Rubens, for whom my sister and I are named. They went to Washington, DC, on their honeymoon and brought back a souvenir that we still have—a plaque of the Capitol made from old currency that had been destroyed by the United States Mint. It's a touching reminder of the stock that immigrant families placed in American institutions.

Grandpa Max arrived in America as a child. He and his parents, Grace and Cappell, had quite a pathway to America. From a small town near Grodno in present-day Belarus, they made their way to Liverpool, where they settled for several years. A photo of 6 Mela Street, where they lived in the 1880s, is as bleak as a Dickens story. My sister even found records showing that Max and his brother Charlie received clothes from a charity "for the poor boys of the Liverpool Hebrew School." (Their sister Polly, as a girl, did not qualify, though she attended the same school.) They left for America in 1886 on the ship *City of Hope* and settled in Salem, Massachusetts. A few years later, they went back to Liverpool, but left for good in 1891, settling in Jersey City, New Jersey.

Max earned his living in the wholesale grocery business, carrying around heavy grocery samples in a Gladstone bag. He was able to buy a row of five brick three-family houses on Summit Avenue in West Hoboken, a German neighborhood where our mother spent her childhood. From my mother, we know that Max was a great music lover and had a very good ear. At about age twenty, he learned to play the violin. Grandma Ettie also loved music; she played the piano, and they often played duets. They listened to classical records on their Victrola, a lot of opera, especially Caruso, Max's favorite, and they went into New York City for live opera and theater.

Grandma Ettie passed on high expectations for learning to all her children, whom she raised alone after Max died in 1922. It was expected that my then sixteen-year-old uncle Louis would leave school after Max's death to go to work, but Ettie insisted that he finish high school before joining Hudson Wholesale Grocery, where he thrived for the rest of his life. My mother, Charlotte, graduated from Dickinson High School in 1925 and from New York University in 1929, in an era when relatively few women attended college. Grandma encouraged Aunt Florrie to train as a teacher and my aunt Gertie to attend a business secretarial school.

Grandma Ettie's emphasis on education helped make her successful as a mother. The city's public schools shaped her and reinforced her sense of what her children and grandchildren could achieve. My mother held her parents up as models of what America offered "if you applied yourself"—with the key word being *if*.

My father, Bill Bloomberg, was born just outside Boston, in Chelsea, in 1906, to parents who both came from Vilna, Lithuania. His mother, Rose Bernstein, arrived in 1891 as a twelve-year-old with her mother and four siblings; four more were born in America. Rose's father, Gedalia, had arrived two years earlier, following some of his own siblings who braved the way. Some of them are listed in an 1881 Boston city directory as living on Nashua Street, not far from the current Museum of Science, an institution that gave me my love of science and learning and taught me how to think.

In 1900, Rose married Elick Bloomberg, who arrived in America in 1896 as a twenty-year-old. Two years later he filed his intention to become an American citizen, "renouncing allegiance to foreign sovereigns, especially and particularly to Nicholas II Czar of Russia." Elick and Rose also took their honeymoon in Washington, DC. We still have the porcelain bowl with a color image of the White House they brought back to grace their home. Together, they raised six children.

Grandpa Elick was learned in the Old Testament, Jewish history, and liturgy. For decades, he was the Torah reader at Chelsea's Walnut Street shul. Though he served variously as a peddler, justice of the peace, notary public, and insurance salesman, my sister, Marjorie, and I knew him as a teacher, strongly committed to Jewish learning. While we were growing up, he earned his living preparing boys for bar mitzvah. Students often came and went when we visited. Sometimes we heard their lessons from another room.

Rose's father, Gedalia Bernstein, was one of the first Jewish residents of Chelsea and a founder of the first local yeshiva. Rose's sister Sarah was also a pioneer, an advocate for the legalization of birth control and a supporter of Margaret Sanger, a leader in the movement. When Sanger was standing trial in federal district court in 1916 for circulating birth control information, she wrote and signed a letter to Aunt Sarah thanking her for her "interest and financial help" and imploring her to do what she could to "keep up the agitation" by writing to the district attorney, the president, and the judge. It's fair to say that our family's commitment to women's rights and the responsibility to participate in public life dates back at least one hundred years.

Our family story is very much an American one. Our ancestors were courageous in uprooting themselves from everything they knew, risking ocean crossings and making new homes in a strange new land. They and their families came from shtetls in Russia's Pale of Settlement, the area to which Jews were restricted. Their towns in Kovno, Vilna, and Grodno are listed in the Valley of Lost Communities at Yad Vashem, remembered because the Jews living there perished in the Holocaust.

No matter how challenging or dangerous their lives were elsewhere, it was not easy to start over. My parents didn't talk about the struggles their parents and grandparents faced as immigrants, or the persecution they may have faced in their home country. But they did teach us that we had a responsibility to give back to the country that embraced our ancestors and that made our lives possible. I remember asking my father why he was writing a $25 or $50 check—which was a lot of money for us—to the NAACP, and I've always remembered what he told me: discrimination against anyone is discrimination against everyone. I have tried to live up to his example, and the values my grandparents and great-grandparents exemplified, through my work in public service, philanthropy, and advocacy for a just and humane world.

My ancestors came to America at a time when immigration—to my great good fortune—was virtually unrestricted. Those days are long gone, and national security demands that we control our borders, but that does not preclude a reasonable and generous immigration policy. I've worked my entire public career to promote legislation that will allow current and future generations of immigrants to contribute to this wonderful nation into which I was born.

I was privileged to serve as mayor of the world's immigrant capital for twelve years. I doubt that my grandparents and great-grandparents could ever have imagined that one day a member of our family would hold that position. I hope that I am repaying some of the debt I owe them by working to keep America's opportunities open to all people, of all colors, faiths, orientations, and backgrounds. We owe a similar debt to our shared American future. There is no way to tell which New York City schoolchild or, eventually, which of their children or grandchildren, will lead this city and country in her or his own time—but I know we are all made greater because one of them will.

Joseph Bower

Professor Joseph Bower taught for over fifty years at the Harvard Business School.

My memories of my grandfather Morris Turitz begin with a friendly, hard-of-hearing old man in a dark three-piece suit and a tie sitting in an armchair in the library of my parents' home smoking smelly cigars. He lived with us in our apartment on Central Park West. He devoted a great deal of time to reading the daily *Forward* and later the *Compass*. He was kind to me and taught me to play pinochle, a game he played when friends of his would visit.

He presided over a family of seven children, whom he was very proud of. He was also a central character in his larger extended family—including among his cousins, whom I would meet at large Passover Seders on the second night when everyone spoke Hebrew out loud at their own pace—and which went on forever, to my young eyes. On rare occasions I was taken to a large meeting of cousins—the Hirsch Mordechai Society—named after my grandfather's grandfather, which consisted of Vilna cousins—the Sachses, Markses, Zizmars, Levins, and Turitzes. This group of families still communicates in a network of many hundreds.

Later, well after my grandfather died in his late eighties, I learned of his accomplishments and wondered why I never had been told about him earlier so that I could learn more. Born in Vilna, Lithuania, he grew up moving among nearby towns as his father's income waxed and mostly waned. In his memoirs, he remembers mostly his Talmud studies and his family's economic struggles. Evidently, he was a brilliant student, for his progress was marked by increasingly important heders and yeshiva. After he survived a serious illness that left him deaf in one ear, Morris's father bought him a ticket to Boston.

There begins his impressive American story. Starting as a peddler— selling sundries to the goyim acted as his English immersion training— the yeshiva *bocher* worked to support his mother and sisters. Soon he gave that up to work for tiny wages in hellish conditions at a felt hat factory in Haverhill, Massachusetts. In 1891, he and other workers organized the workmen's educational society, which grew into the Socialist Labor Party and eventually into one of the foundations of the American socialist movement.

In order to improve his circumstances, this socialist learned cigar making and then decided to go into business for himself. With that foundation he moved to start a business distributing kerosene. He was able to make more money and then eventually to become a US citizen.

My grandfather continued to be very active in the socialism movement, taking part in the establishment of a Yiddish newspaper called *Emmes* (Truth). Later he was a delegate from Boston to the convention that established the Jewish daily *Forward*, and was active in the meeting when Eugene Debs established social democracy. Later he helped to found the ILGWU. David Dubinsky would eulogize Papa at his funeral.

My grandfather married in 1899, and because his wife was longing for New York, they moved there soon after, both to make her happy and to be with the big shots of the socialist movement in New York City. Selling his business and moving to New York seemed crazy, but he did it. A friend of his in Boston had a business supplying clean towels as a service to barbershops. His friend made good money with this business, so my grandfather decided it was something he could try. Lacking experience, he looked for a partner. His choice would end up becoming a lifelong friend. They worked together for twenty-eight years building strong businesses that provided the core of what became known as Consolidated Laundries.

Many milestones marked their progress, but three in particular stand out. Through a conversation with a customer sitting in a barber chair, the idea of renting linen for restaurants as another service business came up. Rapid expansion followed. Milestone two was the building of a purpose-built laundry service that had water-based air cooling—a first for the laundry industry and a model studied by the Labor Department and visitors from around the world. The business also paid a minimum wage well above the industry standard and provided stools for the workers—"Why should they stand if they can sit?" They also had paid vacations, and their drivers and foremen were given stock in the company. Grandpa had a Cadillac, but he parked it blocks from the plant so as not to show off in front of the workers.

After World War I, there were attempts at industry consolidation, but it wasn't until the Roaring Twenties that a merger finally occurred with an investment bank. My grandfather sold his business, took his family on a magnificent trip to Europe, and never looked back. Social causes and politics were always his focus. The crash lessened his wealth, but his support for workers and progressive politics remained a constant for the remainder of his life. That and his family.

His wife and children were the jewels in his crown. My mother was the oldest of his seven children. Interested in music, she was brought up with tutors, then studied at the Institute of Musical Art (later referred to as Juilliard) and then for six years in Europe. His wife presided over this large brood with a strong hand favoring the socialist sentiment in her husband's life. She was famous for her soups, and in the shtetl tradition she boiled the finest cuts of meat. Their daughters married professionals: a lawyer, a professor, a composer, and a doctor. Their sons married social workers. My children and the children of my cousins are friends, often celebrating holidays or milestones together.

It is a wonderful legacy of education and caring. What is most remarkable, though, as I look back from my life in business, education, and management, is that my grandfather understood in the most profound way that business could create wealth so that it provided a good life for all involved. He had the intelligence and ambition of an entrepreneur, but he never saw his progress as something that would happen at the expense of others. To the contrary, he saw science, knowledge, and commerce as a way of making life better, and the fruits of his business progress as something to be shared as part of business, not as charity.

His life is also an exemplar of Jewish history. A family whose records in the town hall of Vilna told a story back to the exodus from Spain scrambled for a living in the shtetls of Lithuania supported by family and neighbors. In America, that energy and study provided the foundation for making a living and then building a profitable business. But at the same time, he saw the need to provide for the community in the way it had provided for his family when the need was there.

In recent years, I have told stories of my grandfather to my HBS students. It was not just the climate of his laundry that could be a model. In a time when business is seen as increasingly transactional and amoral, his humane approach to life is an example for all.

Andrew Cuomo

The Honorable Andrew Cuomo is the Governor of New York.

Most of America met my grandfather on July 16, 1984, when he was already three years gone. That night, my father, who was midway through his second year as the governor of New York, delivered the keynote address at the Democratic National Convention. It was an interesting political time, a time when my father's brand of liberalism had been set back on its heels. Not only was President Reagan's popularity at its apex, but his pro-market approach to the economy had unleashed a flashy materialism among the haves, while his shrinking safety net policies pushed the have-nots into the corners.

To counter all that swagger, my father enlisted his parents, Andrea and Immacolata Cuomo of South Jamaica, Queens. President Reagan had used the metaphor of "a shining city on the hill" to evoke his idea of America. Against that shimmering citadel, my father posed the salt of the earth.

"[The] struggle to live with dignity is the real story of the shining city," he told an auditorium of emotionally flat Democrats at San Francisco's Moscone Center, "and it's a story, ladies and gentlemen, that I didn't read in a book or learn in a classroom. I saw it and lived it, like many of you. I watched a small man with thick calluses on both his hands work fifteen and sixteen hours a day. I saw him once literally bleed from the bottoms of his feet, a man who came here uneducated, alone, unable to speak the language, who taught me all I needed to know about faith and hard work by the simple eloquence of his example. I learned about our kind of democracy from my father. And I learned about our obligation to each other from him and from my mother. They asked only for a chance to work and to make the world better for their children, and they—they asked to be protected in those moments when they would not be able to protect themselves. This nation and this nation's government did that for them."

My grandfather, Andrea Cuomo.

Unfortunately, the Democrats still lost that election, but the speech reminded them that victory alone is not what makes a fight worth fighting. The speech, in which my father was able to weave his family's story into America's story, then acquired a life of its own. Many years after that event, I met a lawyer whose family was from India, but who, like me, grew up in Queens. "My father hung your father's picture in our kitchen," he told me.

I would say that my family had a typical immigrant experience, but with a little wrinkle: both of my grandfathers were born in the United States. In the late nineteenth and early twentieth centuries, about four million Italians immigrated to the United States. Unlike the members of earlier groups, many of them planned to stay only for a short while, earn some money, and return to their towns and villages. Both my great-grandparents had that plan, but in their brief stays in America, something else happened: they became fathers.

Twenty-odd years later, those babies—Andrea Cuomo and Charles Raffa—came back to the United States, American by birth, Italian in every other way. Leaving his pregnant wife, Immacolata, at home in the mountainous Campania region south of Naples, Andrea arrived at Ellis Island in 1926, just twenty-four years old; Immacolata, clutching my uncle Frank, followed the next year.

In the great poem on the base of the Statue of Liberty, Emma Lazarus gave us a vivid image of the people who came to America: "Give me your tired, your poor, your huddled masses yearning to breathe free." If nothing else, the verse tells us a lot about the conditions those people abandoned. At the same time, I wonder if she might not have more accurately written, "Give us your ambitious, your industrious, your clever, imaginative, dauntless dreamers yearning to build a better tomorrow." Neither Andrea nor Immacolata had skills or education; in Italy and in America, they were *cafoni*—rubes—residents of the lowest economic and social strata, but they desperately wanted to be here. Each of them did something remarkable and unique in their lives: they each broke a promise to their families not to go to America. Of all earthly things, they valued nothing more than family. That tells me how deeply they wanted to come to America.

Andrea toiled as the classic pick-and-shovel immigrant. He dug ditches and cleaned sewers and became one of the millions of men upon whose broad backs urban America was constructed. He and Immacolata lived in Jersey City until the work ran out, at which point a friend introduced them to a man who ran a corner grocery store located at 95-40 150th Street in Queens. He hired my father and even better, he rented Dad the rooms behind the store, and for seven years my grandparents and their children lived in those rooms.

But while the habitat was small, the neighborhood was cosmopolitan and filled with German, Italian, Irish, Jewish, and Polish families. For my grandparents to join such a neighborhood must have taken enormous courage; as they assimilated into a mixed community, they faced many circumstances of discrimination with a confidence of eventual acceptance.

They taught their children to embrace the open society into which they had moved. At an early age, my father experienced something his parents were only just learning: how to live with people from other lands. On Friday nights he was a Shabbos goy, lighting the stoves of his Jewish neighbors. Queens wasn't Italy, and Andrea and Immacolata Cuomo wouldn't raise their children as if it was.

After years of eighteen-hour days, the family's circumstances improved with the acquisition of the grocery store where he had worked.

*The grocery store that my grandfather eventually
acquired at 95-40 150th Street in Queens.*

My grandfather's benevolence and humanity, extending credit to patrons during tough times and free supplies during the war, was repaid by customers with loyalty. He sold the business at only fifty-three years old and moved to the other side of the tracks into a comfortable home with a yard and a big, beautiful spruce tree.

In later years, after its service to the Cuomo family was over, the building became at various times a butcher shop, a Jamaican restaurant, and a storefront church, a constant vessel of immigrant visions.

An anecdote special to my father is—today—particularly meaningful to me.

One day, my grandfather and uncle and father were out together. A big storm was sweeping the area, and when they came back, they were shocked to discover that the wind and the rain had toppled the beautiful tree in the front yard. They were all aghast, but what's done was done, and there didn't seem to be any point to standing around in a storm looking at a downed tree. The boys started to go inside. "Where are you going?" my grandfather asked sharply.

"Pop, it's gone," my uncle Frank replied.

"No," my grandfather said angrily, "we gonna push him up." The boys didn't know what he meant, but they knew better than to argue. They waited while my grandfather ran into the house; he came back a moment later with some rope and a couple of wedges of wood that he pushed into the sodden ground. "We're going to push him up," he repeated, looping the rope around the tip of the tree. "Push him up." With Frank pulling on the rope and Andrea and Mario pushing against the trunk, they managed to slide the fallen tree and its severed roots back into the hole it had evacuated. Then they covered over the hole with dirt and rolled a couple big rocks against the trunk, and waited to see if it would take. Today, more than sixty years later, you can drive past that house and see that tree, its wide branches still shading the family within, a living testament to Andrea Cuomo's determination.

None of us ever has the privilege of knowing our parents, and certainly not our grandparents, in the rosy glow of their youth. But I did get to know what made them happy—family. My grandmother at the center of big Sunday dinners, my grandfather at the pond he had built in his backyard. It was made of concrete, about twelve feet in diameter, with a waterfall, and full of goldfish. At either end of the pond were a pair of castles, each four feet tall, that he built out of stones he collected on the beach during the winter. At the tip of each he had constructed a turret, atop which he had placed an American flag.

The callused, hardworking shopkeeper that my father introduced to America is one part of Andrea Cuomo, and one part of his life. His

American castle is another. The worker and the dreamer: you have to know both parts to know the whole.

Today one of those castles sits in the backyard of my home. I have no prouder possession.

Ben Freeman

Ben Freeman, a native of Liberia and a Hemings family descendant, is the author of Careysburg: Freed Negro American Settlers' Quest for Freedom and the Impact on the Social and Cultural Relationship With Indigenous Africans in the St. Paul River Settlement of Liberia, West Africa.

Throughout the seventeenth and eighteenth centuries, an increasing number of people of Negro descent were brought across the Atlantic Ocean as slaves during the transatlantic slave trade and were mainly slaves in North America up until the mid-1860s. But while many of the stories we hear or read have been those not mired in slavery by immigrants from other parts of the world who came to the United States, I begin with the story of my ancestors who were emigrants from the slave plantations of the antebellum South to Careysburg, Liberia, West Africa, and then look at my own journey back to America.

I was born in Careysburg, Liberia. I resettled in the United States of America in 1994 as a result of the 1990 Liberian civil war, which at its roots was caused by the sociopolitical structure of the country and involved the relationship between Americo-Liberian settlers and indigenous Liberians.

Oftentimes when I mention that I am from West Africa, the question I'm asked is "What African language(s) do you speak?" Of course, my answer is always none. Then I narrate the story. I was born in Careysburg, but my non-African linguistics can be traced back to the antebellum South (during the time before the American Civil War).

Liberia was first settled by indigenous Africans, who migrated mainly from northeastern Africa (Sudanic belt) due to the Arab invasion of
that region. In the 1800s, the American Colonization Society, a philanthropic and missionary society, began returning freed slaves back to
Africa. In 1847, the freed Negro settlers gained their independence and
Liberia became one of two independent African nations (the other was
Ethiopia). After independence, ACS continued to settle freed blacks
in Liberia until the late 1800s. In 1856 Careysburg was founded, due
to its topography, climate, the absence of deadly mosquitoes, and the
potential for agriculture.

Careysburg was built by these freed Negro settlers, and up until
the 1960s one could view many colonial-style homes in the city. The
homes were built with planks, timbers, or logs with framed and zinc
sidings. Some of them were built on large whitewashed stones, piled
up as pillars. My childhood years, the early 1960s, were spent with my
grandaunt, Nancy Anna Freeman-Wordsworth. Every morning, she sat
on the back veranda just between the newly renovated indoor kitchen
with the icebox and wood stove and the modern bathroom with its lux-
urious amenities. Prior to the renovation, we took baths in buckets or
zinc tubs with water drawn from the well. The house had a generator for
electricity, which operated before I was born in 1956, but most people
used kerosene, oil lamps, or lanterns for lighting.

Education was a luxury, as most of the population was illiterate—
even within the American Negro settlers' communities. This trend continued during my childhood and adolescence. In the 1960s, I remember helping to carry sand in a wheelbarrow for the foundation of the
Careysburg Public School, which was under construction. The United
States government under President John F. Kennedy had sent Peace
Corps teachers to Liberia, and there we were in Careysburg enjoying
the luxuries of American education. For the first time, we had a school
library. Thus, the impact of Western education continued to influence
my philosophy (life, liberty, and the pursuit of happiness within a

democratic society) along with that of many other Liberians. I went on to graduate from Cuttington University in Liberia and worked for the Liberian government as an economic analyst until the civil war began in 1990.

My story of how I got here is twofold. From the 1600s to the 1800s, slavery coexisted with freedom. You had nonblack immigrants seeking freedom coexisting with the transportation of slaves to be auctioned in North America. But freedom dominated the human soul, whether you were slave or free. It was this quest for freedom that led my forefathers back to Liberia, West Africa—the land of the free.

Our family's ancestry goes back to the Hemings family of Monticello, home of the American president Thomas Jefferson in the 1700s and early 1800s.

Shortly after he was elected president in February 1801, Thomas Jefferson hired John Freeman, a Negro slave, from Dr. William Baker of the state of Maryland. John Freeman worked at the White House during Jefferson's presidency, waiting tables, taking care of the halls and dining area, and sometimes personally attending to the president (Stanton, Lucia C., *Those Who Labor for My Hopelessness*, p. 50, 2012).

John Freeman often accompanied Thomas Jefferson on his vacations to Monticello. During one of his visits, Freeman became engaged to Melinda Colbert, a granddaughter of Elizabeth (Betty) Hemings, the matriarch of the Hemings family of Monticello, and niece of the most famous member of the family, Betty's daughter Sally Hemings. John Freeman and Melinda Colbert eventually married and lived at the White House.

In March 1809, as Thomas Jefferson was preparing to depart the White House, he sold John Freeman to James Madison, the fourth president of the United States. James Madison assigned John Freeman as the dinner room servant in the White House. Melinda Freeman worked at sewing curtains and drapes.

Later, both of them became free and were among the first free black families to reside in the District of Columbia. John and Melinda

Freeman, who had at least eight children, were active in the antislavery endeavors of Washington's free blacks. One of their sons, John R. Freeman, immigrated to Careysburg, Liberia, in 1860.

According to the *African Repository and Colonial Journal*, Volume 34, 1860, Mr. John R. Freeman, a worthy young man of color, who sailed from Baltimore, Maryland, for Liberia, wrote in a brief note, just as the ship was leaving the Savannah River, May 25, 1860:

> "I cannot fail to express my obligations for your interest in my behalf, and for letters to President Benson and others. Your councils will remain with me as precious jewels. Pray that the mercies of God may follow me, and that his arm may defend me, and that it may not be amiss for me to say, that as the mariner steers his vessel from port to port by the needle of the compass, faith shall conduct me to the haven of eternal peace, even though it be against head winds and through stormy seas, at all times will I cast my cares upon God, content to be His—whether I live or die. As I expect inquiries to be made for me in Washington by some of my friends, please assure them that I am well, doing well, and hope to do better."

John R. Freeman was among the list of emigrants sailing on the *Mary Caroline Steven* from Baltimore, Maryland, in April. He became controller of the Department of the Treasury of Liberia in 1868, according to Supreme Court reports, under Liberia's president James Spriggs Payne. At the beginning of Payne's second term, in 1876, John R. Freeman became secretary of the treasury, but he died that same year.

My aunt Nancy Anna Freeman-Wordsworth recounted the story, tracing her ancestors to the 1800s through her Liberian-born father, Reverend Benjamin G. Freeman Sr. (whose ancestors came from Washington, DC), and his wife, Mary Urey (whose ancestors came from Kentucky). She told us that we had a connection to Thomas Jefferson. My research now looks farther, to the 1700s, to Elizabeth Hemings's (1735–1807) daughter Betty Brown, whose daughter was Melinda

Colbert (niece of Sally Hemings), and who married John Freeman (Jefferson's White House servant).

In 1948, my grandfather Benjamin G. Freeman II, a member of the National Legislature from 1939 to 1951, and Speaker of the House of Representatives from 1943 to 1951, served as member and chairman of the Liberian delegation to the United Nations General Assembly. During that 1948 UN conference, Liberia's was a decisive vote in obtaining the partition of Palestine and leading to Israel becoming a nation in its own right. On June 1, 1948, while in New York, Liberian Speaker Benjamin G. Freeman wrote the Liberian president, William V. S. Tubman, to say he would be leaving for Washington to stay a week with his relatives.

During this trip to the United States, he made a significant connection with the Washington descendants of John Freeman and Melinda Colbert-Freeman.

On his visit to Washington, DC, in 1948, Benjamin Freeman II took a photo (opposite, in white suit) with John Freeman/Melinda Colbert-Freeman's Washington, DC, descendants, thereby connecting the dots of the African and American families. In 2013, I met Jeanne Cupid, Isaac and Minerva Cupid's daughter, in Washington, DC. Jeanne and Isaac are on the far right of the photo, in the back row. Jeanne died in October 2015. Since meeting her, I have been in contact with the Washington family.

But the irony of it all is that Betty Hemings was born into slavery, probably in Chesterfield County. According to her grandson Madison Hemings, she was the daughter of an English sea captain and an enslaved woman, possibly born in Africa.

Thus, our journeys have been back and forth and interrupted by various factors (slavery, freedom, separation of families, faith, economics, and civil war). As I look back, I can share that my family was seeking the opportunity for the true promise of freedom. While this freedom with God's ascendency lies in the opportunities for education, economics, faith, and philosophies, it is incumbent upon me to share those same opportunities with others, especially the less fortunate in developing countries, including Liberia.

A visit to Washington, DC by the Liberian relatives. Benjamin G. Freeman II (seated, in white suit), his niece, Eugenia Stevenson (standing fourth, from left to right), and her husband George Stevenson (far left) with their American relatives, who are descendants of John and Melinda Freeman (1948).

Peter Blair Henry

Peter Blair Henry is the WR Berkley Professor of Economics, and Dean Emeritus of New York University's Stern School of Business.

I forgive people for wondering just how, exactly, a boy from rural Jamaica wound up not only as a professor of global economics but also dean at a top business school in New York City. It sometimes seems incredible even to me. It would not be incorrect to say that the story of how I arrived in the United States, became a naturalized citizen, and found my professional calling hinges on the actions of a fledgling nation's prime minister and, separately, a twelve-year-old girl who happened to be my sister. At its most elemental, however, mine is a story driven by the desire of one generation to give greater educational opportunities to the next, and as such it is perhaps one of the most common journeys taken to America.

This story begins with the fact that my parents, George and Caroll Henry, each belonged to the first generation of their families to attend university, for which they both received scholarships—they could never have gone to college otherwise. Born to humble beginnings, my father's earliest memories of school were lessons that his mother, a teacher, delivered from her "classroom" beneath an acacia tree that sprang from the red dirt of Pedro Plains, Jamaica. A dedicated student, my father's academic excellence was rewarded with a scholarship to Cornwall College in Montego Bay. The pride in such an education manifested when Dad returned to Pedro for the holidays. He was easy to spot: a gangly, six-foot-two, 150-pound youth strolling through the dust and searing heat, sweating beneath his red-and-gold woolen Cornwall blazer. In 1958, he matriculated at the University of the West Indies. There, on the Mona Campus, he studied chemistry, participated in sports, and met his match—Caroll Easter Rose, the young lady from Kingston who was every bit my father's equal in intellect, integrity, and determination. Eventually my parents arrived in the United States for the first time, on scholarships and student visas to pursue their doctorates—his in chemistry at the Illinois Institute of Technology, hers in biology at the University of Chicago.

Despite being third in birth order, I was the first among us four siblings to be born in my parents' native Jamaica. My sister and older brother were born in Chicago and Ontario, respectively, first while my parents completed their PhDs, then thanks to a job my father took with a Canadian company. But in 1962, Jamaica gained independence, and like many scholars of their generation, my parents wanted to help build a better Jamaica during those heady early days. They returned to their island home.

I was born in Kingston in 1969; soon after, my younger brother followed. In 1973 our family moved to an idyllic property in the rural village of Hampstead, in the parish of Saint Mary—the heart of Jamaica's cocoa-growing district. As an oil chemist, my father formulated and supervised the manufacturing process for transforming cocoa beans into chocolate for Cadbury Foods in the nearby town of Highgate. (Imagine: a father who worked in a chocolate factory!) My mother conducted research on cocoa and vegetable pathology at an agricultural research station called Orange River.

Growing up in Jamaica was extraordinary. In Hampstead we lived on nineteen lush acres, in a two-story house situated high on a hill with a postcard view of the Caribbean Sea. We lived in such a rural area that we didn't have a phone—but we had no shortage of books. We also had dogs, chickens, and goats, fruit trees of every variety, our imaginations, and plenty of freedom for youthful adventures. When the power went out, as it did frequently, Dad told stories as we clustered around his knees in the dark. He told duppy stories, which are Jamaican ghost stories. These contained lively bursts of patois, but my father equally enjoyed the King's English. I remember him reciting Coleridge's "Rime of the Ancient Mariner": *Water, water, every where, nor any drop to drink.* Prophetic for an island on the brink of political and economic ruin. Within five years of moving to Hampstead, our family's dream of a thriving Jamaica ceded to parental worries over their children's future: the American dream would soon be ours instead.

In a now famous speech given in 1975, Jamaica's prime minister at the time, Michael Manley, declared that Jamaica had "no room for millionaires." For those who desired individual prosperity, he suggested one of the country's "five flights a day to Miami." Having chosen careers as scientists, getting rich was never a priority for my parents, but Manley's antibusiness rhetoric and policies produced consequences that eventually forced them to take his advice. By 1977, due to the rising costs of doing business in Jamaica, Cadbury had moved operations to West Africa. My father took another job in Kingston, but the hundred-mile commute pitted the cost of gas against food for the family. My mother's work also became difficult, as import restrictions and a lack of funding required Herculean efforts to obtain research equipment and personnel.

When my parents learned that our local school was going to close because of financial problems, they decided that immigrating to the US with a family of six and few assets provided a better chance of educating their children than soldiering on in a country in economic free fall. Sponsored by my twelve-year-old sister, who was an American citizen due to her birth in Chicago, our family drove to the embassy in Kingston and waited with crowds of others trying to leave the island. We obtained the necessary documents and left Jamaica on February 28, 1978.

The question of why standards of living are higher in some countries than in others—and what can be done about it—is one of the great mysteries of economics, and it's been my professional obsession across the better part of four decades, since my arrival in the US. To settle in our adoptive country, my parents made the typical educated immigrant choice: they found the cheapest house in the best school district they

Me (second from right) with my siblings in Jamaica on the day of our one-way departure to the United States (February 28, 1978).

My parents and maternal grandfather (same day).

could afford in the Chicago area, and we moved to the suburb of Wilmette. This move quickly taught me, first, that winter in Illinois is a lot colder than in Kingston, and second, our middle-class neighbors in the States had a great deal more disposable income than middle-class families we knew in Jamaica, ours included.

Our life in the US wasn't hard by most standards—I certainly don't pretend we were poor—but it was different. Thrifty by nature, my parents were determined not to spend money on anything that wasn't related to basic needs and the development of their children. Our house was a very modest two-bedroom ranch style. My parents slept in one of the bedrooms, my sister in the other. My brothers and I crammed into a space that was meant to be a study and that opened onto the living room. My dad hung a secondhand bamboo screen, and that was that. Then there were the cars: clunkers that my father rehabilitated in our front yard. I felt mortified when he pulled up in front of my posh public high school or a friend's driveway in another noisy old green Ford sedan. The contrast between Dad's jalopies and the luxury automobiles in which everyone else seemed to be chauffeured could make things nearly as hard for a boy trying to assimilate as his foreign appearance or manners. It's fair to say that at the time I attended, my high school was not very diverse; I was aware of my outsider status.

Moving from Jamaica was no piece of cake for Mom, either. For a long time my mother's principal employment consisted of working in a department store, wrapping gifts and doing other things for which a University of Chicago PhD made her vastly overqualified. When my mother finally landed a position as a tenure-track professor at Chicago State University, it was a ninety-mile round-trip commute from Wilmette. (My father promptly bought our family's first new car for her. He also spent many hours helping her format her first paper for publication using our outdated computer.)

Of course, we also had good times. We no longer swam in rivers, but Wilmette had nice public pools that we enjoyed each summer. We might have heard fewer stories, since the power almost never went out, but there are distinct advantages to having a reliable power supply. There were baseball, basketball, and football games, trips to Wisconsin Dells and to the Great America amusement park. We also had fun just clowning around in that tiny, overstuffed house with the old cars in the driveway.

And no matter how simple, old, or hand-me-down our house, cars, computer, or clothes might have been, my parents were first-class in the things that mattered. They walked tall, heads high. When they spoke to our neighbors or interacted with teachers at school, money no longer seemed so important. My parents were smart, educated; they had character and good judgment, and everybody knew it. With every word, they leveled the playing field around me that much more. This is the power of an education: my parents had a sense of self.

There's a Caribbean saying I heard many times as a child, and from my father as a refrain to accompany my teenage years: *long road draw sweat, short cut draw blood*. Doing something the right way—creating results of lasting value—requires hard work; shortcuts end in pain and suffering.

My parents' thrift and sacrifices, our family's immigration story, paved a long road from Pedro Plains to Wilmette, but the efforts paid off through the value of the education my siblings and I received. To this day, not a week goes by that my mother does not remind me to count among my blessings the opportunities that my adoptive country afforded. She's right. Without our journey I would never have won scholarships to attend the University of North Carolina at Chapel Hill, the University of Oxford, and MIT, let alone earn tenure at Stanford and end up as dean of the NYU Stern School of Business. Indeed, the role of education in my family history has bestowed a personal appreciation for the power of education to make or break a young person's chances in life and has driven me to raise money to create scholarships for high-achieving undergraduates who would not otherwise be able to attend college.

Yet for all the hallowed halls in which I have had the privilege of studying, and of opening doors so that others might also study, life in the rugged hills of Hampstead still formed the core of my character. Although my family left the island that was our home, I remain connected to it emotionally. You can live in many places, but you are only born in one. In a fate at once ironic and marvelous, it took leaving my Jamaican home and embracing my American one to finally absorb the lessons that my birthplace and parents had to teach me.

Declan Kelly

Declan Kelly was US special envoy to Northern Ireland. He is the founder, chairman, and co-CEO of Teneo, an international consulting firm.

My journey to becoming a citizen of this most incredible country was enabled by two things—love and luck.

When I was a child, the idea of even going to visit America seemed like an impossible dream. I grew up in a small village called Portroe. The house we lived in was a three-room cottage—not three bedrooms but three rooms in total. When I was seven years old, that house burned to the ground one night when we weren't there, and my parents lost virtually everything they had in the world. We were left only with the clothes on our backs, a dog covered in soot called Tiny, and a loving extended family that opened their homes to us for a year while we built a new house from the ground up and began to rebuild our lives.

That was 1975, a year when unemployment in Ireland was heading rapidly past 7 percent, inflation was at almost 20 percent, and emigration was a booming industry.

My father built us a new house with his bare hands, and my mother worked three jobs for several of my formative years to ensure that my brother and I could have an education. That gift of education was what they devoted their lives to; our house was full of books, music, discussion, and laughter. Every spare penny went into further education and tuition to ensure we could achieve the best possible life.

That backdrop is important, because from an early age my parents drilled into me that you can achieve almost anything if you work hard enough and never take no for an answer. They also instilled in me a belief that the vast majority of people want you to succeed and achieve your dreams, and that belief in humanity is an enabler, a force multiplier, if you choose to use it that way.

Nowhere is that more evident than in America, a place where success is applauded, failure is met with the belief one should get back up and try again until one succeeds, and, above all else, hard work is rewarded.

Growing up as a boy and then a young man, I was always curious to know whether the things I had been able to achieve in my life while living in Ireland would be achievable if I ever got the opportunity to ply my trade on the biggest stage of all: America.

I never thought that opportunity would come in reality, but, as life has a habit of showing us all, sometimes things happen when you least expect them. And that's when my wife, Julia, literally and figuratively walked into my life, in a random place at a random time, and my whole world changed forever. She was the reason I came to live in America, to have the opportunity to build a new life with someone who viewed the world through fresh eyes and a perspective that aligned with mine.

Her story and that of her parents made me realize that only in America are you truly given the opportunity to remake yourself in a positive way if you are prepared to do the work and dedicate yourself to the task. Her parents were political refugees who escaped from Moscow and proactively elected to come live in America. They were highly accomplished individuals in their own right and came here with $200 in their pockets, ready to start all over with nothing. Two aerospace engineers, my father- and mother-in-law started life in America handing out flyers for three dollars an hour and mending dresses for something similar, while at the same time learning how to speak English. A bit of a sea change from helping design the simulator for the Russian space shuttle and launching satellites into space, which they used to do when they lived in Russia. And their daughter, the first Russian woman ever to be admitted to the University of Pennsylvania, waited tables and worked in kitchens to put together the money to buy the tickets that would help them escape Russia. Seeing all of this made me realize very quickly that what I saw as risks or insurmountable obstacles to my dream of living in America were nothing by comparison.

And so I left Ireland behind and came to America to start all over again and build a new life.

The Irish have always been integral to the American social fabric, and so New York quickly felt welcoming to me for that reason. Two amazing men, the late Don Keough and my great friend John Sharkey, mentored and looked out for me in ways that would take an entire book to describe. Their endless kindness and support are something I will never forget and made everything that has happened to me since then actually possible. It was my good fortune to meet them at a time when I needed help the most, and together with the love of my wife I managed to build a new life in this country.

Don Keough used to say that he tap-danced into life every day, and he really did. Only in this amazing country is that truly possible. Where a kid who had no running water in his home in Ireland for the first seven years of his life gets to do the kind of things I have been so fortunate to do.

I feel blessed to live here. I am deeply honored to have been able to serve the American government and do some public service along the way. One of the proudest days in my life was the day I received that blue passport that meant I could finally call myself an American as well as an Irishman.

Our two beloved children, Adrian and Charlotte, are now making their own dreams. All they know is the New York and America they see today. I tell them every single day how lucky they are to be born in this country. Ten times a day I find myself saying, "Only in America."

Only in America.

Jackie Koppell

Jackie Koppell is a political satirist, writer, and producer.

Turns out, my ancestors were pretty badass. It took international tragedies to get them to leave their homelands. They resisted originally, but the Irish potato famine and the rise of the Nazis were eventually enough to do the trick.

I'm the proud product of Irish and German immigrants. (And yes, that means I'm extremely pale. I like to think my inability to tan is a choice, but who am I kidding?)

It may sound a bit odd to think of these two groups as immigrants, since today they're just part of the melting pot of modern American life, but back then they weren't exactly welcomed. For those of you who weren't around in the 1800s through some of the 1900s, signs were often found in store windows saying "No Irish Need Apply," and in 1939, the US refused to allow a boat of Holocaust refugees to dock. (Sent away, many of them died in concentration camps.) The Irish and German Jews of the last century were sort of like the Central American and Muslim immigrants today: people in search of a better life, eager to contribute to the United States in return. The stories of my family are like those of so many other immigrants and refugees, past and present.

My father's parents arrived in the US after fleeing Nazi Germany, although they did so separately. They first met when my grandmother interviewed my grandfather for a magazine while on an airplane. (Flying was a big deal at the time.) As she put it, she lost her heart and head in the air that day. Back on land, they dated for a while, but it was clear to my grandmother Gabrielle Kaufman, or Oma, as I called her, that my grandfather wasn't ready to settle down, so they split up.

(Commitment issues were a thing back then, too.) Around the same time, the increased violence and discrimination that accompanied the rise of the Nazis was impossible to ignore. Oma fled Germany in 1932 and moved to England, followed by the US. In one of the most inspiring actions of her life, my grandmother was the first leader of the Kindertransport, bringing German Jewish children fleeing Hitler from Germany to America. Transporting these children helped save their lives and offered them the opportunity of a future.

When my grandfather fled Germany, he went to Palestine but took getting shot at by a group of Arabs as a sign that he probably shouldn't stay there. So, he moved to the US, and, just as my grandmother felt she was moving on, my grandfather arrived on her doorstep. They created a family together while working to contribute to their new country.

My grandfather had been a book publisher back in Germany, so with this skill, and conscious of the dangers of Nazism and Communism at the time, he made it a point to publish books that helped Americans understand the evils that were being committed in Europe. (At the time, Americans were reticent to get involved in the war; an isolationist campaign was led by an organization called the America First Committee to keep the United States out of WWII. Its members were America Firsters. Two of the books that my grandfather published helped Americans understand what was really happening: *Out of the Night* by Jan Valtin and *The Revolution of Nihilism* by Hermann Rauschning.)

I promise there was a lighter side to my grandfather's publishing ventures—much lighter side! He helped my father establish the hugely successful Let's Go travel guidebooks. As an undergraduate, my dad was president of Harvard Student Agencies, and it was through this student organization that he created these travel guides at the suggestion of my grandfather. Millions of copies of the Let's Go books have been printed. If you're ever walking around a foreign city with a guidebook (or website) called Let's Go, you have an immigrant named Henry Gunther Koppell to thank for preventing you from getting lost or getting food poisoning… or staying in a hotel with a coin-operated shower.

On my mother's side, there's more of a mystery. The families of my grandparents are somewhat shrouded in... well, they're not shrouded, we just don't know very much. In fact, I really only know a little about my mother's father's family. Irish immigrants were a tough breed—not ones to talk much about their feelings and definitely not known to be the most communicative people in the world. (Guinness apparently didn't make the tongue slippery!) But what I do know about my family is awesome.

My great-great-grandfather Bernard Coyle was born in Ireland and moved to the US in the 1850s, likely because of the potato famine. He settled in Brooklyn, married a nice Irish girl named Catherine Comiskey, and had six kids. Two cousins of Bernard fought in the Civil War and were imprisoned in Libby Prison in Virginia. One member of the family was a chief rigger for the Brooklyn Bridge during its construction. Another was a customs inspector, working on the docks checking cargo listings and making sure taxes were paid. Though my relatives started off new to the United States and were conscious of being Irish (it wasn't cool back then) they were grateful to be here and proudly helped weave the fabric of America today.

Though I try to approach my family history with humor, the impact each of these individuals had on American society is not lost on me. Millions of people have traveled and discovered new corners of the world, finding opportunities for greater communication and understanding with each other. Today, thousands of people benefit because my grandmother not only saved herself from the Nazis but helped save others. Those refugees went on to have families and children of their own, each of them making a mark on our world. Millions of people have crossed the Brooklyn Bridge, opening up opportunities for work, travel, and growth throughout the New York metropolitan area. Yet the lives of these relatives can also be measured by the countless actions they took that further served their communities on a more local level, through volunteer work with their churches, synagogues, nursing homes, etc. This legacy of service has been carried on by my parents. My mother,

Lorraine Coyle, is a strong female role model who put herself through college and law school, owns her own law firm, and has devoted time to political causes, tutored inner-city children, volunteered to help victims of rape and sexual assault, and so much more. My father, Oliver Koppell, has dedicated his life to the law and public service, owning his own law firm as well as being a thirty-year public servant, elected first as a New York state assemblyman and then rising to become attorney general for the state of New York, followed by many years as a New York City councilman. Just a generation or two removed from the hardships of immigrant life, my family has been able to find the best kind of success: providing for their families while giving back in return.

Every contribution that my immigrant ancestors made enriched others' lives. Though they are gone and won't get acclaim at this point, I am so proud of the contributions they made to this incredible country of ours.

Funa Maduka and Nonso Maduka

Funa Maduka and Nonso Maduka are sister and brother. Funa is a film executive and filmmaker. Nonso is a senior product manager at NerdWallet. Each served as co-presidents of their respective classes at Harvard Business School.

We stood quietly in my mother's bedroom doorway as she reviewed our report cards. She was taking it all in, reading every single teacher's comment. After she finished reading one she would place it on the bed. Like gladiators awaiting the emperor's verdict, we anxiously awaited her response. Our eyes were fixed on her every movement. Finally she said, "You tried, my dears. Next time it should be all As. I don't want to see Bs."

Since emigrating to the United States from Nigeria, excellence had always been the ringing refrain from our mother. An Eastern Region Area Chemist with the Nigeria National Petroleum Corporation, she left Nigeria with three children under the age of three to join our father, a medical doctor, as he completed his residency in Virginia. Upon arriving in this country, companies required her to "recertify," in a sense. She took hourly jobs and enrolled in Howard University to complete her second undergraduate degree in chemical engineering. Impressed by her performance, Howard granted her a full scholarship to continue her studies in their master's program.

In Maryland, our parents divorced. My mother was forced to embrace a new challenge: raising four children on her own in a country still new to her, while building a career for herself. Throughout grade school and beyond, it seemed as if our mother created time out of thin air. She woke us up at five in the morning to begin getting ready for the day. We presented ourselves downstairs within the hour and often would be sent back upstairs to iron out wrinkled collars or sleeves. To this day we have a complex about wrinkled clothing. As we ate breakfast, she'd pack our lunches.

Before leaving the house, there was always prayer. She never wanted us to forget the guiding hand that God had in our lives. She'd walk us to the bus stop (later on we'd walk ourselves) with firm reminders along the way about behavior and, again, excellence. During those days her fragrance of choice was Trésor by Lancôme. The scent held us almost as tightly and reassuringly as she did as we pressed ourselves into her for the morning hug goodbye. Unbeknownst to us at the time, after getting us on our way to school, there were mornings when the car wouldn't start and she'd have to figure out how to get herself to class.

And speaking to her now, she'd tell us there were nights she didn't sleep because she was studying for exams and that, when she woke us up at the crack of dawn, she'd just finished going over her last chapter. We don't know how she did it, but we do know there's only one response to "how I got here" for the Maduka children—our mother, Helen Uju Umeadi Maduka.

In reality, though, *how* she did it is much less important than *why* she did it. Our mother did not leave a top-tier job at an oil company in Nigeria for the sheer challenge. Our mother left because she is defined, as America is defined, by a virtuous instinct for betterment. But betterment, in her eyes, is never selfish and never without impact. In our prayers every morning before school, our mother always emphasized service. Even when times were hard—one winter we all slept in one room to save money on the heating bill—we'd stare in amazement as my mother faithfully wrote checks to charity causes every Sunday.

Her unyielding sacrifice, day in and day out, inspired us to achieve. Our brother, Ifediora Maduka is a venture capital advisor who won two state championships in high school for excellence in oratory. Our sister,

Uzoamaka Maduka, is an editor-cum-filmmaker, named twice to the *Forbes 30 Under 30* for a magazine she co-founded. Collectively, we've garnered multiple degrees from top-tier institutions, worked for top companies and foundations, and committed ourselves to serving our respective charitable causes. But one of the most enduring lessons that our mother taught and continues to teach us is that excellence solely for excellence's sake is not excellent at all.

Each new arrival to this country's shores weaves their own story into the fabric of the country's larger tale. No one comes to America to be average. One's desire to enter this country is tantamount to one's acceptance of the challenge to be better and do better, not just for oneself but for one's family, community, and country. Our mother still says to us often, "Charity begins at home, and should not end there." She lives by this credo, as do we. By investing so tirelessly in us, she made her greatest contribution to the country she loves. She raised citizens and believers who pay it forward. It was her efforts that opened the doors for our success. Her high standards helped us actualize the potential that we sometimes did not know existed. As her children we're still writing our story, and through it, working to leave blank pages on which others like our family can boldly write theirs.

Mario Neiman

Mario Neiman is a driver for a car service in Northern Virginia.

It was early 1904. Moshe Neiman and his family were patiently waiting in line to disembark the ship that had brought them from Odessa, in faraway Ukraine, now docked at Ellis Island in New York. They had arrived to America at last, and their hopes and prayers were about to be answered.

The line was moving slowly as they advanced to the plank that would bring them ashore. Suddenly a nervous murmur started to grow in front of them. What! No more people from this ship! Says who? Why? This can't be true! But it was indeed true. Somebody at immigration had decided they had enough, a quota had been filled, and they were not going to admit anyone else from this ship.

And now what? What's to become of us? Where do we go? Well, the boat continues down to Argentina, in South America, and they say immigrants from all nations are welcomed. Back in Odessa they had heard of Jews going to Argentina a few years before and doing well there. So, faced with no alternative, Buenos Aires became their new destiny.

Going back to Ukraine was out of the question. The Russian armies of the czar were getting ready to fight the Japanese and were drafting Jewish men en masse, almost a death sentence for the unlucky ones. Moshe had avoided the draft and now, with his wife, Ite Arstein, and his two young children, Shlomo, aged four, and Lev, barely three months old, was facing an unknown future in far and remote South America.

The rest of his story is a good one. He was a smart man and soon, in spite of not knowing the language or the local customs and thanks to his inventive and hard work, he was able to save some money and open up a small tire shop in La Plata, a new town thirty miles south of Buenos Aires. The year was 1909, and it is hard to imagine why he thought selling tires would be a good idea then, when cars were just beginning to hit the roads. Obviously, he saw something in the business, because not only was his tire store the only one in town for the following thirty-five years, but in 1937 the family business Moises Neiman e Hijos (and Sons) won an award from the Goodyear Company for being their largest volume seller *in the world* outside the US. He became a very wealthy man, but he never forgot his roots and helped a great number of other Jewish immigrants settle in this new land. He founded the local Jewish community center and died in 1938, in his midseventies, a well-respected and honored elder of the community.

I was the first grandson born after his death, and, following the Jewish tradition, my given name in Yiddish is Moshe, honoring my grandfather Moshe Neiman, that courageous and industrious man who never looked back and, with his young family in tow, faced the uncertainty of a new life in the Americas.

The other side of my family, headed by my great-grandfather Dovid Shmuckler, had arrived in Argentina twelve years before, in 1891. They came from a small village near Konstantinov in western Ukraine. They became Jewish gauchos (cowboy-like field hands) who settled in fertile regions of Argentina in agricultural colonies established by the Jewish Colonization Association, which was founded by Baron Maurice de Hirsch, a Jewish-French industrialist. Deciding to help Russia's Jews emigrate and improve their lives, the Association bought more than 198,000 acres of land in Argentina to distribute among the settlers.

Dovid first brought his two eldest sons to help him, as well as a young niece to cook and clean house. It took them two long years to mark and prepare their land and build the basic facilities to bring the rest of the family from Ukraine, which they did in 1894. That's when my grandfather, six-year-old Shlomo Shmuckler, arrived in Argentina.

Shlomo grew up in the colony, learning about farming and all related chores. His teachers and companions were the local gauchos and his friends from other Jewish families. It was named Colonia Mauricio, in honor of their benefactor, Maurice de Hirsch, and eventually became the most successful of all the Jewish colonies in Argentina. They created the first farming cooperative in Latin America and introduced the sunflower from seeds they had brought from Russia. Unknown in the country before, sunflowers are now one of the main farm crops cultivated in Argentina.

Shlomo, now Salomon, became a true gaucho. He tamed horses, handled cattle, and excelled in the chores of a field hand. The only difference with his Catholic friends was that instead of attending church on Sundays, he would go to the synagogue on Fridays. He married Sofia (Sonya) Lerner, from Moisesville, the largest and most important Jewish settlement in Argentina, and had three daughters. My mother Emilia (Ethel), born in 1909, was the eldest. Her education started in a one-room school where her classmates were country folks of all ages from nearby farms. She used to talk about this big twentyish native boy whom she helped learn to read and write and who became one of the good friends of her childhood. After Emilia took third grade three years in a row (that was as high as the school went), and with their two younger daughters coming of age, Salomon and Sofia moved to Buenos Aires, the big city, so that the girls could have the proper education all Jewish families wanted for their children. All three girls got college degrees, and more.

In 1934, my mother, Emilia Shmuckler, married Luis Neiman, that three-month-old baby, Lev, who didn't get off the ship in New York in 1904. I was born in 1944, the third of four siblings. We all had a solid education, and my mother made sure we studied languages, especially English, which I did since kindergarten.

I always had a fascination with the United States. In my childhood I started a pen pal exchange with a distant cousin living in Cincinnati to whom I wrote in English and who helped me polish my writing. I also remember going periodically to the American Embassy's library to pick up travel brochures and magazines, especially one with an abridged history of the United States in the format of a comic book. I can still visualize the image of the patriots, disguised as Indians, throwing the tea into Boston Harbor.

Music also accompanied me all my life. I sang in family gatherings since my early childhood, mostly in English. Lullabies, cowboy songs, and, naturally, rock and roll hits. Bill Haley, Elvis, Sinatra, and many others became my ever-present companions. In 1971 I picked up my guitar and started my journey north. My best friend had left a few months before and was already in Paris playing in the Métro and passing the hat, which, in those youthful days, sounded like a great adventure. After a few months in Mexico, where my wife, Alicia, had joined me, and on our way to Paris we decided to make a quick stop in Washington, DC, where another Argentinian friend was staying. We did, and before we knew it, twenty years had gone by. We had become immigrants.

A few months after settling in DC, we took a trip to New York—I for the first time—to visit a friend staying there. We were happily cruising along the NJ Turnpike when, suddenly, approaching Manhattan and after a sharp curve, New York City came into full view. The Big Apple appeared in front of us in all her splendor. To this day I cannot quite explain what happened to me then. The emotional impact of that image was so strong that I just couldn't go on driving. I was trembling. I had to pull over to the shoulder to calm down and get ahold of myself. I was here! I finally had arrived! Broadway, the Empire State Building, Times Square—all my life I'd been hearing stories and reading about them, watching movies, imagining what it would be like to be there, and now, finally, here I was. We crossed the tunnel, and soon I felt I had come home. Like an old yearning fulfilled at last. Almost seventy years had to pass until I, Mario Neiman, the grandson of Moshe Neiman, could finally reach his original destination and come to America, to New York, the land he dreamed about and where, in spite of being so close, he was barred from ever setting foot.

Today, my American-born son, the grandson of Lev, that three-month-old baby who didn't get off the ship in 1904, is also named Luis in his honor and lives a fruitful and productive life in New York City. So does his sister, Victoria.

And the journey goes on…

Tim Scott

Tim Scott is the junior United States Senator from South Carolina. He was elected to the US Congress in 2010, appointed to the Senate in 2012, and in 2014, became the first African American senator elected in the South since Reconstruction. He was elected to a full six-year term in 2016.

After my parents divorced while I was still in grade school, my mother moved my brother and me from Michigan to South Carolina to live with my grandparents. We moved to a small, two-bedroom house that we called home for most of my childhood.

It was in our small home that I really got to know and appreciate the story of my grandfather Artis Ware, who to this day continues to be my hero and biggest inspiration. One of my most vivid memories of my grandfather is watching him read the newspaper every morning at the kitchen table. He looked like an executive or an attorney, setting an incredible example for his two impressionable grandsons. It was from him that I first learned to appreciate the importance of education, and how literacy could help open doors of opportunities.

Years later I came to find out my grandfather actually could not read. He was simply pretending so that he could impart an invaluable life lesson to his family. My grandfather was born in Salley, South Carolina, in 1921, a much different time in our beloved Palmetto State. My grandfather was forced out of a segregated school in the third grade and went to work in a cotton field so he could earn fifty cents a day to help his family. My grandfather persevered and went on to raise a family where he instilled in us the values of hard work, compassion, and the will to never give up.

Sadly, we lost my grandfather in 2016. But he lived long enough to see one grandson elected to Congress, another grandson rise to command sergeant major in the army, and a great-grandson graduate from college and start graduate school at Duke University.

That is the power of opportunity in America. In a single lifetime, families can go from not being given a fair chance to learn to read to graduating from college. We only need a level playing field to start from, a fair chance to succeed, and an appreciation for education and hard work.

There have been times in our past when the playing field did not seem as level. Our nation has a provocative history when it comes to race. There was a time when the color of your skin would determine your fate in life. But I thank God for the trailblazers who rose up and fought relentlessly for equality. I stand on the shoulders of giants who risked their own safety, so that generations upon generations of African Americans could live out the true American ideal and God-given right that "all men are created equal."

It is necessary to remind ourselves of where we've been. I hope that all Americans can understand the depth of the pain, agony, and tragedy of slavery and inequality. I hope that, from time to time, the weight of the past will slow your gait and bow your head. And as you consider history, I hope that the sense of freedom and a sense of expectation will overwhelm you. And that you will feel individually responsible for making America even better for every single citizen in our land.

Mary Skafidas

Mary Skafidas is Vice President of Investor Relations and Corporate Communications for Loews Corporation.

My family's origins begin at the birthplace of civilization, philosophy, and wisdom—Greece! At least if you believe the Greek supremacy portrayed in the movie *My Big Fat Greek Wedding* that's true.

The movie is often quoted in my house and while it's a caricature of Greek-Americans—loud, brash, talking over one another, food-focused and family-oriented—it hits the mark almost on the bullseye. Not just for Greek families, the portrayal is reminiscent of other immigrant families as well—Italians, Jews, Russians, Turks, or Persians to name a few.

My father's family is from Mani, Greece. A dry, harsh, mountainous area that creates people just as harsh—with unbending wills and indomitable spirits. In other words, a swift kick to the head by a mule wouldn't begin to dent the craniums of the people from Mani. It's often said that all the bad-tempered Spartans (legend has it Spartans left deformed infants out in the wilderness to die rather than be burdened with raising them) were sent to Mani. So, you can just imagine what my father's side of the family is like.

My mother's side of the family is from Kalamata, Greece, known for its olives. In contrast to my father's side, my mother's family is as smooth and polished as olive oil made from Kalamata olives. They say opposites attract, and the contrast between my mother and my father, and their families, has made for some very interesting family dinners.

My parents' journey to America took place more than forty-five years ago. They simply boarded a plane and arrived. They were lucky enough to have family in the US that sponsored them to become citizens. Their physical journey, unlike earlier immigrants, was a non-event. It was the emotional journey they took after their arrival that really defines my family.

I'm sure my parents have—on more than one occasion—questioned why they left behind their comfortable middle-class surroundings to move to the United States. When I was a child, my family and I lived in Sunset Park, Brooklyn—complete with gangs, tiny apartments full of roaches and mice, and a gaggle of teenage mothers. Overlaid on top was constant street noise—yelling, loud crashes, fists hitting—I remember as a little girl sitting in the corner of the room with my hands over my ears trying to block it all out, trying to find a minute's worth of peace.

While those early years were hard on all of us as we acclimated to a new culture, I am thankful every day that my parents choose to come here, that they saw the writing on the wall for Greece's future. Every time I speak to one of my relatives in Greece currently facing years of recession with no recovery in sight, I know they made the right decision.

Growing up first-generation, straddling two countries, was not easy. Only someone who has lived this can understand what I mean. You are raised with the moral guidelines of a country you know nothing about. My parents where moored in Greece's archaic societal norms, never progressing their thinking with the country they lived in. Luckily, their old-fashioned thinking didn't extend to education, more specifically a woman's right to education. My parents, especially my father, believed that girls had just as much right to an education as boys. Would their thinking have been altered if I'd had a brother? I will never know. But I was one of the lucky ones, able to receive the tools I needed to make my own way in this world and not be reliant on a man. Others of my cohort were not as lucky.

As a first-generation immigrant I was very aware that I was Greek-American. Not of one country, but of two. I have tried to take the best of both—the rich history, beauty, and tradition of Greece and marry it to the fierce, forward momentum of the United States. I felt that Greek food deserved its own mention in this essay. Not enough good things can be said about Greek food and what a gift it is to the rest of the world!

I am blessed with two beautiful boys, the second generation (at least on my side of the family and more like the sixth on my husband's side). Their last name is Jones and while I dreamed of such an Americanized name as a little girl, today the name seems like white toast—dry, with no flair. That's why the middle name for both is Skafidas. It adds a little spice back into their names, makes them interesting, gives them a history and a story. A story that could only be written in America.

My boys' lives are the perfect blend of all the generations that have come before them. And as our family gathers to roast a lamb on Easter (which has mercifully moved from the front yard to the back), our family Greek, Jewish, Irish, Russian, Polish, and Welsh all come together to eat and celebrate that we are all Americans.

Jane Wang

Jane Wang is Vice President and a senior executive at Loews Corporation in New York.

As I stood with my head down in front of my class of fifty-two students in Shanghai, my second-grade teacher reprimanded me, "Where is your red scarf?" (It was a requirement to wear our Communist scarves every day in school.) "You think I'm going to help you with getting free lunch at school if you can't obey the simplest class rules?" Lesson learned: standing out, bad; blending in, good.

My mother and I came to the US shortly after that incident, when I was seven years old. My father had immigrated a year earlier for a PhD program at the University of Tennessee in Memphis. With $200 borrowed from relatives in his pocket, he came to the US on a student visa during the beginning of Deng Xiaoping's "opening up" of China. At a stipend of $10,000 a year, he and my mother had to work extra jobs for $2.50 an hour to make ends meet.

Both of my parents are part of the Lost Generation of China, a period during which the Communists shut down secondary education and forced young, able-bodied adolescents to the countryside to farm crops and manufacture goods. My father's father was a high school history teacher who, during the Anti-Rightist Movement in 1957, had raised criticisms against the Communist party and was cast to the countryside for "reeducation," leaving his wife and four kids to fend for themselves. My selfless and kind grandmother, having raised her children for ten years alone, ultimately passed due to lack of proper medical treatments during the Cultural Revolution. My father and his older sister had to take care of their younger siblings. When the Communists shut down the schools during the Cultural Revolution in 1966, he spent ten years of his life toiling away in the countryside, working with farmers and eating nothing more than a bowl of rice each day. When colleges and universities finally reopened, he was thirty years old. Instead of going to work at a blue-collar job, he never gave up his dream for higher education. He studied for the college entrance exam and entered college with peers a decade his junior. Even though he received BS and MS degrees as a highly honored student at top colleges in China, it still wasn't enough. He decided to come to America at the age of forty to continue his dream of being a higher-level scientist and providing his daughter a better education and more opportunities.

My mother's father was a technician at a steel plate printing company in China. He visited the US from 1944 to 1946 to study money-printing techniques in Washington, DC. During the Cultural Revolution, he was labeled a traitor for having traveled to "enemy" America and was captured by Mao's Red Army. They tried to beat a confession out of him until he jumped out the window in a suicide attempt. He survived but used a wheelchair for the remainder of his life. My grandmother's strength throughout this period greatly influenced my mother to be independent and capable of overcoming any situation. When my mother came to the US at the age of thirty-five, she had to learn a new language, work odd jobs, and, at the same time, study to become an accountant, the job she had in China.

Both of my parents' experiences during the Cultural Revolution taught them to keep their heads down, avoid unnecessary attention (as any attention was negative attention), and work hard. Education was their road map for success—and this was the single-minded focus under which I was raised.

My parents achieved the ultimate American dream. My dad graduated with a PhD in medicinal chemistry, designed drugs for treating glaucoma and age-related macular degeneration, and achieved more than thirty patents and research articles as a top scientist at the Novartis Institutes for BioMedical Research. My mother worked as an accountant until they both retired recently. They sent me to Stanford University and are now enjoying watching their grandchildren get a dual-language education at a private school in Manhattan.

Coming full circle, my daughter is now seven years old, the same age I was when I came to the US. Rather than commanding obedience and rote memorization, her education cultivates curiosity, fosters creativity, and even challenges authority. It is the American way.

The Survivors

/////

Adem T. Bunkeddeko

Nataliya Demchenko

Misha Galperin

David Harris

Daniel Lubetzky

Stephanie Murphy

Jane Swift

Andrew Tisch

Jan Vilcek

My mission in life is not merely to survive, but to thrive;
and to do so with some passion, some compassion, some
humor, and some style.

— Maya Angelou

Survival—it is the most primal instinct.

Our heroes in this chapter come from all over the world—Ukraine, Vietnam, Uganda, Libya, Czechoslovakia, and Iran. These are all stories of people who saw danger and chose to leave the impending destruction behind. However, when they arrived in America they did more than survive—they thrived.

Adem T. Bunkeddeko

Adem T. Bunkeddeko is a resident of Crown Heights and a member of Brooklyn Community Board 8.

There is a proverb in my parents' mother tongue that roughly translates as "being generous is not easy; generosity reveals a noble mind." The core ethic of this simple aphorism has traveled with me from my ancestral land of Uganda all the way to the hallowed halls of Harvard Business School.

I am the son of Ugandan refugees who fled the country's civil war to enjoy the peace and freedom of the United States. When my father arrived in America from war-torn Uganda in 1980, he was eight thousand miles away from his birthplace and family. Paving the way for my mother, who stayed behind, my father's first stop was an immigration and naturalization detention center in Elizabeth, New Jersey, where he spent several weeks in an eight-by-eleven-foot cell before being granted asylum. Five years later, he returned to Uganda—with its conflict still raging—to save my mother. Together, they would settle down and successfully raise their American-born children in a one-bedroom apartment in Queens, New York, which, despite being infested with cockroaches and mice, represented their American dream.

My parents worked two or three jobs each as social workers to keep a roof over our heads while also helping our family in Uganda. They were never discouraged by life's hardships and gave me a sense of what matters and what truly sustains—giving back. I spent many nights sharing the top of a secondhand bunk bed with my younger sister to accommodate the myriad relatives and family friends who poured in from the mother country. As a welcoming host, I spent many early mornings before school tutoring these guests in English as they readied themselves for job interviews seeking positions such as janitors or security guards. My afternoons and evenings were often spent helping to wire money to their children back in Uganda, many of whom wondered whether or not their parents would return to see them again. Although it was a demanding role for a child, I always knew I was helping family members whose situation was separated from my own by nothing more than fate.

My upbringing seared into my conscience a deep commitment to assisting others who were even less fortunate than my family. Many people view growing up poor to be a curse, but in hindsight, it has proven foundational for establishing some of the key tenets that drive me to this very day. That my family, despite our relative hardship, could find a way to lend a hand of assistance to those even needier than themselves has left an indelible mark on my psyche. It etched the theme that giving is not solely the province of the well-off and that by so doing we are all creating stronger, more resilient communities of mutual interest.

These themes inspired me to pursue public service as a means of broadening this communitarian ethic by helping forgotten communities and gave me a unique perspective on the problems besetting them. I have spent most of my career in community development and organizing as a means of helping these communities. Unfortunately, despite my efforts and those of countless others like me, these communities suffer tremendously because of a lack of financial investment, crippling social issues such as unequal educational opportunities and significant health disparities, and devastating cycles of poverty wrought because of high rates of unemployment.

My desire to make a difference in these communities motivated my decision to leave finance and join the Bedford Stuyvesant Restoration Corporation. As a leadership fellow, I helped form a collaboration of social, private, and public-sector partners to create an infrastructure of community assets to improve the educational and social outcomes of low-income children in central Brooklyn. I subsequently took a role at the Empire State Development Corporation helping to create public-private partnerships to revitalize distressed communities in Brooklyn. After receiving an MBA from Harvard Business School, I came right back home to take a job at Brooklyn Community Services, helping them evaluate their programs geared toward underserved populations.

In all, I am grateful for my family's struggles and for their moral example. As their son, I am fiercely proud of them. Just as my parents equipped those in need, I hope—as the second member of my immediate family to graduate from college and the first to earn a graduate degree—to equip the forgotten with the resources and knowledge that will empower them to end their cycle of poverty and despair.

Nataliya Demchenko

Nataliya Demchenko is an oncology nurse at Weill-Cornell Medicine. She had been a journalist in Ukraine.

As an oncology nurse, I look at the world from a different perspective. The field I work in, which does not play games or wear masks, humbles the most powerful people. Nothing can touch me more deeply than kindness, loyalty, and the will to fight and find joy in the present moment, no matter what. When it comes to cancer treatment, status and name become irrelevant, and love, sincerity, and family support step in to make the magic happen. Those values have given me strength and will always guide me in my life decisions.

On my father's side, my roots go back to the time of Catherine the Great, who at one point invited an architect from Greece to work in the Russian Empire. It was winter, and the architect and his wife did not know how to properly use the Russian stove to heat the house. As a result, the couple were asphyxiated by toxic fumes, but their son, sleeping in another room, was rescued. He was then adopted by a wealthy landlord named Goreloff from the city of Kaluga, ninety miles from Moscow. The boy who survived was my great-great-grandfather.

My mother's family, of Jewish heritage, came from the Khertson and Odessa regions of eastern Ukraine. Unfortunately, due to German as well as Soviet persecution, they never shared any family stories with their descendants.

Running from the Communists in the early twentieth century, my father's family bought some of the famously fertile land in Ukraine. However, between 1932 and 1933, this put them squarely in the path of the Holodomor, also known as the great famine. After that struggle came conscription, and by 1941, all the men in their region had left to fight in the Second World War.

My paternal grandfather was interned in a concentration camp in Germany, but he escaped and served in the Russian Army until the war ended in victory, returning home as an amputee but also a hero of the Soviet Army.

The trauma trickled down to younger generations—my paternal grandfather, Volodymir Demchenko, lost both his parents and grew up in the care of a stepmother. After high school, Volodymir left his home village for good, carrying only a backpack with some bread. This bright and ambitious young man was admitted to the Agriculture Academy of Kiev, and he graduated with honors as a doctor of veterinary medicine. At the age of twenty-six, he was the head of a farm and later CEO of the biggest chicken factory in the Kiev region. He shared his success with my grandmother Olga, a schoolteacher who has been his wife for fifty-five years.

My father, Yuriy Demchenko, grew up in a powerful and strict Soviet family that was carefully attuned to social norms and expectations. A creative soul, he found his escape and passion in music. He met my mother, Olga, at the Kiev Conservatory. In the 1980s, after fifty long years of fear, wars, and political repression, the Soviet people began to live in peace—but this was short-lived for most, including my family. In 1986, we escaped from the Chernobyl nuclear disaster to eastern Ukraine, where I would finish my schooling. Then in 1990, with the collapse of the Soviet Union and perestroika, we and all our country-men awoke, essentially, to find worthless paper in our savings account instead of money. In this turbulent new political and economic environment, my grandfather was coerced into leaving his position as CEO of the chicken factory by a so-called New Russian businessman. Despite everything, my family started over again and supported each other through it all.

This all seems long ago now. In 2002, I was accepted to the National Technical University of Ukraine's Igor Sikorsky Kyiv Polytechnic Institute. Knowing I carried a legacy of courage and hard work on my shoulders, I did my best at school. During my summer breaks, I joined the study abroad programs Camp America and Work and Travel USA, working as a camp counselor in Springfield, Missouri, and a hostess at West Gate Resort, Orlando. Being abroad was a valuable experience, but I could not wait to return to my home country and share my experiences.

My career as a journalist began during my freshman year in college. I was passionate about writing and driven by the opportunities and influence that the media afforded me. As a senior, I was one of five hundred students from the National Universities to be offered a government job in the press and media department for the mayor of Kiev. Unfortunately, my excitement and pride dissolved when it plunged into reality—the administration of my nation's capital turned out to be a corrupt bureaucracy. I felt like an outsider. This disappointment fueled my new and better dream—to become a documentary filmmaker and reveal the truth. To pursue it, I left the administration and began honing my skills at script writing and editing at a TV station. I wrote my first documentary, about J-1 visas and the jobs they provide for international students. At the same time, I was actively involved in politics and the Orange Revolution.

In winter 2010, I landed in Newark, New Jersey, to finish my last interviews for the TV documentary I was working on—this was my seventh trip to the USA for work, in addition to many more travels in Europe. This time, I never used my return ticket back to Kiev. In January, while I was in the USA, the results of the presidential election back home shocked Ukrainian nationals, including me. At twenty-five, I was successful in Ukraine. I had already bought my own apartment in Kiev and had a promising career there as a TV journalist. But I Skyped my parents and announced I had made the decision to stay in America, where my own children could someday grow up with a rule of law that protects honest, hardworking people.

It was difficult to start again from scratch in New York. I had a few hundred dollars to my name and no relatives, connections, or even work authorization, but the hardest part of all was to be at the bottom of the social ladder. My grandmother's words—"act honorably, everybody in town knows what family you come from"—rang ironically in my head in this country, this city, where I lacked any social capital. Still, I knew I had to uphold my family's values and beliefs and build a strong reputation. I started by gathering all my journalistic work and asked the American government to allow me to stay on the basis of my commitment to the truth. On June 17, 2010, after a successful interview with a homeland security officer, I started my second life in the USA.

At this point, I knew nothing but journalism, but in this new life path I could no longer rely on my main skills of public speaking and writing. I turned instead to visual communication; because I had professional video and editing equipment, I was able to find work as a wedding and event videographer and editor at a Brooklyn studio. This job dovetailed nicely with my filmmaking ambitions, but I knew I needed higher education to go farther. As fate would have it, though, when I submitted my application to film school, I unexpectedly fell into a different career entirely.

At that time, I met a woman whose life story inspired me to become a nurse. My new friend was a cancer survivor and a mother of five who, despite her illness, had transformed from a poor Irish girl from the Bronx to a successful businesswoman. I enrolled in prerequisite courses and was eventually admitted to a few accelerated nursing programs for second-degree students.

At this point, my personal life was put on hold. I could not afford to be homesick or to sleep in on weekends, and I never owned a TV set. My brain burned after studying hours of anatomy and microbiology in a foreign language. To pay my bills and tuition, I worked ten different jobs, starting with nanny, waitress, hostess, film extra, and nurse's aid, and continuing with documentary editor, producer, and videographer. As an example of my average week, I was a corpse on *Law and Order*, wedding guest on *Gossip Girl*, fashion channel producer covering the *Wall Street: Money Never Sleeps* red carpet, and on top of that, changing diapers for a newborn as a nanny, helping eighty-six-year-olds take a bath as a clinical nursing assistant, and finally greeting guests at Lavo or Buddakan as a hostess. The holiday season was the hardest time for me as an expat, so I was lucky if I could find work on Thanksgiving to keep my mind busy.

In January 2014, after four challenging years in New York, I flew south and started an accelerated nursing program at the University of Miami. This was essentially a one-year boot camp where even the most promising students are put through the wringer; your GPA is pulverized, your confidence is quashed, and you are constantly aware that failing one class will lead to dismissal from the program with no second chance in the whole country. In other words, you can study hard and still end up empty-handed—except, of course, for your huge student loan. Professors tried us physically and psychologically.

In April 2014, I was studying for my first finals in rooms I rented on Airbnb because I still could not find a permanent place to live. And Ukraine was on fire. My parents had been hiding the truth from me, avoiding political conversations when we spoke. During this time, sweet childhood memories of summer trips to Crimea were smeared by political speculation. My Russian coworker, a documentary filmmaker, committed suicide amid the political conflagration. I could not afford the luxury of tears, however. I had to stay strong and pass pathophysiology while figuring out how to rescue my family.

Unfortunately, I failed—I failed my leadership course, and it felt as if something within me had died. After years of sacrifices, I was exhausted and financially drained—and I wasn't the only one. Each semester, fewer and fewer students were keeping up with the program. I needed a miracle, and one came down from the dean of the School of Nursing, who let me stay and continue the program. I was one semester behind, but I progressed well, working for the Sylvester Comprehensive Cancer Center and later getting an internship at Memorial Sloan Kettering Cancer Center. In 2015, I finally graduated with a bachelor's degree in nursing, and I also ran my first New York City Marathon to support cancer research.

Today I am proud to be an oncology nurse. Every day I give thanks to those who believed in me and helped me succeed, and I repay their generosity, energy, and passion forward to my amazing patients. Nursing is a very rewarding profession, because I get to make a difference every day. I am still fighting for truth, justice, and healing the way I did as a journalist, only with a different skill set. And recently, another dream of mine came true—on October 3, 2016, my parents landed at JFK so we could have a family reunion. I had the best Thanksgiving I could ask for with my amazing hospital team, my patients, and my family.

Misha Galperin

Dr. Misha Galperin is founder of Zandafi Philanthropic Advisors. He has been engaged with Jewish communal organizations for many years.

He told me this story when we were standing on a railroad platform, in the bitter cold, on November 14, 1975. We were in the town of Kashovitze in Czechoslovakia, watching our suitcases that had been offloaded from a train that had taken us out of the Soviet Union a few short hours earlier.

My little sister, my mother, and my grandmother sat in the relative warmth of the train station while my father and I stayed outside. He was smoking a cigarette, and I was wishing I could admit that I wanted one, too. We had planned to travel directly from Odessa to Vienna, but our plans got completely derailed (pun intended) when Soviet border guards took us off the train in Chop, turned our luggage inside out, strip-searched my seventy-four-year-old grandmother, and terrified my eight-year-old sister by pulling at the tiny diamond studs in her ears. After enjoying their due, the guards let us go—but our train had already left and we now had to change in Kashovitze and then in Bratislava. So my father told me this story, the story that had haunted his dreams almost every night for thirty years.

A rabbi in a long, dark coat is being dragged out of his synagogue by the beard. He is made to walk over a Torah scroll rolled out onto the street. His congregants and other Jewish residents of the small shtetl of Tomashpol—in the Vinnitza region of Ukraine in the former Pale of Settlement—are being herded by the SS einzatztroopen to the edge of town. A six-year-old boy wants to run up to his father, the rabbi, and the rest of his family, but his grandmother sternly gestures for him to stay away. So he follows the crowd to the ravine, just outside of town, and climbs a mulberry tree. And then he watches as four hundred people are massacred and their bodies piled into the ravine.

My father was the six-year-old and the rabbi was my grandfather.

Somehow my father survived the war and was eventually adopted by a relative in Odessa. He met my mother, who, as the daughter of a prominent physician and scientist, was fortunate enough to be evacuated to Uzbekistan in Central Asia during the Nazi occupation. They met in college and made a family and a life for themselves in Odessa—but he always, always wanted to leave. He wanted to be part of a Jewish community that was permitted to exist and to thrive and to remember.

In 1974, when the doors of the Soviet Union opened up a crack, my parents applied for exit visas. As was almost always the case in those days, they lost their jobs. A couple of months after the applications were filed, we received a package with a foreign set of stamps and an address in English. It came from somewhere in Europe, and inside were some sweaters, stockings, and—oh, joy—a pair of genuine Levi Strauss blue jeans. The jeans were every Soviet boy's dream. They guaranteed dates and admiring glances of friends and rivals. I was sixteen and very excited. But the jeans were not for me. They were to be sold at the flea market—they cost as much as my father used to earn in a month. These jeans and those packages were how we survived without other means while waiting to get our exit visas.

Years later, when living in Washington, DC, I was lucky enough to meet the man who came with this idea and this program—the then president of American Jewish Joint Distribution Committee, the Joint—Heinz Eppler. But back in 1974 in Odessa, it just seemed like a miracle. People who did not know me or my family reached behind the Iron Curtain to give us the help we needed. Those were the people from the community of which my father so wanted to be a part, that his father and his family were a part of before being murdered.

When we ultimately arrived in the US, I wanted to fulfill my dad's dream for himself—to continue the rabbinic legacy of his father and his forefathers before him. I went to study at Yeshiva University, and while I quickly realized that the rabbinate was not my calling, I discovered the field of clinical psychology while assisting a psychologist working with an immigrant family; I was an interpreter as part of my work-study scholarship. I would go on to earn my doctorate from NYU and do my research and clinical practice with refugees and immigrants, helping them and those who worked with them deal with the traumas of transitioning to a new life.

And then, when restarting my Jewish studies as part of the Wexner Heritage Foundation program, I had a truly transformational moment. I learned that the commandment of *pidyon shvuim*, or redeeming captives, is, according to Moses Maimonides, the highest religious duty for a Jew. Why? Because saving a life is a supreme value in Judaism and saving someone who may be tortured and murdered, and whose family is tortured because of the captive's suffering, is even more important.

And there I was—redeemed from captivity myself by the Jewish community, by the American people who put pressure on the Soviets to "let my people go," who welcomed me and my family and hundreds of thousands of others like us to this country and shared it with us. And I was helping now as well, volunteering, working for the community. But after that revelation—that the Jewish communal services system, and many of the values upon which the United States itself stands, stem from ancient Jewish values—I decided that I would devote my professional life to this cause.

And so I went on to work for and run social service and educational institutions in the Jewish community, including the Jewish Board of Family and Children's Services, the Educational Alliance, New York

Association for New Americans, UJA-Federation of New York, the Jewish Federation of Greater Washington, and the Jewish Agency for Israel.

My father passed away at fifty-six, but he knew the path that I had embarked upon. And he approved.

David Harris

David Harris is the Chief Executive Officer of the American Jewish Committee.

For my family, America meant, quite literally, rescue, salvation, and rebirth. Nothing less.

In our case, we don't have to go back several generations or multiple centuries. In fact, as I am the first person in our extended clan to be born in the United States, everyone older than me was from somewhere else and had harrowing stories to tell about their lives before seeing New York Harbor—and the unforgettable image of the Statue of Liberty—for the very first time.

Let's begin with my mother, Nelly.

She was born in Moscow in 1923, during the early Bolshevik period. It wasn't a good place to be a human being with any democratic instinct, much less a Jew.

She and her family were among the lucky ones, though. By 1929 the family of four, having managed to trade an apartment for passports, was en route to Paris. They were fortunate: the Soviet exit gates slammed shut pretty soon afterward, and unimaginable horrors were to ensue, beginning with Stalin's Great Terror of the 1930s.

Life in Paris was a welcome change from the situation in Moscow, though it wasn't easy to start over—new language, new culture, new everything. But this family was resilient, even in the face of the taunts about being Russians and Jews.

Eleven years later, the tsunami arrived. Despite French confidence that the Maginot Line would prove a bulwark against possible German aggression, and that therefore the invasions of 1870 and 1914 would not be repeated, in the end it proved worthless. By June 1940, the Nazis had occupied France, finding eager local collaborators along the way.

For my family, like so many others, the only hope was to flee south, trying to stay ahead of the aggressors. But, ultimately, it meant trying to leave France altogether and finding refuge in a faraway land where the Nazis couldn't reach them.

At the time, American immigration policy was appallingly restrictive, especially when it came to Jews. After months of effort, a guardian angel appeared in the form of Congressman Ivor Fenton of Pennsylvania, who successfully arranged US entry visas for fourteen members of my extended family.

And thus, on the eve of Pearl Harbor, my eighteen-year-old mother and her relatives arrived in New York. Once again, they started from scratch—new language, new culture, new everything. But, to say the least, it was worth it.

America saved them from the same fate as six million Jews in Europe. America gave them a new start. America restored their dignity. And they reciprocated with a love of America that defined them ever after. In fact, as I look back, it's amazing how rapidly and unconditionally they integrated into American society.

My father was born in Budapest in 1920. In 1936, he entered the Institute of Chemistry in Vienna, but two years later, after the Nazis arrived to an enthusiastic welcome and incorporated Austria into the Reich, he was expelled for the simple reason that he was a Jew.

For the next seven years, until the war's end, he served in the French Foreign Legion, was imprisoned in a French Vichy camp in Algeria for three years, managed to escape, and joined the OSS, the US wartime espionage agency, where he had one dangerous assignment after another for the last years of the war. After the defeat of Germany, it was the OSS that brought Captain Eric Harris to the US.

He became a US citizen and, like my mother, felt he owed a lifelong debt of gratitude to this country for the new start it had given him—and, no less, for helping save the world, and him, from Hitler's dream of a "thousand-year Reich."

Ironically, in 1975, the Institute of Chemistry in Vienna, the same one that threw him out, invited my father to come back and receive an honorary doctorate for the work he had done on the synthesis of the heavy hydrogen atom from 1936 to 1938, when he was still a teenager. But for the Nazis he was a Jew, therefore targeted for annihilation, and nothing else mattered. Austria's loss became America's gain.

This was the ambience in which I grew up on the West Side of Manhattan. My family's story was not unique. It sometimes seemed to me that, among my friends at school, it was more or less the norm. Many of us were first-generation Americans, and sooner or later we came to understand that, but for this country, in all likelihood we wouldn't be alive.

Later, I had a third up-close experience with understanding what America means to a newcomer. My future wife, Giulietta, and her family—including her parents and seven siblings—had also been refugees, but in their case, not from the Bolsheviks or Nazis, but from Arab extremists.

The family had lived in Libya for centuries, part of an ancient Jewish community that dated back to the Roman period, long before the Arab conquest and occupation of the country. But by 1967, despite guarantees purporting to protect minorities in the country, the Jews were not only treated as permanent second-class residents, but also as convenient targets for periodic pogroms.

Giulietta and her family were fortunate to escape, but not before enduring weeks in hiding. Some of their Jewish neighbors weren't so lucky. Today, incidentally, there are no Jews—literally none—in Libya. They were all driven out by blind hatred and fanaticism.

Ask my wife what America has meant to her since she arrived in 1979, and she is likely to call our country the last great hope for humankind, the ultimate bastion of democratic, pluralistic, and humanistic values, and the one country that gives newcomer and native alike the chance to pursue their dreams.

Apropos, where else could a Henry Kissinger or Madeleine Albright rise to the highest ranks of American society, even though they were born and raised elsewhere? America, to its everlasting credit, is not only about the second and third generations, but also about the first.

Perhaps it's only those who came to this country from places where their fundamental rights were trampled on—like my mother, father, and wife—who can truly grasp the ultimate gift of America, the blessing of freedom, and, yes, the shared responsibility to defend it.

We must not, dare not, ever take that precious gift for granted.

Daniel Lubetzky

Daniel Lubetzky is the founder of KIND.

I was born in 1968 in Mexico City. My three siblings and I grew up in the sheltered Jewish community there, which numbered about fifty thousand. My mom, Sonia, stayed home to raise us. She grew up in Tampico, Tamaulipas, a cattle-ranching region where her family was one of only a handful of Jewish families.

My mother's father, Don Marquitos Americus, was born Marcos Merikansky. He immigrated to Mexico from Lithuania early in the twentieth century to escape pogroms. He started out selling religious trinkets and eventually became a respected cattle rancher. (After being conscripted into the Cossack Army, he had become an excellent horseback rider.) He was about five feet tall but strong and tough; he seemed to be built of steel, even when I knew him in his seventies. What I best remember is his humility and kindness, how he always helped the farmers who worked with him, how he sat, ate, and slept next to them and treated them as family.

The family prided itself in preserving Jewish values and traditions while incorporating Mexican flavor: upholding the Jewish tenet of *tikkun olam*—to heal the world—by always helping fellow ranchers; and they adapted Jewish holiday dishes such as the traditionally cold and bland gefilte fish into a warm red snapper delicacy in a spicy red *veracruzana* sauce. Sometimes there is great value in diversity!

What I learned from my grandfather—and from my mom and her siblings, who were influenced by his values as well—was the importance of modesty in business and life. He did not attribute his accomplishments to his own genius or even his own talent. He seemed to understand that hard work and skill are essential, but that success is greatly a function of luck and circumstance. My relatives had fled persecution; they worked enormously hard, but they considered themselves lucky (not entitled) to have survived and flourished.

My father, Roman, was born in 1930 in Riga, Latvia, and raised in Kovno, Lithuania, where my grandfather Sioma had a small business making corsets.

As they grew up and war approached, my father and his older brother, Larry, frequently got into scrapes with local kids who would shout anti-Semitic taunts and otherwise bother the Jewish kids. When the Nazis invaded Lithuania, life for the Jews quickly worsened. My dad was nine years old when the war started, and his brother, Larry, was fourteen.

Massive pogroms swept Lithuania as the German occupation took hold. A huge percentage of the Jews were killed at the time, mainly by Lithuanian paramilitaries but also by the Nazis. My father, his family, and the remaining Kovno Jews, some forty thousand, were herded into ghettos, where they were kept under horrible and humiliating conditions. Those who survived were sent to a nearby concentration camp. That was where my father and his family ended up.

Just before the Nazis left Lithuania to the Soviets in 1944, they loaded many of the camp's prisoners, including my family, onto the infamous cattle cars and shipped them by rail back to Germany, where even worse camps awaited them. At one point, the overcrowded train stopped and with no warning the Nazis took all the women off, including my grandmother. She had no time to say goodbye to her husband and sons.

My father, his brother, and my grandfather continued on to the Dachau concentration camp, where starving inmates were kept in sub-human conditions and forced into slave labor. Despite their suffering, the three were able to stay together, and my father credited my grandfather with helping him survive.

Just before the end of the war, in 1945, the Nazis marched the prisoners in my family's section of Dachau out of the concentration camp and toward the nearby mountains. It was freezing, they had no food or warm clothing, and the prisoners were in very poor health. As they approached a steep ravine from which the Nazis intended to push them to their death, a snowstorm overtook the group, and my father found himself huddled with his brother and father under a thick blanket of snow. When the storm stopped, they emerged to find the Nazi guards gone. For the first time in years, they were free. The group straggled back out of the mountains and into a village in search of food.

Suddenly, they saw tanks approaching. Afraid it was the Nazis, they were relieved to discover American soldiers, who liberated them. I've always been grateful to American servicemen, because if it wasn't for them I wouldn't be around. Countless Americans sacrificed their lives to stop Hitler and save people they had never met.

After the war ended, my uncle joined the US Army as a translator in Berlin and helped start a reunification program for survivors who were trying to reconnect with their missing family members. He also discovered that his mother, my grandmother, had survived the war.

She had gone back to Lithuania after her own liberation from the concentration camps to search for her missing family, not knowing that they were in Germany. She was unable to get across the border between the Soviet-controlled and US-controlled areas. Trapped, she supported herself as a piano teacher, trying repeatedly to get out of the USSR. It took her from 1945 until 1955 to obtain a visa to travel from Lithuania to Mexico, where she was finally reunited with her husband and sons after twelve years.

After the Allies found them near Dachau, my father and grandfather were sent to recuperate at St. Ottilien for a year. After a short stay in France to await visas, my father and my grandfather went to Mexico, where one of his uncles and an aunt had emigrated before the war; later, my uncle Larry joined them. My dad was sixteen and spoke Russian, German, Yiddish, and some other Slavic languages. He taught himself Spanish and English by watching movies and reading books. He educated himself by buying used encyclopedias and reading them cover to cover and by devouring used books of all sorts. In spite of only having a third-grade education—after the German occupation, he never went to school again—he was one of the most erudite men I ever encountered. Eventually he spoke nine languages and had read thousands of books.

In Mexico, the family had little money, and my father started off working multiple shifts at factories. But he felt incredibly lucky to be alive, and he always tried to help others. My dad had the rare strength of being able to recall that dreadful chapter of his life without letting it embitter him. He lived a life that was fulfilled, optimistic, and positive, and, as much as it emotionally drained him, he frequently spoke about his Holocaust experiences, so that we might never permit such tragedies to befall humanity again.

After some time in Mexico, he started working in a jewelry shop and learned that trade. Then he and his father opened their own small jewelry shop and traveled to Switzerland. My grandfather and my dad spoke Swiss German quite well and were able to get a business started. They began getting the concessions to represent some of the best watch brands in the duty-free channel and in Mexico, starting with Bulova and then Cartier, Audemars Piguet, and Rolex, among others.

Many years later, my dad partnered with three other Holocaust survivors to build one of the most successful chains of duty-free stores along the US-Mexican border, called International Bonded Warehouses. The company later went through several mergers and was acquired by Duty Free International and since then by several other companies.

When I was in high school, there were some anti-Semitic incidents in Mexico. By that time most of my dad's business had shifted to Texas, so my family decided to immigrate to the United States in 1984.

As you might imagine, transferring from a Jewish day school in an insulated Jewish community in Mexico City to Robert E. Lee High School in San Antonio, Texas, was an adjustment. There was a lot to learn about the language, culture, and styles, but I quickly came to embrace all that my new home had to offer. I discovered and have hence always cherished many of the things that we, as Americans, sometimes take for granted, like the rule of law, the free enterprise system, meritocracy, democracy, freedom of expression, and a moral fiber that makes our society vibrant.

Since finishing law school in 1993, I have endeavored to leverage those forces to create companies that are both economically sustainable and socially impactful. Through these ventures, which I call "not-*only*-for-profits," I strive to build bridges between people in order to prevent what happened to my dad from happening again. These include Peace-Works, which fosters cooperative ventures among neighbors striving to coexist in conflict regions, so far mainly through food ventures; Mai-yet (which I cocreated), a fashion brand that partners with artisans to promote entrepreneurship in developing economies; and Kind Healthy Snacks, whose Kind Movement celebrates purposeful acts of kindness and aims to inspire our community to improve the world through small and big kind acts.

My entrepreneurial journey was not always an easy one. I made a ton of mistakes, but I learned from them and, in the process, came to realize the United States is an incredible environment in which to start a business. According to the Partnership for a New American Economy, about 40 percent of Fortune 500 companies were founded by immigrants or the children of immigrants, and that doesn't surprise me. As immigrants, we appreciate the unique opportunities that this country has to offer. We don't take them for granted because we recognize what society would look like without them. I am very proud, honored, and grateful for what America has provided me, and I am committed to ensuring that others have the same opportunities that I did.

Stephanie Murphy

The Honorable Stephanie Murphy is a Congresswoman representing Florida's Seventh Congressional District. She was born Dang Thi Ngoc Dung in Vietnam and is the first woman of Vietnamese descent to serve in Congress.

On November 8, 2016, I became the first Vietnamese American woman ever elected to serve in the US Congress. As a refugee who arrived in this country as an infant, my story is one that almost didn't happen, but one that could have only happened in America.

I was born in Vietnam in 1978 following a very prolonged and destructive war. During the war, my mother worked on Tan Son Nhut Air Base in South Vietnam, which the Americans had used for decades, and my father worked for the South Vietnamese government.

When the war ended with the fall of Saigon in 1975, many Vietnamese families like mine faced uncertain futures as the Communist regime began to consolidate power.

Hundreds of thousands of people associated with the former government of South Vietnam were rounded up and sent to reeducation camps, where they endured torture, starvation, and disease while being forced to perform hard labor.

As you can imagine, my family was concerned about my future and the future of my eight-year-old brother. So in 1979 they, along with hundreds of thousands of families, fled Communist-controlled Vietnam—mostly by boat—to escape persecution, seek refuge, and find a better life for their families. All of us refugees during this time became known as the Vietnamese boat people.

*My family greeting members of the Virginian Lutheran church
that sponsored our passage to the United States.*

It was a treacherous journey, and many didn't make it. Most fled
without proper documents, crammed into tiny, flimsy boats with only
limited supplies and little fuel. Some were lost in storms, others robbed,
raped, or killed by pirates. And some, like my family, simply ran out of
fuel—dangerously adrift at sea with no means of getting to safety.

However, one event occurred that forever changed my life and put
me on a trajectory that led me to where I am today. A US Navy ship
discovered our small boat adrift at sea but could not take us on board.
Out of the kindness of their hearts—and representing the generosity of
America—those sailors refueled and resupplied us and pointed us to
Malaysia, where we eventually made it to the safety of a refugee camp.

My family stayed at that refugee camp for a few months before a
Lutheran church in Virginia sponsored our passage to the United

States. Once here, they helped us find housing and helped my parents find jobs.

Because of my parents' relentless hard work at multiple jobs here in America, my brother and I were the first in our family to graduate from college through a combination of scholarships, Pell Grants, and student loans. After earning a bachelor's degree in economics from the College of William & Mary, I began my career as a strategy consultant at Deloitte Consulting in Washington, DC.

Boat family gets gift car from church

A few months ago, Dang Hieu Liem and his family were adrift on a barge, fleeing their native Vietnam, their futures uncertain.

Now, Dang and his wife are making strides at a new life in America. They have learned to drive, and, thanks to members of St. Peter's Lutheran Church in Stafford, they have something to drive: a standard-shift Ford Pinto.

Christ Lutheran Church is sponsoring the family in the initial adjustment period. James Brockman of the church helped teach the couple how to drive. Dang had driven a jeep in Vietnam, but his wife, Luu Thi Ho Phach, had never sat behind the wheel. So eager was she to master the skill, however, that she learned in one day, and both have now received their Virginia operator's li-

One example of the generosity of the church that helped
my family adjust to life in the United States.

Then another pivotal moment happened in my life. On September 11, 2001, the country I owed everything to—the country that had saved my family and had given me so many opportunities to succeed—found itself under attack.

I could no longer ignore my sense of duty to serve and help protect this great country. So I left the private sector to earn a master's degree in foreign service from Georgetown University and eventually became a national security specialist at the US Department of Defense, where I earned numerous awards for distinguished service, including the Secretary of Defense Medal for Exceptional Civilian Service.

It was the honor of my life to serve alongside our men and women in uniform to help protect and serve the country that had rescued my family so many years before.

After I'd been at the Pentagon for a few years, my husband had the opportunity to start a new small business in central Florida, so we relocated and made Florida our new home.

But that calling to public service never left me. I sought to serve and give back to my community through charitable work with various nonprofit organizations and by becoming an instructor at Rollins College in Winter Park, Florida. However, I still felt there was more I could do.

When my children were born, I began to think about the future—their futures and the futures of children across this country. I grew concerned that the uniquely American opportunities that allowed my family to seek a better life were becoming out of reach for too many families, that too many obstacles were preventing children from achieving their dreams. At the same time, I grew incredibly frustrated by our elected officials' inability to work together in a meaningful way to fix these obstacles and keep America as the land of opportunity. So I decided to run for Congress—and I won.

However, I almost didn't run. To be honest, I was worried about telling my immigration story in the midst of a campaign—especially since the 2016 presidential campaign featured so much anti-immigrant rhetoric.

Luckily, I have an amazing older brother who helped me to be unabashed about who I am, where I came from, and what I have achieved. He helped me realize that our story was truly an American story—one that should be shared with the public and one in which we should take pride. I will always love him for that.

Our family's story never would have happened had America not held true to its founding principles—to be a beacon of hope, light, and freedom to those escaping tyranny or religious persecution around the world.

America's greatness is born of a unique blend of power and principle. This is not an abstract concept to me. I did not discover it simply from eloquent words on a page or soaring lyrics in an anthem. Instead, my patriotism is the product of a life lesson, one instilled by US service members bestowing grace upon desperate strangers.

In fact, one of my life's proudest moments was as a teenager, standing alongside my mom when we took the oath of citizenship. My mom and I had studied together, and I had helped improve her English skills. We quizzed each other on the citizenship test and practiced our oaths together.

So, there we stood, waving little American flags after having taken the oath, proud to be citizens of this great country. More than twenty-five years later, on the floor of the US House of Representatives, my six-year-old son stood by my side and waved that same little American flag as I took a second oath—the oath to become a US congresswoman. It was another proud moment for my family and me on a journey that could have only happened in America.

Jane Swift

*The Honorable Jane Swift is an education executive, the Executive
Chair at Ultimate Medical Academy, and the former Governor of
Massachusetts.*

Every year as I welcome a new group of students to my course on political leadership on the campus of Williams College, a mere six miles
from the modest home where I grew up and where my parents still
live and have lived for my entire life, I share the same story. I tell them
that my parents, Jack and Jean Swift, are more impressed that I have
been invited to teach a course at Williams College than that I served
as Massachusetts' first (and to date only) woman governor and the first
in our nation to give birth while in office. The six-mile distance from
42 Olds Street in North Adams, Massachusetts, to Hopkins Hall on
the pristine Williams Campus and the 120 miles to the state house in
Boston are only part of the story of how I got here. The spunk, tenacity,
and determination passed down from my great-grandmother Maria
Santa Vivori, an immigrant to the United States, and the courage and
work ethic of my grandmother Alma Antoinetta, who arrived in North
Adams as a nine-year-old girl, are the traits that propelled my unlikely
ascendance in politics and academics.

Pietro Bertoldi and Maria Vivori lived on a beautiful estate in Bolo-
gna d'Arco, Province Trento, Austria, in the early 1900s. Pietro was
employed as a winemaker and spent his time outside in the fresh air in
the foothills of the Italian Alps on the shores of Lago di Garda. Maria
was the treasured governess for the estate owner's children. Their love
story was aided by Maria's industriousness. When Maria knew Pietro
was in the wine cellar, she would encourage the housekeepers to drop

a rug out of the upper-floor windows, and she would quickly volunteer to retrieve it—along with a kiss from Pietro! Pietro and Maria were married in 1910 in Arco, Austria, at the church of Santa Maria d'Assunta and honeymooned in Venice. Their first child, Enrico (my uncle Henry), was born in 1911, and my beloved noni arrived in 1913. Their life was ideal except for the chilling events impacting southwestern Europe and the world.

In November 1913, seeking a better and safer life for his young family, Pietro boarded the *Philadelphia* and sailed to New York, arriving on Ellis Island. Like many other young, strong men from Austria, he traveled to the coal mines of Pennsylvania and, along with his brother, found work as a coal loader. After spending his life outdoors in the vineyards, he would lie flat on a rail car each day with the ceiling of the mine only four inches above his head to be transported miles into the earth. The work paid good money, and it was the fastest way to earn enough to bring Maria and the children to America.

World events conspired to separate Maria and Pietro for seven long years. A year after Pietro's departure, with a war raging all around them, Maria and her children found themselves loaded into a freight car with other displaced refugees heading to a relocation camp. The danger of that trip was real when Maria and the other women found themselves under attack by a group they described as gypsies. My great-grandmother would often share the story of one of the attackers attempting to steal my grandmother, forcing Maria to attack the woman with a hatchet, cutting off her foot, retrieving the baby, and defying anyone to touch her or her children!

Maria and her two children spent the next five years being moved from one refugee work camp to another on large farms from Bavaria to Moravia. Maria's tenacity and determination were what allowed them to survive. My grandmother would share, proudly, the story of her mother going on a night raid to a local apple orchard—needing to find food for her starving children. She knew that the owner would shoot her if she was caught and that she would have to scale the metal fence protecting the apples from the hungry prisoners. Maria dug a hole under the fence and hurriedly collected apples in her skirt, only to be attacked by two guard dogs. With the dogs ripping out clumps of her hair in the pitch-black darkness, Maria found her entry hole and escaped—with all the apples still in her skirt (but much of her hair missing)!

Finally, in 1918, when the war ended, Maria and the children returned home to find their farmhouse badly damaged and that they were now residents of the enemy—Italy. Maria fought to maintain ownership of the farm so that Pietro could find her when he returned home. When the family was reunited, my aunt Gina (Jane) arrived—delaying the family's departure to America. But in March 1922, the family sailed from Genoa to the Coast Guard Station in Philadelphia on the *San Rossore* and settled in North Adams, Massachusetts, in a section known to this day as Little Italy.

Like many who worked in the mines, Pietro developed black lung disease. After so many years working and struggling to bring his family to America, he died in 1928 at the age of forty-five, leaving Maria with four children. Maria's survival instincts and determination weren't left in the old country. She became a successful wine and grappa bootleg-ger (or as she called it "the family business making product"). Henry became a high school football star, demonstrating that his mother's fierceness could be translated to the playing fields. He was also the first Italian American to be elected president of his high school class. He played both football and baseball on a full scholarship at Syracuse University. The opportunities and expectations for girls in immigrant families were different. My grandmother went to work at age sixteen and worked on the assembly lines of local factories for forty-eight years. Her speed on the assembly line was well known, and I remember her bragging to me about the other workers being mad at her for "bending the curve" because she assembled so many more parts than the next fastest worker.

My mom, Jean Mary Kent, was the only child of my grand-mother Alma and grandfather Leslie Kent. They adored their four grandchildren—convincing us at a young age that lollipops magically grew on the pine tree in front of their modest one-story home. My mom, a beloved kindergarten teacher, Girl Scout leader, PTO president, and catechism teacher, made sure we understood and admired the sacrifices each of our grandparents had made to provide us with the solidly middle-class life we lived in North Adams.

When I was encouraged to run for the State Senate in 1990 by the incumbent who was retiring, my dad—who had volunteered and run other successful campaigns—wisely urged me to register for the ballot as Jane Maria Swift. Many political observers were surprised when I upset a well-established incumbent state representative in that first campaign when I was twenty-five years old and a few years out of college. Some believe, perhaps correctly, that my narrow victory was due to a surprise event on the Friday before the election. The extremely popular congressman Silvio Conte, who never endorsed candidates in local races, agreed to meet me with a reporter present to make a personal donation to my campaign. With a wink and a smile, he told the reporter and photographer it was a contribution, not an endorsement. He then quietly asked me how my grandmother was and if I would please tell Henry he said hello...

That is how I got here.

Andrew Tisch

Andrew Tisch is co-chairman of the board of Loews Corporation. He is widely engaged in the business, political, and philanthropic communities.

More than one hundred years ago, my grandfather Avraham Titenskaya stood as a young child in the big room at the new immigrant arrivals hall on Ellis Island. He took the same oath virtually every American immigrant has taken. Avraham and his family had come from Dniepro-Petrovsk in Ukraine sometime around 1904, through Odessa on the Crimean Peninsula. Half the family turned left and went to Tashkent in Uzbekistan, and the other half, including my great-grandparents Shlomo (Solomon) and Dinah, my grandfather, and his sisters Shirley and Jean came here. We think distant parts of the family had already come to America. None of us knows what became of the Uzbek family.

That's the family lore, but research by the Statue of Liberty-Ellis Island Foundation shows my great-grandfather Shlomo arriving from Hamburg on February 12, 1904, and the rest of the family arriving on September 30, 1904. Presuming the ships' records are more accurate, it would make no sense for them to go to Odessa to get to Hamburg, so the family lore is probably somewhat faulty!

Although I'm not sure why the family left Ukraine or why they decided to come to the United States, I can surmise that part of it had to do with the fact that they were Jewish and felt vulnerable living in what was then part of czarist Russia. One story has it that the Russians were drafting young Jewish men for the Czar's army, which was equivalent to a death sentence.

Jean, Abraham, and Shirley Tichinsky, 1912. Abraham became Al Tisch in 1918.

I imagine they came for the same reason that so many others came to these shores: for the opportunity to live a better life than they could in their place of birth for themselves, for their children, and for their future generations.

My grandfather's given name was Avraham Titenskaya when he arrived at Ellis Island. The old family lore was that our name was Tischinsky and we were table makers, because Tisch means "table" in Yiddish. However, that seems too simple an explanation. But the ship manifest showed Titenskaya. Whatever our family name was when my great-grandfather left Dniepro-Petrovsk, it became Tichinsky on Ellis Island.

I believe my great-grandfather was a tailor specializing in fur. The family first moved to the Bronx to be near American relatives. Shlomo, now Solomon, set up his tailor business in his home. Dinah was a founder of the Ladies' Day Nursery which, in some incarnation, is still in existence and provided early daycare services for working women in the borough. Then they moved to Brooklyn, before Brooklyn was fashionable again, and my grandfather and his two sisters went to public school, where they learned English.

Larry Tisch, Shlomo Tichinsky (nee Titenskaya), Alan Medoff, Bob Tisch circa 1943.

My grandfather went to the City College of New York, where he did well academically and was captain of the school's basketball team in 1917–1918. Avraham Tichinsky's nickname was Al, but Tisch was the nickname used for basketball cheers, because no one could pronounce his other names. The cheer "Go Tisch" was certainly catchier than "Go Tichinsky." The nicknames stuck, and he carried that name for the rest of his life. Al Tisch married Sayde Brenner, whose family was from Poland. They had two sons, and he worked hard in the garment business, making boys' corduroy knickers in partnership with a man named Handelsman, whom he later bought out.

Al Tisch never loved the garment business, so he took advantage of a great American right—the right to change your mind. He and my grandmother tried their hand at the real estate business by buying a pair of summer camps in Blairstown, New Jersey, which they operated for ten years. Their two sons, Larry and Bob, spent their teenage summers working at the camp.

They bought the camp with a five-thousand-dollar loan from Al's father, Solomon. It was successful and provided a nice income for the family.

Among the campers was one of their Brooklyn neighbors, Belle "Bubbles" Silverman, who went on to change her name to Beverly Sills; she became a great opera star and stayed a close friend of theirs for her whole life.

Al and Sayde's sons, my father, Larry, and uncle Bob, fought in the army in World War II. Larry grew up doing the cryptograms in the newspapers and became a cryptographer in the OSS. He was due to be sent over to Myanmar (Burma in those days) but developed hepatitis and finished the war in a hospital in Washington, DC.

The boys took advantage of another opportunity afforded them in the United States—a good education. Before World War II, my father went to New York University's School of Commerce and graduated at age nineteen. After the war, he used the GI Bill to get a business degree from Wharton and began his studies at Harvard Law School. However, Larry dropped out of Harvard to join the rest of the family in the hotel business. In 1946, Larry and Bob, along with their parents, leased a hotel in Lakewood, New Jersey, called Laurel-in-the-Pines, which they ultimately bought and parlayed into a chain of hotels in New Jersey, New York, and Florida. Together, the family took advantage of the opportunities allowed them by the American dream and capitalism.

Through good sense, excellent timing, and a positive vision of what can happen in America, they created a business that, today, is listed on the New York Stock Exchange and employs nearly twenty thousand people in hotels, insurance, oil exploration, natural gas pipelines, and packaging.

My father met my mother, Billie, on a blind date in June 1948 while he was just getting into the hotel business. They dated for a couple of months before getting engaged and then married on October 31, 1948. Mercifully, I was born nine months and two weeks after they were married. Billie and Larry went on to have three more sons, my brothers, who are my closest friends and business associates to this day.

I grew up as a hotel brat, moving every year or so to wherever the newest hotel was located and finally to New York at age ten. I have four children, a boy and three girls. My wife, Ann, is a journalist and educator who is working to make the world better by reintroducing single-gender education as a choice into the public education arena. Her efforts have helped thousands of young girls attend college and achieve their own American dreams. My children are all more-than-productive citizens making their own marks in society.

Throughout my life, community and philanthropy were key elements reinforced by my parents, my aunt and uncle, and my grandparents. I don't know where this spirit came from, but I know it was a key element in the way our family lived. The family was always most important, but we never lost sight of the needs of the community. We were taught to be generous, to be participants, and, no matter what the consequences, to do the right thing.

In all, we came from many different places. My father's family was from Ukraine and Poland, my mother's family from Lithuania and Germany. My wife Ann's family came from France, the United Kingdom, and Hungary. Their countries of origin are just reference points, because we are all Americans.

Two of the great attributes of this country are the rewards it offers for taking advantage of opportunity and risk. Throughout our family's experience in America, we have had opportunities presented to us. None of them came without risk, but at many important junctures, my forefathers and foremothers were able to assess the risks involved in taking advantage of the opportunities. When doors were opened, we were in the fortunate position of choosing many of the right doors to walk through. No one predetermined what we could or could not do or be. Instead, we had the opportunity to make our own luck.

My grandfather Avraham Tichinsky can count not only his two sons, but seven grandchildren, twenty-three great-grandchildren, and seventeen great-great-grandchildren and growing. All American and all committed to the American dream of peace and opportunity in a better world.

America is filled with Al Tisches—boys and girls of every ethnic origin from every corner of the world. I know how hard families work to become citizens of this great country. And to each of you, I want only to say, "Welcome to the United States."

Jan Vilcek

Jan Vilcek, MD, PhD, is an educator, researcher, inventor, and philanthropist. He is a professor of microbiology at the New York University Medical School.

October 10, 1964

Marica and I stepped out of the car and embraced.

"We made it," I said, my voice trembling. Marica nodded, wordless, her eyes glistening with emotion.

We were on a deserted two-lane highway, about a half mile from the border between Czechoslovakia and Austria. The border was part of the Iron Curtain—equipped with watchtowers, minefields, and electrified wire fences—separating Communist countries from the free world. The remarkable fact was that we were on the Austrian side of the Iron Curtain, not in Czechoslovakia, the country of our birth and where we had always lived. Moments earlier we had waited in trepidation as Czechoslovak border guards examined our papers, hesitating for the longest minutes of our lives before they let us pass to the other side. Would they become suspicious because we were carrying heavy winter coats for our three-day visit to Vienna in early October? Would they search the contents of our two bags and find that we had packed more than three shirts and three sets of underwear? The guards opened the car trunk to make sure we were not smuggling someone out of Czechoslovakia. They inspected the underside of our car. But they ignored the winter coats and they were not interested in how many shirts or pieces of underwear we were carrying.

Only two weeks earlier we had learned that—much to our surprise— the Czechoslovak authorities had approved our application to visit an

Austrian colleague of mine in Vienna who had invited us to spend a weekend with him and his family. Marica and I had gotten married some two years earlier and, ever since, we had been trying to find a way to get out of Communist Czechoslovakia and settle in the West.

We were not political activists, and our lives were no worse than those of the majority of other local citizens. But we were increasingly desperate: tired of the daily inundation of primitive propaganda promoting Communist ideology, the restrictions on our personal freedoms imposed by the regime, and the extreme limits on our possibilities for professional and personal development. Because of constraints both on travel abroad and on what was allowed inside our border, we could not see and get to know the wider world of which we wanted to be a part. Books we wanted to read, films and plays we wanted to see were often banned. We both had university degrees—Marica as an art historian and I as a physician and medical scientist—and we had relatively comfortable jobs, but in our short professional careers (I was thirty-one, Marica about to turn twenty-eight) we had already achieved all that we could in the small, closed world of Communist Czechoslovakia.

When we received the permit to visit Austria, we knew that our secret desire to leave Czechoslovakia was about to be fulfilled. The immediate challenge was to contain our excitement and not arouse anybody's suspicion about our plans.

Once on the right side of the border, the free side, we were elated. We could begin to shed the fears, not only of the last two weeks, but also of the years before. Vienna was forty miles ahead of us. We could not begin to guess what lay beyond. We got back into the car and drove on.

February 1965

On Monday, February 8, 1965, the fourth day after our arrival in New York City with two suitcases, a tiny amount of cash, and a few thousand dollars in personal debt, I was having my first meeting with Dr. Milton R. J. Salton, chairman of the Department of Microbiology, in his office at the NYU School of Medicine on First Avenue near Thirtieth Street in Manhattan. About three months earlier, while waiting for our immigration visa to the USA in Frankfurt, Germany, I had sent my résumé to Dr. Salton along with a letter in which I inquired about a possible position in his department. Quite promptly I received a reply; Dr. Salton wrote that, provided I could obtain a visa and move to New York within a reasonable time period, NYU School of Medicine was ready to offer me the position of assistant professor of microbiology.

During my first meeting with Dr. Salton, we talked about my research plans, and I told him I wanted to continue working on interferon, a natural protein important in immune responses. We also discussed my teaching responsibilities.

When I came back to see Dr. Salton a few days later, I asked to see my future laboratory. "We had the space cleaned, but I should warn you that it is still not completely ready," he said.

We walked there together. It turned out that my future laboratory was going to be in a space that, until recently, had housed experimental rats and mice. The cages were gone, but not the smell of animal waste. Figuring that the odor would eventually subside, I thought the space was quite adequate.

"Where will the laboratory equipment that I need come from?" I asked. Dr. Salton said that he could find an incubator for me. As for my other needs, I would have to do what everyone else in my situation did in America—write and submit grant applications to secure funds for my research. Once I received the grant money, I could buy equipment and supplies, hire a technician, and perhaps recruit graduate students or postdoctoral fellows.

On my first day at work, Dr. Salton personally introduced me to everyone in the Department of Microbiology, which at the time consisted of about ten faculty members and some fifty other people, including graduate students, postdoctoral fellows, lab technicians, and administrative employees. They were all extremely welcoming. As promised, Dr. Salton had had an old incubator moved into my empty laboratory.

The smaller room—my office—was now equipped with an old metal writing desk and a used desk chair. A reassuring sign of progress was that the foul smell was almost gone.

Circa 1968

One day in our third or fourth year in New York, Marica and I made a radical decision. From that day on we would no longer speak to each other in Slovak. We were going to converse only in English. We made this decision because—not unlike other immigrants—in our conversations we started mixing Slovak and English words, creating our own version of "Slovlish," and we disliked that. We wanted to improve our English vocabularies, to learn to communicate on a more sophisticated level in our adoptive language, and we felt that we could achieve these goals more effectively if we switched completely to English.

The first weeks of the implementation of our English-only policy were difficult—it seemed so unnatural for the two of us to communicate in English; we would frequently slip back into Slovak. Over time we got used to it. I even forced myself to do sums in English, and to my surprise, after a while it became perfectly natural. Then one day I realized that I was thinking in English, and when I spoke Slovak to someone I would be translating in my mind from English into Slovak—not the other way around—and coming up with sentence structures that sounded weird in Slovak. After a few more years, I realized that I was dreaming in English—with a Central European accent, of course!

We did not make these efforts because we wanted to conceal our European origins or appear to be more American than Benjamin Franklin, but because we did not want to feel like perpetual strangers in our new home. We ran into émigrés from Czechoslovakia, most of them exiles who had left after the Communist coup in 1948. They were cultured and perfectly nice people, but after all these years in the US they were still living in the Czechoslovakian past. Most conversations were about the days back in "our country"; for them Czechs and Slovaks were us and Americans were them. They still hoped that one day after the fall of Communism they would be able to return home, where they would regain their lost property and former positions.

We did not see ourselves as exiles, nor did we envisage moving back to Czechoslovakia even if one day the Communist system were to collapse, which, in any case, we knew would not be happening soon. Fortunately, it was easy for us to get used to feeling at home within the multicultural and multiethnic community that is New York City.

February 1, 2013

Less than five months before my eightieth birthday, I was seated in the ornate East Room of the White House along with twenty-one other scientists chosen to receive either the National Medal of Science or, like me, the National Medal of Technology and Innovation.

"Ladies and gentlemen, the president of the United States."

Within seconds of the announcement, President Obama walked into the room—already filled with some two hundred guests.

In his speech, the president talked about the obstacles many of the National Medal recipients had overcome and mentioned four recipients by name. I was one of them.

"One of the scientists being honored today is Jan Vilcek. Jan was born in Slovakia to Jewish parents who fled the Nazis during World War II. To keep their young son safe, his parents placed him in an orphanage run by Catholic nuns, and later, he and his mother were taken in by some brave farmers in a remote Slovak village and hidden until the war was over. And today, Jan is a pioneer in the study of the immune system and the treatment of inflammatory diseases like arthritis."

This text was adapted from Love and Science. A Memoir, *published by Seven Stories Press. Copyright © 2016 by Jan Vilcek.*

The Trailblazers

/////

Tony Bennett

Lisa Birnbach

Eugene Dattel

Mitchell Gold

Irshad Manji

"Mohammed"

Laura W. Murphy

Nancy Pelosi

Mao Ye

The trailblazers in human, academic, scientific, and religious freedom have always been nonconformists.

— Martin Luther King Jr.

The people in this chapter came to America to make their mark. They emerged as leaders, thought provokers, disruptors, and mavericks. They had new and different views about religion, politics, sexuality, race, and the arts. They pursued the cherished prize of free expression.

America has always been fascinated by trailblazers. They are key to American ingenuity and creativity, and are celebrated for their individuality. The Trailblazers sought a place where they could be pioneering and be heard and in doing so they made America into a country of diverse thought and expression.

Tony Bennett

Tony Bennett is a legendary American singer and entertainer.

A few years ago, while filming a documentary about my life, I returned to Podargoni, in the Calabria region of Italy, where my family originated. I found myself on a mountaintop singing "O Sole Mio"—the same mountaintop where, I had been told, my father used to sing and could be heard by the whole village before he left Italy and immigrated to America. It was an extraordinary moment for me—knowing how far both my parents traveled to create our family's life as Italian Americans—to return to the place where it all began.

My paternal grandmother, Maria Benedetto, who was a widow at the time, my father, and his sister, Antoinette, took a steamship from Naples to America just two days before the historic eruption of Mount Vesuvius on April 4, 1906. Maria dressed my father, John (named after his late father, Giovanni), as a girl for the twenty-one-day trip, as otherwise he would have been separated from her in the men's section of the ship's steerage class. My maternal grandparents, Antonio and Vincenza Suraci, had arrived in America much earlier, in 1899, after blight forced many of the farmers of that region to immigrate. Vincenza had two children by then, Mary and Frank, and was pregnant with my mother, Anna, during the trip to New York to start their new life. It is also important to know that my maternal grandmother, Vincenza Suraci, was the sister of my paternal grandmother, Maria Benedetto.

When you think of how the immigrants of that time moved to a new country, many of them with no relatives to greet them or any knowledge of what to expect, it is astounding. Today most of us won't go to a local movie without reading all about it online beforehand, let alone a new country! I have always felt that the immigrants who came to America during this time were the most courageous citizens of all.

The Suracis made it through the harrowing experience of arriving at Ellis Island and took a small boat to Battery Park in Manhattan. They had been given an address of a tenement at 139 Mulberry Street, where they could find lodging, and by September of 1899 my mother, Anna, was born. She was the first in my family to be born in the United States. Over time the Suracis saved money and sent it to Calabria to bring more of my relatives to New York. They took them into their home and helped them find work. By 1906, when my paternal grandmother and father arrived in New York City, they stayed with my maternal grandparents, who had now moved to Little Italy.

Grandpa Suraci was a true example of living the American dream. He worked hard, saved his money, and was able to move the family to a quieter neighborhood on East Twelfth Street between First and Second Avenues in Manhattan. He began a wholesale fruit and vegetable business providing goods to the pushcart vendors throughout Lower Manhattan. Grandma Suraci had the head for numbers, so my father would turn over his earnings each night, and like so many immigrants, she kept their money in a trunk under the bed.

My mother's older brother, Frank, was determined that my mother would get an education. The rest of the family protested, as in Calabria there was no education system. Thankfully, Frank prevailed and my mother, for a short time during her childhood, attended school.

During this time my father's sister, Antoinette, and her husband, Demitri, moved to midtown and opened a grocery store on the corner of Fifty-Second Street and Sixth Avenue. Decades later, I would marvel at the coincidence of my signing with Columbia Records in 1950—the corporate offices were on the same block where my aunt and uncle owned a grocery store in 1918. As they say, only in America!

My father moved in with his sister and went to work at his sister's grocery store. At twenty-four, John Benedetto began to think of marriage, and in those days, arranged marriages were still the norm, so a family discussion ensued and it was decided that Anna Suraci, his cousin, would be the perfect match. In Lower Manhattan on November 30, 1919, my parents, Anna and John Benedetto, were married.

When my sister, Mary, was born in 1920, the apartment on Fifty-Second Street was getting crowded, so my father's brother Domenick suggested they move near them so my father could help run his brother's grocery store. My parents left New York City and moved to a small town in upstate New York called Pyrites. That lasted until my brother, John, was born in 1923, and then my family moved back to Manhattan.

Soon after, Grandpa Suraci told his wife, Vincenza, that he wanted to get away from the city and move to the country and buy a house. My grandmother thought that was a fine idea, and out came her trunk from under the bed. To my grandfather's shock and delight, she had saved $10,000 in cash! So they moved to the country—which in those days was the borough of Queens—and they bought a two-family home on Thirty-Second Street in Astoria. My parents followed them to Queens, and after a few years most of the Suraci and Benedetto family members also settled there. That is how Astoria became the center of my family's life. I was born Anthony Domenick Benedetto on August 3, 1926, at St. John's Hospital in Long Island City, thereby becoming the first person in my family to be born in a hospital.

During my early years in Astoria, I remember sleeping on a pullout couch with my brother, as our apartment had two bedrooms—one for my parents and the other for my sister, Mary, and Grandma Maria, who came to live with us. My father, who had rheumatic fever as a child and was sickly from then on, had to stop working, as he barely had the strength to leave our apartment. My mother took a job as a seamstress in Lower Manhattan and would work long hours and even bring dresses home with her at night. One of my most vibrant memories is sitting at her feet while she worked. She was always very quiet, but every once in a while she would throw a dress over her shoulder in disgust and say, "I refuse to work on a bad dress." It was from my mother that I learned that sticking with quality is important and why I have always strived to only record and perform the very best songs from the great American songbook.

My father was poetic, and he loved music, art, and literature. He sang Italian folk songs around the house—the same ones he sang on the mountaintops of Calabria in his youth. He was a philosopher, and we would sit outside and watch the stars at night and he would tell me about the universe. Tragically, his health deteriorated, and he passed away when I was ten years old.

After my father passed, my mother had to work even harder to support three children on her own. And this is when our immigrant family rallied around her to make sure she was taken care of. Every Sunday they would come to our house and we would have a big Italian meal. Afterward they would form a circle, and my brother, sister, and I would perform for them. Those Sundays in the circle of my family, where I received so much love and encouragement, were the inspiration for my wanting to become an entertainer. It was then that I learned who I was and what I wanted to do in my life. Although it was Bob Hope who changed my given name to Tony Bennett, it was my Italian American family who brought my dreams to life.

Our family name is Benedetto, which means "the blessed one" in Italian, and I know that I have truly been blessed in my life and that coming to America was a dream come true for my family and for so many other immigrant families just like ours.

Lisa Birnbach

Lisa Birnbach is author of The Official Preppy Handbook *and a comedy writer and playwright.*

My father, Maks Birnbach, was a two-time immigrant. Born in Frankfurt, Germany, in 1920, he and his family escaped to Palestine in 1933, within a month of his bar mitzvah. His mother, Regine, was heartbroken to leave her beautiful life in her beautiful house in her family's country. But his father, Michael, felt they should leave—at least temporarily—until the Nazi Party was toppled. The decision to leave was swift, and forty-seven members of my dad's extended family left by train, struggling to seem like nonchalant picnickers who weren't all traveling together.

The Middle East was nothing like Europe. My father didn't know Hebrew or Arabic, was accustomed to wearing ties and jackets to school (translation: "tease this kid"), and enjoyed long winters with snow. Now he was living in a desert, with kids who lived much more informally, more brusquely, and without the cultural niceties of Western Europe— no violin lessons or visits to the symphony and art museums.

By the time my dad came to New York in 1948, it was his second time arriving in a new and vastly different land with a new language, new alphabet, and new culture. He came not as an immigrant, but as a fundraiser for Menachem Begin's underground force, the Irgun—seeking support of all kinds from American Jewry. He came under a nom de guerre, Moshe Jacobi, as he was then—technically—a guerrilla.

Jacobi made speeches—haltingly at first, in very broken English. (When Begin singled him out for this job, he asked my father how strong his command of the language was. "I don't speak English," he confessed.

"Good," said Begin, "Americans love an underdog.") He spoke at huge dinners with daises three levels high at the Waldorf Astoria, he spoke at little house parties in Atlantic City and Florida—wherever there was a minyan of interested Zionists.

After statehood was declared, my father decided to split his time between Israel, where his family lived, and America, the land of opportunity. He dated like crazy, having been seized by Jewish parents for their daughters. He had charm, height, an unusual accent—the melding of German and Hebrew—and a great sense of humor.

The early '50s were a time of blind dates. A mutual friend suggested he call my mother. He did. She said, "I know a girl named Barbara Birnbach. Why don't you call her? She won't have to change her monogram." He called Barbara. She was engaged.

Eventually my parents met in person. I mean, they had to, on behalf of my brothers and me.

My mother was a fourth-generation New Yorker, whose grandparents were born in New York.

My brothers and I considered them the Jewish Lucy and Ricky from the classic TV comedy *I Love Lucy*. If they had, let's say, a gentle dispute, she'd get loud, and he'd get more foreign. When I was a child, he seemed to speak in various tongues much more than in English. (Dad spoke seven languages, including English, and in his earlier years in America he was often more comfortable in the other six.) My mother, when asked by one of Dad's Viennese friends, "*Und* how many languages do you speak, my dear?" answered, "One, but I speak it beautifully." So, yes. The Birnbachs were the Ricardos if the Ricardos spent Friday nights not at the Tropicana nightclub but in a dining room with Shabbat candles and the glow of a large, gleaming sterling silver menorah that had somehow been stuffed into the bottom of a picnic basket in 1933.

When my father died in 2007, we had his tombstone engraved with "Cherished Husband, Father, Grandfather. Israeli Patriot, and a Real American."

Eugene Dattel

Eugene Dattel is a former investment banker. He is a financial historian, author, and lecturer.

I knew my paternal grandfather, Harry Dattel—Big Papa—the immigrant, well. Now I regret the unasked questions—about the family in Riga and Tukum, Latvia (then officially classified as part of Russia), his immigration to the US around 1900, and his first impressions of his new country. Perhaps I would have met with the same reluctance to speak about the old country that my older brother Jerome encountered when he probed. The prospect of conscription into the Russian army, the Russian czar Nicholas II, and anti-Semitic pogroms were the probable causes of his decision to leave. His older brother Jake had preceded him to America. Details about the journey from New York City to the Delta are sparse and vague. Importantly, why on earth did these Eastern European Jews settle in a most unlikely place—the cotton country of the Yazoo-Mississippi Delta? Harry Dattel came as a fourteen-year-old with no knowledge of English and an abbreviated education at a heder, a Jewish secondary school. His wife, Pauline Rubenstein—Big Mama—also came from Latvia around the same time.

My maternal grandfather, Joseph Marks, came from Hungary, and his wife, Rose Balkin, arrived from Lithuania. Rose's brother Sam Balkin had settled in the Delta, become prosperous, and brought several family members, including my grandmother, to America. Sam Balkin was business partners with William Crump Sr., a Protestant, whose son William Crump Jr. liked to go to Hebrew classes with his Jewish friends!

The Delta became their new home. The immigrants' Yiddish accents were replaced in the next generation by soft Southern accents.

What was the Delta that shaped my grandparents and their descendants? It bore no resemblance spiritually or physically to New York's Lower East Side or to the urban centers that became home to most Jewish immigrants at the turn of the century. It was part of Mississippi but a distinct, different part. The Delta was a subregion—a sociological and geographic entity—flat and fertile and prone to flooding. According to the Jewish Delta native author David Cohn, it extended from the lobby of the Hotel Peabody in Memphis to Catfish Row in Vicksburg, Mississippi. Still 90 percent virgin forest after the Civil War, the Delta attracted whites and blacks to clear the land and plant King Cotton. A series of small towns connected by rivers and railroads dotted the landscape in this majority-black region. A Delta native, when asked where he or she is from, will invariably say "the Delta" rather than the name of a town. The Delta became the epicenter of cotton farming after the Civil War. The cotton world was a risky commodity-based economic roller coaster. My family's cotton legacy led to fascination and my book *Cotton and Race in the Making of America*. Some have accused me of having cotton in my DNA.

The frontier Delta was opening, and enterprising people like Jake and Harry Dattel, probably by Jewish word of mouth and contact with relatives, heard about an opportunity and found their way to the Delta. Harry Dattel peddled and then purchased a store in Sunflower, Mississippi, and then bought a much beloved farm, Lonesome Pine, nearby. In Sunflower (population five hundred), Dattel's Grocery and Market with an adjoining dry goods store was born. Delta towns needed a commercial class, and Jews were welcomed. Towns in the Delta were divided into two categories—those with stores on only one side of the main street and those with stores on both sides. Sunflower had stores on one side only—mostly Jewish owned—Dattel, Borodofsky, Liebowitz, and Siegel. Big Papa had two sales clerks, one white and one black. The black sales clerk, Mose Miles, determined early that communication with my grandfather was best accomplished in Yiddish.

*Dattel sign remained in 2006, decades after the store had
closed and the demise of Sunflower, Mississippi.*

Big Papa lived in the present, not the past. Big Mama was quiet, gen-
teel, and always catered to me. Their son, my father, Isadore Dattel, was
born in 1912. Big Papa was avuncular, solid, always smiling, and a constant companion on my visits. I was with him from our early-morning
breakfast and then a trip around the farm before we arrived at the store.
He was always impeccably dressed in a tailor-made three-piece suit.
From an early age, I liked hanging around the store with its smells and
stream of customers. Until the 1950s, there was a vacant lot used for
parking mules, not cars. I pilfered candy and locked myself in our car
to consume my plunder—much to my parents' consternation.

Big Papa was elected alderman in Sunflower, succeeding his Jewish
predecessor, Sinai Brownstein. At the town board meeting on May 1,
1951, "a motion was made by H. Dattel and seconded by W. J. Martin
and voted in the affirmative… to elect H. Dattel pro-tem mayor." It
hardly needs translation. The confident immigrant nominated himself
for mayor. His brother Jake would win a seat on the Rosedale board of
education. Later, my brother Richard was elected alderman in Sunflower, and my uncle Mickey Dattel would become mayor of Rosedale—
both won contests in majority-black towns after African Americans
were reenfranchised. Big Papa as well as my father served on the boards

*Dattel store opening in Ruleville, Mississippi. Family
members surrounding the cash register (1951).*

of local banks. My grandfather's first business partner was a Protestant,
his neighbor Charlie Holland.

My maternal grandfather, Joseph Marks, died at age fifty in 1917 and
by all accounts was a well-educated man who even visited the old country. His hero was Theodore Roosevelt. Rose, my grandmother, had the
challenge of supporting two young girls, my mother, Elsie, and her sister, my aunt Hannah. She ran the family store in the Delta river town of
Rosedale. She then moved with Elsie and Hannah to Webb, Mississippi,
and started another store. Rose was a wonderful cook, and baking was
her specialty. Fortunately, the trait was passed along to my mother, who
always made sure that delectable pastries were in the house.

Education was paramount. My father had to travel a couple of times
a week by train to the larger town of Greenwood for violin lessons;
eventually, he forsook the violin for saxophone and a jazz band. He was
sent off to the Gulf Coast Military School and then to Washington &
Lee for a brief stint shortened by the Depression. He came home to run
a farm and a business. Mother went to the Webb public school, where
she was very bright and an accomplished pianist. She would travel with
her friend Margaret Webb to Clarksdale for piano lessons taught by a
graduate of Juilliard. The baccalaureate ceremony for her high school

class of eight students was conducted by Rabbi Rabinowitz from Greenville, Mississippi. After a few years working in Memphis, she married my father and they lived in Sunflower. In 1946 when my bored older brother kept climbing out the window of the one-room schoolhouse in Sunflower to go home, my parents moved ten miles away to the larger town of Ruleville (population fifteen hundred).

Sunflower still loomed large in our lives. Big Papa had purchased a home—formerly owned by the family of food critic Craig Claiborne, on the banks of the Sunflower River. There was a huge vegetable garden that extended toward the river. It was great fun to sleep in the screen porch room. Mary Long, our black cook, was a disciplinarian, and knowing how prone to mischief I was, watched me carefully. She was especially attentive at Passover, when Jake Dattel's family would come to Sunflower. The patriarchs—Harry and Jake Dattel—would sit at the end of the table and mumble in Hebrew. Big Papa would make gefilte fish from scratch. Mary Long was well acquainted with Passover, having worked for the Sinai Brownsteins. I remember sitting in the backyard watching black baptisms on the other side of the river and listening to spirituals. The racial chasm was depicted physically, not metaphorically, by the river.

Judaism was alive and well in the Mississippi Delta. My grandfather was one of the founders of our temple in Cleveland, Mississippi. Almost all Jews were members of a congregation—the result of peer pressure from living close to our religious Christian neighbors. In the 1920s, one Jewish merchant in Indianola (the town where B. B. King grew up), did not close on the high holidays. A group of Christian leaders entered his store and asked him why his store was still open on an important Jewish holiday. He said that he didn't want to close. They informed him that this was a religious community and that people should take their religion seriously. He complied.

We trooped to Sunday school ten miles away in Cleveland, where our Rabbi, Moses Landau—a scholar who mastered German, Hebrew, French, Latin, and Greek before English—presided with humor and a real love of history. His interests extended beyond Judaism—in particular to Abraham Lincoln and the German classes he taught at the local college, Delta State. In one town at the beginning of the century, the Torah for the recently constructed temple was met by the townspeople at the train station; a parade led by a band proceeded triumphantly to the new house of religion.

Ruleville had stores on both sides of the street. Daddy's store was on Floyce Street. As in many Delta towns, Jews owned most of the dry goods stores. If you wanted to buy clothes in Ruleville, you went to stores owned by Jews—Baker, Turner, Sklar, Dattel, or Orlansky. Jake and Harry Dattel helped other family members come to America and start businesses; there were Dattel stores in twelve Delta towns at one point. Dattels who were not equity owners would appear at store openings as a symbol of unity.

My parents were fully integrated into the town's civic activities—president of the Rotary Club, officer of the PTA, and several volunteer organizations in addition to board member of the Adath Israel congregation, and head of the Temple Sisterhood. The store was both a great learning experience and a source of entertainment. Working there on Saturday night was exciting. African American farm laborers filled the town, and they were my customers from an early age. One became sensitized to the needs and wants of poor people. The stores, like my father's, in small towns were an integrated place within the separate racial experience. I would walk around Ruleville's few streets. Front Street—home to Chinese grocery stores, white-owned stores, a random blues musician, and Mack's Café, a lively juke joint—was packed with African Americans. I then would check out the businesses on Ruby Avenue and Floyce Street. There again, everyone, black or white, knew I was the "Dattel boy." I generally had dinner alone at the Lebanese-owned Eddy's Café when the store was very busy.

Mother taught her black employees how to cook. One started her own restaurant. Another left Ruleville and began her own catering business in Oklahoma. Years later, I would find out that her menu was mostly from my mother's kitchen. So the recipes traveled from Eastern Europe to Mississippi to Oklahoma and from white to black. Fried chicken, corn bread, turnip greens, and coconut cake were the undisputed first choice of meals in Ruleville.

As Martin Luther King Jr. often observed, despite the oppressive overt racial segregation in the South, the contact between blacks and whites, unlike in the North, offered hope for the future. As a young person in a very small town, a kid learned to navigate among groups—middle-class (there were no rich people) and poor, old and young, white, black, and Chinese. There was no anonymity; you saw the same people a lot.

Assimilation among whites was the norm. In Mississippi, one of the most sacred ecumenical events was the Friday-night high school football game. The coach would check the dates of the high holidays before planning games. If a high holy day occurred on Friday, the coach would accommodate the Jewish athletes by scheduling the game on Thursday. Rabbi Landau would hold Shabbat services early so that congregants could arrive at the high school games on time during football season. Our neighbor Esther Florence Silverblatt's parents were religious Jews; nevertheless, Esther Florence (Flo) had a beautiful voice and would alternate Sundays singing in the Baptist and Methodist churches where her friends worshipped. Maurine Weinberg Lipnick, as a Jew in the 1920s, was president of the Methodist church youth group in Indianola; she would become an active member of her Jewish congregation, a merchant, head of the Indianola Chamber of Commerce, and beloved Latin and algebra teacher. In Greenville's Temple Israel, some Christians attended Shabbat services. One of whom, Mr. William Moose, is commemorated with a yahrzeit plaque, a Jewish tradition that remembers someone on their passing. The highest civic award in three towns— Cleveland, Greenville, and Indianola—was named for a Jew.

In his 1940 tale of life in the Delta, the Greenville author William Alexander Percy wrote of the Jewish intellectual tradition:

> "Every American community has its leaven of Jews. ...I was talking to one, an old-timer, not too successful, in front of his

small store. He suddenly asked in his thick Russian accent: 'Do you know Pushkin? Ah, better than Shelley or Byron!' Why shouldn't such a people inherit the earth... because of a steadier fire, a tension and tenacity that makes all other whites seem stodgy and unintellectual."

The Delta continues to be an indelible part of me. In 2003 I sponsored an oral history and art project for a group of elderly black women in the famous all-black Delta town of Mound Bayou. When I was introduced to the group, one woman stood up and said that she had bought her wedding dress from my father's store. Then she began a conversation about him. A hundred years after my grandfather had settled in the Delta, the stores still remained a connective tissue.

In Europe, the family was Jewish; in America, we were Americans who practiced Judaism. Big Papa told us many, many times, "America is the greatest country in the world." After all, he had traded a despotic Russian czar and a terrible fate for one of his heroes, Franklin Roosevelt, and the promised land of possibility.

My grandfather, Harry Dattel. Memphis, Tennessee (1940s).

253

Mitchell Gold

Mitchell Gold, cofounder and chairman of Mitchell Gold + Bob Williams, is a different kind of man running a very different kind of business. In every aspect of his personal and business life, he strives to make a difference.

People immigrate to America for a variety of reasons. America is often referred to as the land of opportunity and many come for that very reason. Some also come to escape persecution and oppression. My ancestors came for both.

Many of my fondest memories while growing up in Ewing, a suburb of Trenton, New Jersey, are of time spent with my grandparents. My father's parents, Max and Helen Goldstein, lived in an apartment above a neighborhood grocery store, which the family owned and operated.

Both of them immigrated to the United States to escape anti-Semitism. Helen came from the city of Kalisz in central Poland and moved to Brooklyn with her parents, Rose and Harry, and her siblings. A significant event that triggered the move was the rape of Rose's sister. It was the straw that broke the camel's back in a world where life for Jews was precarious. Just the thought of this horrible incident reminds me why people are not only willing, but find it imperative to leave oppressive countries. Especially countries where there is little or no opportunity. Upon getting settled in America, the family started a business sewing clothes, and Helen worked as a seamstress. Her father, Harry, later opened a notions store.

Max Goldstein was born in Romania. After settling in America, he met and married Helen. He started his own hat manufacturing facility in Queens, New York, and the couple later moved to Trenton, where he had family, and started the grocery store. Max adored his wife. I remember vividly how he lit up when she walked into the room. As I think back, I guess it is part of why as a gay youngster I felt like there was a hole in my life—I thought I would never get to experience the joy of having a spouse that could make my life so whole. More on that later.

I was always so excited to visit my grandparents and remember having to ring the downstairs buzzer so they could let us up to come inside. There was always incredible food and a big room for the entire family to gather. While I never had the opportunity to meet my great-grandparents, I do recall seeing photographs of them. I never knew much about them, as my grandparents rarely spoke about their parents or the old country. Now I understand why—they were trying to forget the past and live for the future.

The same was true of my mother's parents, Joe and Sarah Lavine, who lived in a beautiful garden apartment in Trenton. According to family accounts, Joe came from Russia with eighteen dollars in his pocket, likely given to him by a Jewish charity at Ellis Island. He moved to Trenton where there were other family members, and started a fruit and vegetable business that supplied restarurants from Trenton to Lambertville. His wife, Sarah, was born in America and contributed by taking in boarders, which was a good fit as she was a terrific cook, kept a clean and orderly house, and was good at enforcing rules. A real taskmaster!

Whenever we visited them, there was also good food to be had—traditional Jewish fare, like brisket and mashed potatoes, and my grandmother's sponge cake, which has not been duplicated to this day. Poppy Joe and Nannie Dear, as we knew them back then, also never spoke of their parents or the country from which they came.

Looking back, I think my grandparents chose not to speak of the past because their parents' lives were so oppressed. They immigrated to the United States from Eastern Europe, where life was really tough, and even more so if you were Jewish. While they didn't speak much about the past, they held on to traditions and holidays, like Passover, which we always celebrated as a family. As the youngest child, I always looked forward to these times with family, especially during the Seder meal, which, according to Jewish tradition, meant that I got to ask the Four Questions.

While my grandparents held on to these and other traditions, they also wanted to be modern. This meant dressing like the new country and not the old country—especially for their children. My father, for instance, shopped in Princeton and maintained a preppy, Ivy League sort of look. I think dressing in this way was part of his yearning to be as American as possible.

The family's difficult history also had an impact on my parents, Jacob and Rhoda Lavine Gold. My father, Jack, tried to have his last name changed from Goldstein to Gold while going into the military service. This was during World War II and a time when there was still a good bit of anti-Semitism in America. For some reason, it didn't get changed in time, so he ended up going through service and too often being referred to as "Jakey Goldstein" in a teasing and sometimes humiliating manner.

While I was growing up, both of my parents were liberal Democrats and very much in favor of equality and civil rights. I attended Ewing High School, which during the late 1950s and early 1960s was predominantly white and not Jewish. In fact, less than 5 percent of the students there were Jewish, and less than 5 percent were African American.

It was a prejudiced environment, and while I didn't think that much about it then, I can remember the African American kids trying to steer clear of the white football players, even moving out of their way when walking down the hall, because they didn't want to get in a fight. There were plenty of bullies at my school, and they were always ready to pick a fight. I tried to keep on the down low and didn't let myself get caught in the middle of anything. These bullies would say prejudiced things all the time, whether it was the N word or "dirty Jew," which I was called. I was also made fun of because of my name—Mitchell Gold—which was a very Jewish name in a very Bill Smith and Jane Darling kind of school. Of course, today I love it and think it makes a terrific name for a home furnishings business. Had my grandparents not been able to immigrate to this country and enjoy the opportunities it offers, there wouldn't be this company that employs more than a thousand people today.

I once asked my parents why they were so involved in supporting civil rights, and my mother said to me, "Because we come from an oppressed background. We always have to fight for the oppressed." Her words really resonated with me and left me with a sense of responsibility and an obligation to stand up for the oppressed as well. She reminded me that while living in America was—and still is—not perfect, it was far ahead of what Germany was like during the days of Hitler's rule. My mother also believed that because her and my father's life was much freer than that of their ancestors, they had a responsibility to elect public officials—like John F. Kennedy and Lyndon Johnson—who would pursue a civil rights agenda and fight for the oppressed.

At the time, I didn't really understand that this being in my DNA would be so integral in the fight for my own equality as a gay man. While I've had too much trauma in my life realizing my sexual orientation and trying to adapt to a life with this burden, I've also found it energizing as I've been witness to so much change. My life is so fulfilled, especially because I have someone who lights up my life when he enters a room, my husband, Tim Gold.

For the past two decades, I've been on the front lines educating people about why it is imperative, and the American thing to do, to afford full legal and spiritual equality to all lesbian, gay, bisexual, and transgender people. Especially teenagers who are at a much greater risk than their straight peers for mental anguish that too often results in severe depression and even suicide.

The importance of family in one's life and feeling connected is a consistent theme, whether you are emigrating from Russia or Poland, Mexico or Ethiopia. One of my observations is that whether a person is Christian from the South, Jewish from New York, Muslim, Puerto Rican, Mexican, or Canadian, there is this strong sense of obligation and connection to family. Every ethnic group, every community, has a certain sense of family. This is why families must also understand and fully embrace their innocent, vulnerable children no matter how they happen to be born.

Throughout my travels I've seen how family is a unifying trait and an important connection for feeling safe and protected. For example, when traveling in taxis, hearing drivers talking on the phone might drive you crazy, but if you listen and pay attention to whom they're talking, it's their little girl. You start to see that there's a real sense of obligation to family, no matter their culture or ethnic background.

That understanding of how important a person's family can be is one of the reasons my company supports Exodus Homes, a nonprofit in Hickory, North Carolina, that helps connect ex-offenders and recovering addicts who are homeless with housing and other resources, like education and employment. While working with this group, one of the things I have noticed over time is that when people don't have a healthy family or a support system of any kind, they are more likely to become incarcerated or struggle with addiction. A lot of us take that for granted—having a mother and father, or other family members, to keep us feeling connected.

One of many reasons I believe America needs a robust immigration program with strong support policies and equal rights protection in place is because people who come from immigration experiences are more likely to face prejudice and discrimination. They need to be welcomed with open arms into the family called America.

And that is what makes America great. To be on a quest for equality for every citizen, every day.

Irshad Manji

Irshad Manji is an author and founder of the Moral Courage Project. She is an educator and advocate for a reformist interpretation of Islam.

The Statue of Liberty bears more than a passing resemblance to my Muslim grandmother. Both women came from Egyptian stock—yes, even Lady Liberty! (You'll see what I mean in a moment.) Both spent years in Europe. Both settled into their final homes after crossing the Atlantic. Above all, both taught me the power of wonder.

Conventional history has it that France gifted the Statue of Liberty to a fellow lover of Enlightenment values, the United States. Well, yes and no. It's true that a French sculptor, Frédéric-Auguste Bartholdi, designed Lady Liberty. But he conceived of her in Egypt, at the opening of the Suez Canal.

Awed by ancient Egyptian architecture and inspired by the Suez as a passage to possibility, Bartholdi let his imagination loose. He envisioned a monument, taller than the Sphinx, radiating *noor*—Arabic for "light"—as ships entered the Suez en route to Asia.

Bartholdi thus knew his mission: to erect "the likeness of an Egyptian peasant woman holding aloft a torch of freedom," writes the historian Michael Oren. (By the way, Oren is a former Israeli ambassador to the United States. I mention this in case any reader suspects me of putting an Islamist spin on American history.)

Having found an Arab philanthropist to finance the lady of light, Bartholdi began sculpting her.

But the dream very nearly flamed out. Bartholdi's donor went bankrupt. Crestfallen, broke, and bereft of a plan B, the artist needed distance from the woman who almost was. So he set sail for America.

Unexpectedly, Bartholdi felt ecstatic as he cruised into New York Harbor. *This*, he realized, *is where the torchbearer belongs.* He landed more financing. He also secured an American chief engineer who had once served in the army that tried to liberate Egypt from her British colonizers. It seems you can take the lady out of Africa, but not the other way around.

Which brings me to my grandmother Leila Noor Nasser. She was the daughter of dirt-poor farmers from Egypt. At the time, Britain ruled much of Egypt and transported hardworking families like hers to its colonies in East Africa, where their labor could be exploited for immediate benefit of the empire.

Leila Noor wound up raising her family in still another colony, the Belgian Congo. However, in the early 1970s, wars of independence spread across much of Africa. My grandmother fled to Belgium with her youngest children. But no beacon, no *noor*, greeted Leila. Most Belgians didn't want exiles like her. Indeed, she would wait many more years to find home.

One afternoon, my grandmother noticed me messing around with my BlackBerry, an early version of the smartphone. She zeroed in on the mobile screen and asked, "Is that a TV in your hand?" It hadn't even occurred to me that my device could someday play video. Leila Noor's question foretold my mission—not unlike that of Frédéric-Auguste Bartholdi—to communicate the wisdom of being, and staying, open.

My grandmother found her welcome in Canada, the country that also embraced me and my family as refugees from East Africa. There, we enjoyed enough psychological safety to become curious about the wider world. Leila Noor once confided to me her endless fascination with *Amrika*. At the time, I had no clue that this was where I'd wind up. Today, I'm the holder of a green card, which puts me on the path to become a dual citizen of Canada and the United States.

How I got to America matters far less than who got me here. Never will I forget that an Arab peasant woman lit my way—as she has for generations of seekers, strivers, and survivors. May many more of us discover the full glory of Lady Liberty's story.

"Mohammed"

Anonymously submitted under the name Mohammed to protect the individual.

For over three centuries, my family has lived in the same Arab village in the mountains of the lower Galilee in northern Israel. Two thousand years ago the Romans planted olive trees in my village that survived the test of time. My family continues to harvest these trees today. Throughout the years, my village was a serene place where all the three Abrahamic religions coexisted peacefully. When Israel celebrates its day of independence, the Palestinians mourn their catastrophe. It wasn't until the 1948 war that my family was separated from our home for the first time. Whether they were kicked out of their home or fled out of fear looking for safety, my village woke up one morning in 1948 to a whole new reality. Overnight, the villagers became refugees, leaving behind centuries of history and roots in Palestine as they joined the 750,000 Palestinian refugees in southern Lebanon. Weeks after settling in a refugee camp, my grandfather returned to our village seeking safety and livability after the 1948 war. He was caught by Israel's military rule and never had the chance to reunite with his family and friends, who all remain in refugee camps in southern Lebanon today. And since all of his land, including his home, was confiscated by the new state, my grandfather became homeless in his own land.

I grew up on the Palestinian narrative with a strong sense of victimhood, fear, and injustice. I spent my childhood exploring the magical serenity of those ancient olive groves and often pondering the past, trying to make sense of it all. The past surely looked bleak and felt like a missed opportunity, yet the present and future did not look any brighter. I always felt a deep attachment to my homeland village, to the rich soil of the olive grove, to the crevasses of the mountains' limestone rocks, to the fresh smell of wild mint and za'atar, and the taste of figs, pomegranate, and cactus pears.

I was born in the post-1948 reality—a reality of modest economic means, poor educational background, and limited opportunities, not to mention the difficulty of being treated as a second-class citizen in one's very own country. In this regard, I felt rudderless—countryless in my own country, and homeless in my own home. True, there is a great sense of comfort that comes with historic and geographic familiarity with a place. Yet that sense of comfort vanishes when home is not a place of hope, inspiration, opportunity, and the possibility to live up to one's fullest potential.

The great American poet Ralph Waldo Emerson said once that "America is another name for opportunity. Our whole history appears like a last effort of divine providence on behalf of the human race." Those very same words have always echoed loudly in my life and led to a personal transformation and, thus, a life I could have never imagined, not even in my wildest dreams. When I was a child, two American philanthropists, a rabbi and a businessman, visited my village to learn about the challenges of the Arab minority in Israel being treated as second-class citizens. It was my first time ever meeting Americans, and I was amazed at the extent to which they showed genuine interest to learn about the cause of "the other" and support my village in means far beyond financial. They literally explored my village's narrative and communicated it to their American constituencies.

Their generous philanthropic efforts helped create the first organization in the Galilee that fosters coexistence and equality between Arab and Jewish Israeli citizens. As a young activist at age eleven, I became fully engaged in the organization's activities, going through peace camps, dialogue groups, and workshops that brought young Arab and Jewish Israelis together. Seven years later, my life changed forever when I became the recipient of a prestigious full academic scholarship to Tufts University. The scholarship was created by one of these two American philanthropists. It really wasn't until I landed in America and started my studies in the fall of 1998 that I discovered my own ability to dream… and dream big. I've always seen the world with wonder, but America helped me expand my horizons and find my voice to uncover what is possible. I honestly exceeded my very own expectations in that I flourished academically and went on to successfully earn three MA degrees from American Ivy League universities; I launched a career that started with social entrepreneurship and morphed into investing with a double bottom line.

My adult life continued to resemble that of a nomad, physically and mentally wandering between two concepts of home. The first was the birth home, where my roots sprouted deep into the rich and rocky soil of the ancient olive groves. This is a home of insecurity and limited opportunities, where the daily struggles of life often bring out the worst human traits… a home feels hopeless and helpless buried deep under the horrors of past wars. The second was a home of enthusiasm, inspiration, opportunities, and prosperity, a home where, with hard work and dedication, dreams and desires become reality. A home where a group of total strangers found strength in their diversity through shared values and a common goal.

I always thought to myself that the latter concept of home is what makes life worth living. Indeed, the more I lived in America, the deeper I understood its essence—that each and every one of us, no matter how humble our background, can live up to our fullest potential. I recall the words of President Barack Obama describing America, saying that "in the unlikely story that is America, there has never been anything false about hope." This very sense of hope coupled with an unwavering desire to seek opportunities and create a better life for us and those around us is the foundation of the American dream.

My decades-old dream of becoming an American was realized when I recently had the great privilege of becoming a citizen and swearing the oath of allegiance. I joined almost five hundred other individuals to go through the naturalization process and a moving oath ceremony conducted in, of all places, Faneuil Hall, America's cradle of liberty. It was a somewhat surreal moment to find myself sitting in the same great hall where, two and a half centuries ago, some of the most legendary Americans, including Samuel Adams and James Otis, delivered speeches calling for independence and liberty. Listening to a Massachusetts district court judge give a meaningful oath ceremony address, I couldn't help but feel the energy in the hall and notice the joyously eager faces of those individuals around me, all coming from different corners of the world and listening attentively, waiting patiently to receive their certificates of naturalization and the flag of their country.

America remains the land of immigrants and opportunities. We came into Faneuil Hall strangers to each other, coming from various ethnic, cultural, academic, and socioeconomic backgrounds, and all left the hall united by a common identity and a shared vision. And with such privilege comes a great deal of responsibility to give back and contribute to our communities and to the well-being of our global society. Most immigrants retain a connection to their birthplaces, and there lies the opportunity to help create a positive change across the globe. To me, becoming an American is not just about having individual freedoms, opportunities, and shared values—it is about adopting a powerful identity and acquiring an influential passport that allows me to travel the world freely and enter countries forbidden to me thus far. I've always dreamed of helping advance peace through business between Israel and the Arab world, and becoming an American gives not only the credibility to be the bridge, but it also allows me to travel to the Arab and Muslim world freely. In this sense, the Faneuil Hall oath ceremony carried a much deeper sense of belonging and relief—it was like finding the home that will help me find my place in the world.

Laura W. Murphy

Laura W. Murphy is a national civil rights and civil liberties leader with over thirty years of public policy, government relations, and management experience at the local, state, and national levels.

The migration of my ancestors started over two centuries before Ellis Island opened its doors. Some of my ancestors came here voluntarily, and others were brought against their will to these shores as African slaves. My little-known story is about the distinctly American confluence of law, custom, and heritage that made me the successful African American woman I am today. As the first woman and first African American to serve as the director of the American Civil Liberties Union's Washington legislative office, and having served some forty years as a leader in the civil and human rights movement, I value the remarkable stories of my ancestors that shaped me and my family.

Although I knew a great deal about my storied African American family history, a key part of my white ancestry came to light in 1994. That is when my family traveled to upstate New York to support my mother, Madeline Murphy, a writer, artist, TV personality, and civil rights leader from Baltimore and my nephew Christopher Rabb, the family genealogist and a recent graduate of Yale College. My mother had kept letters sent to her in the 1950s from her aunt saying that we were related to a prominent New York family, "the Livingstones" [sic], which turned out to be an understatement. Two years of research by my mother and nephew proved those letters correct.

After a yearlong correspondence with a member of the Livingston family, we were invited to the Livingston reunion to meet and make a presentation about our shared lineage. As a history major, this was an event that I could not miss.

I remember the tension I felt when my nephew rose to tell our story. He stood at a lectern under a huge billowing tent, filled with over one hundred of our white Livingston cousins, situated on a large green lawn on the majestic grounds of Clermont (now a state park) overlooking the Hudson River. This was the storied home of seven generations of Livingstons—a founding family whose patriarch, Robert Livingston, son of a Scottish minister, first immigrated to precolonial America in 1673. The property where we stood that day was part of 160,000 acres granted to Robert Livingston by the king of England—a sum that far exceeds the typical resources most immigrants have when they come to America.

Chris led the gathering through our Livingston lineage. A Livingston son, Philip Henry Livingston, impregnated my great-great-great-grandmother, Barbara Williams, a woman born into slavery from Jamaica, producing a daughter, Christiana Williams, my great-great-grandmother. This was news to the people gathered, because the Livingston family lore and most of the history books had erased any mention of the fact that the Livingstons not only owned hundreds of slaves in New York and Jamaica but also owned ships that transported human cargo from Africa. So, there it was laid bare—irrefutable documentation of slavery, miscegenation, and adultery. The icing on the cake was the fact that our family directly descends from Philip Livingston, one of the signers of the Declaration of Independence.

I felt transported back into history and, for a moment, relived the pain and terror that made up the everyday life of a slave—not being able to control your destiny, your own body, or your family's safety. I remember thinking how my family survived and even flourished in spite of, not because of, our Livingston ancestry. We came to Clermont with something to prove, and yet we had nothing to prove. We came to establish our lineage, not seeking inheritance or reparations, only acknowledgment.

Even though the news of our connection at first landed like cold water on our cousins' faces, no one took issue with the facts. As we stayed through the evening, the environment became more hospitable, as few of the Livingstons could resist the collective charms of my highly successful, educated, and affable black family. It was clear that the white Livingstons had never met African Americans who were as accomplished as us. Our delegation included a noted surgeon, an author, a director of the Department of Fine Arts for the city of Chicago, a judge, an inventor, and a civil liberties leader and graduates of Yale and Stanford Universities and Wellesley College, to name a few.

Our ancestor Christiana Williams, cast off to make her own way, was remarkable, and she had her own successes. She was born on the Livingston plantation in 1812 but was freed as an adult well before the Emancipation Proclamation of 1863. She relocated to Brooklyn, New York, around 1830 and learned how to read and write. She became active in securing the escape of other slaves and was married to a noted abolitionist, Amos Noe Freeman. She survived the Civil War, raised a family, and lived to the age of eighty-six. Her obituary said that she was a "wealthy Negro" who was a highly esteemed member of the Christian Science church.

Her children and great-grandchildren produced college professors, noted artists, and civic activists, who, even after the passage of the Thirteenth, Fourteenth, and Fifteenth Amendments, survived nearly a century of repressive forced segregation and exclusion from the benefits of citizenship under a legal regime known as Jim Crow. They somehow managed to flourish notwithstanding this form of white supremacy established through law and custom. Even though Caucasian blood—"blue blood"—also coursed through our veins, our African blood made us less than equal in the eyes of the law.

My mother was born Madeline Wheeler in 1922. She and her two siblings all went to college. Her father was a teacher and her mother graduated from Cambridge Latin, an academically rigorous high school in Massachusetts. In 1932, as a ten-year-old, my mother traveled to

Europe with her aunt Evangeline Rachel Hall, the third African American woman to graduate from Radcliffe College. Mom was treated to the trip as a reward for her good grades, and this instilled in her a passion for education and travel, something that she passed on to me. Later in life, in her seventies, after raising five accomplished children, writing a book, and having a career in politics, my mother went back to school to study watercolor and painting at the Maryland Institute College of Art.

My mother was so steeped in the arts because of another aunt, Laura Wheeler Waring (for whom I was named), born in 1887. She was a classically trained painter who graduated in 1914 from the Pennsylvania Academy of the Fine Arts in Philadelphia. Upon her graduation she received additional training in Paris and later taught at Cheney State University. She was a highly successful artist who, in her heyday, won a gold medal competition that financed the painting of portraits of acclaimed African Americans. Five of her works, including a painting of the opera singer Marian Anderson, are now displayed in the Smithsonian museums.

When my parents married in 1942, it was a merger of two influential, highly educated African American families who prevailed despite slavery and Jim Crow.

My father, William H. Murphy Sr., born in 1917, was the son of prominent Baltimoreans. He and his five siblings all went to college, at the insistence of his father, who ran the colored school system in Baltimore. My father graduated from Oberlin College, because his state school barred the admission of African Americans for many generations. He later became the third African American to be admitted to the University of Maryland School of Law, as a result of the efforts of Thurgood Marshall. Dad later went on to be the longest-serving district court judge in Maryland state history.

Dad's mother's side of the family owned a prosperous catering company. The Hughes Catering Company started soon after James Hughes married Mary Lee in 1873. Despite all of our research, we cannot figure out how or whether the two were born into slavery. The couple had five daughters and established their successful Baltimore catering business that lasted seventy-four years. They amassed so much wealth that when James died in 1921 during the height of the Great Depression, he left his wife well-off, gave each of his daughters $5,000, and donated thousands of dollars to charity.

Dad's paternal grandfather founded the Afro-American Newspapers in 1892. The family-owned *Afro* is still publishing after 125 years, having covered ubiquitous lynchings of African Americans, white race riots, African American service in the armed services from the Civil War to Afghanistan, the breaking of sports barriers by figures such as Jackie Robinson and the coverage of historic figures such as Madame C. J. Walker, W. E. B. DuBois, Marcus Garvey, Malcolm X, Martin Luther King Jr., and Barack Obama. I serve on the paper's board of directors.

As I look around my home at Aunt Laura's paintings, as I use the sterling silver handed down from the Hugheses, as I read the *Afro-American* newspaper and as I wear my Livingston-linked Daughters of the American Revolution pin, I marvel at the true story of my forebears who came to these shores. This is a uniquely American case study that might explain much about who we are, how our identities developed, how we are seen, and how we behave toward each other.

Nancy Pelosi

The Honorable Nancy Pelosi is currently the Democratic leader of the House of Representatives. She was the fifty-second Speaker of the House and the first woman to hold that position. She represents the Twelfth Congressional District in California.

One of the privileges of serving as a member of Congress is the opportunity to participate in naturalization ceremonies for new citizens.

Sometimes the ceremonies embody the full and beautiful diversity of the newcomers to our country. Sometimes they represent the fulfilled dreams of a specific community—like the group of Filipino veterans whom I witnessed finally receiving citizenship from the nation they had proudly served in uniform.

Every time, the patriotism of our newest citizens gives new life to the vision of our founders, who created our country and enabled the American dream, which has attracted so many to our nation over the years.

In these ceremonies, we are inspired by the courage, determination, and optimism of the immigrants who make America more American.

They show the enduring power of the idea of America. They make us remember when our own families were the newcomers to these shores—and the challenges our families faced when they arrived.

I grew up as the youngest of seven and as the only girl in a Baltimore family that was devoutly Catholic, fiercely patriotic, proud of our Italian American heritage, and staunchly Democratic.

My father's mother, Antoinette, was born in Baltimore to parents from Venice and Genoa. His father, Thomas D'Alesandro Sr., was born in Abruzzo, a gorgeous region in the center of Italy. As Speaker of the

House, I was presented with a copy of my grandfather's birth certificate, which I treasure.

My mother, Annunciata Lombardi, was a force of nature. Her family loved music, and her grandmother had the first box at the Baltimore Civic Opera. As a little girl, my mother had the honor of giving flowers to Toscanini when he visited and later presented him with a bouquet when she greeted him as first lady of Baltimore.

When my parents were dating, my father, Thomas D'Alesandro Jr., had to enthusiastically court my great-grandmother for my mother's hand in marriage, because as an early feminist, she had other aspirations for her granddaughter.

When he was a little boy, Antoinette took my father to the 1912 Democratic convention in Baltimore, where he saw Woodrow Wilson nominated for president after many ballots.

I think that was probably when my father caught the political bug. I take pride that it was the act of a D'Alesandro woman that may have ignited my family's legacy of public service.

My father went on to run for public office as soon as he was old enough to vote, dedicating nearly five decades to public service: from the Maryland State House to the US Congress to city hall to the Kennedy and Johnson administrations.

My father was one of the earliest Italian Americans elected to Congress—and with his characteristic panache and pride in his Italian American heritage and his Catholic faith, my father boldly broke down barriers of prejudice, enabling many others to succeed.

My father's Catholicism was integral to his pride of heritage, and he boasted that he was not only the first Italian American mayor of Baltimore but also the first Catholic to be elected mayor.

My father was always a fighter for the underdog. His experience with the prejudices that faced Italian Americans and Catholics at that time inspired his fight for other communities that faced discrimination.

He served as a Shabbat goy and learned a good deal of Yiddish, which served him well in his political career. He valued that connection as a

A young Nancy Pelosi holds the Bible as her father, Thomas D'Alesandro Jr., is sworn in as Mayor of Baltimore in May 1947.

New Deal congressman and early supporter of the creation of the state of Israel in Palestine.

As a postwar mayor, he built schools, paved roads, and created jobs and housing as he began the transformation of the city of Baltimore. My brother later went on to serve as Baltimore's mayor, continuing our family's tradition of public service.

We always maintained our strong community connection. My parents raised their family and lived in the same house in Little Italy until their passing.

My husband Paul's father was born in Potenza, Italy. His mother was born in Tuscany. They met and married in San Francisco. They shared my Baltimore family's love of America and opera.

As we discuss immigration in the present, we must always remember the voyages that our own ancestors made to America.

The pride we take in our individual heritage enables us to recognize the beautiful diversity that is the great source of our national strength and energy.

Our nation is a nation of immigrants. We must never forget the constant reinvigoration immigrants bring to our nation and that God truly blesses America with our newcomers.

Mao Ye

Mao Ye was the first Mainland Chinese person to ever be elected as a trustee of an Ivy League university. He is currently Assistant Professor of finance at the Gies College of Business at the University of Illinois.

Sitting down to write the immigration story of my family was more daunting than I had expected. Many people who have stories like mine have made significant contributions to this country and overcome significant obstacles, but my own tale is hardly comparable.

Those who immigrated to the United States centuries ago were some of the most courageous people to have ever lived. My generation is blessed not only by modern transportation but also by an abundance of information. I read a lot about the US before I arrived in 2005, and I even knew people already in the country. I remember that around that time my brother had an album with a song called "Stranger in Paradise," a phrase with which I identified. (I have always suspected that the album came from his first girlfriend, but I have never dared to check with him. Asking him this question requires more courage than moving to the US.)

My story is probably similar to those of many others who arrived in the US in my generation. Education brought me here, as I applied to the economics PhD program at Cornell University and received an acceptance with full financial aid several weeks later. My wife, Xi Yang, was already a PhD student at Cornell, and she was there to welcome me when I arrived on May 14, 2005.

Xi and I are blessed by the globalization of higher education. The knowledge and experience accumulated in other corners of the world can now quickly be applied in the US. We figured that out several days after I arrived at Cornell. When Xi was preparing for her PhD qualification exams, she and I realized that I might know enough to take the exam without taking any courses at Cornell. Xi helped me pass the exam, which was a requirement to advance to the third year of PhD study, before I enrolled as a first-year PhD student. This relief from course work not only helped my research but also gave me more time to understand other aspects of higher education. Xi and I are interested in higher education because it is the way to promote the exchange of knowledge between people with different ideas, upbringings, and origins. We benefit from the globalization of higher education, and we also want to contribute to this positive trend. One day, an administrator suggested, "Mao, to move a step closer to your dream, why not run for trustee of the university?"

My initial response was, "What's a trustee?"

I googled the word and found out that it meant "the president's boss." I thought, *That's good. I like the sound of that.*

I started to run in the trustee election in February 2006, only nine months after I arrived in the United States. My chances looked dismal. I was a new student; I was a foreigner; I only had two Facebook friends, and one of them was my wife. I decided to run anyway and spent the campaign listening to students, faculty, and administrators—anyone who was willing to talk. Things started to change for me. I didn't just survive the campaign—against the odds, I won. And I even gained a hundred more Facebook friends. After the results came in, my parents read about it in the most widely circulated newspaper in China—*The People's Daily.* I had become the first Mainland Chinese person ever elected to serve as a trustee at an Ivy League school.

After several days of excitement, I began to realize that it is hard to win an election, but it is way harder to fulfill the campaign promises made in the election. Fortunately, my mom, Xiaoping Zhu, and my father, Yunyao Ye, gave me one piece of advice before I established my campaign platform: "Make promises only for what you can do, and do whatever you said." They had never been to the US before, but their advice and Chinese wisdom inspired and encouraged me for my two-year term. For example, I proposed to create the first campus-wide award for teaching assistants because I believe that teaching assistants are an important aspect of the education experience for students. Xi and I believe that the best way to convince other people of an idea is to show how much you believe in it. For that reason, we promised to contribute all of our savings to the award at the time of our graduation. With Xi's mental and financial support, we donated $25,000 out of our PhD stipends.

The award was named after our daughter, Cornelia Ye, the first generation born in the US in my family. She was born on October 5, 2008, when Xi and I were both at Cornell University. We moved to the University of Illinois at Urbana-Champaign in 2010 and had our second daughter. We found that Urbana Ye, Champaign Ye, and Illinois Ye were not natural names for a girl, so we finally named her Christine (Tina) Ye.

Many earlier immigrants experienced significant culture shocks upon immigrating to the US, but it is hard for us to recollect anything significant. We are really lucky. Our home country, China, provided a world-class education and the US had become more diversified and open by the time we arrived. My most significant culture shock—which was not even one percent of what the pioneers faced—involved no confrontation at all. In 2006 I was preparing for an interview by the Chinese Central TV station, the biggest TV station in China. I struggled with how to best express Cornell's motto to millions of Chinese audience members. More than a century ago, Ezra Cornell established Cornell University with what was a radical notion in his era. He wrote, "I would found an institution... where any person can find instruction in any study." The translation of this motto into Chinese, however, is hard. A literal translation might let my fellow Chinese think that Cornell is a university with low admission standards and no academic prestige.

In discussion with Xi and my parents, we had an epiphany: the motto is closely related to two famous sayings from the ancient Chinese thinker Confucius. The first one is *"You jiao wu lei,"* meaning, "In education, there is no class distinction." Confucius developed and followed a need-blind admissions system, accepting students from different backgrounds so that education would not be a privilege for just a few people. The second saying, *"Yin cai shi jiao,"* stated that students must be educated based on their strengths, interests, and passions.

Although Ezra and Confucius never met, each man dedicated his entire life to the same goals. I first came to the US to appreciate the diversity between cultures, but ultimately, I found that we are all very similar. All cultures actually share similar dreams, and the only difference is in the way we express that dream. Human understanding is a process of self-help as much as it is one of empathy. Therefore, understanding people of different cultures helps us to understand our own; in respecting people from different backgrounds, we learn to respect ourselves.

I recently followed the debate on whether this country has become more divided. When Cornelia Ye and Christine Ye grow up, will they face a country more divided? When Xi and I reflect on our story of coming to this country and when we compare our story with those of pioneers, we can't help but be optimistic. Our world is very different from the times of Ezra and Confucius, and it is also different from the time when the families of most of the authors in this book arrived in this country. The internet links the world together, and modern transportation can bring anyone from the farthest reaches of the world to this country in just a matter of hours. We believe that technology's advancement will also move our hearts closer. There might be some turbulence along the way, but there are always more and more things that unite us than those that divide us. People in this country will become closer to each other as people in the world become closer to each other.

The Undocumented

/////

Richard Uscher Levine

Erick Meza

Juliana Pérez-Calle

Helen Polychronopoulos

Nasser Yaghoobzadeh

If I cease searching, then, woe is me, I am lost. That is how I look at it—keep going, keep going come what may.

— Vincent van Gogh, *The Letters of Vincent van Gogh*

He or she is the anonymous individual whose hand is plucking an orange from a tree, delivering medicine, placing a plate on your table in a restaurant, or sewing cloth.

His or her face may not register to you, and their singular task may seem insignificant but their impact on American society and to the American economy is immense.

Undocumented immigrants have been coming to America for many generations and a number have risen to the heights of influence. These immigrants write about why they made the fateful decision to come to America without proper documentation, and what it was like to be in America without being allowed to feel truly American.

Richard Uscher Levine

Richard Uscher Levine, MD, is an obstetrician-gynecologist affiliated with NewYork-Presbyterian Hospital and Columbia University.

Unfortunately, the story of my family is shrouded in lost facts, missed opportunities to document our roots and history, and secrecy about events and family members. At the core, it is built on very traditional values of faith, family, generosity, helping others, hard work, the importance of education, and survival despite difficult times. Both my parents came from Eastern Europe, but under different circumstances. They met each other on the Lower East Side of New York in the 1920s, married in 1927, moved to the Bronx, and then in the 1950s joined the mass migration from American cities to the surrounding and growing suburbs. For our family it was Teaneck, New Jersey, designated by the army as a "model American town." Mom and Dad lived through both world wars, the Great Depression, intense times of anti-Semitism, personal bankruptcy, family turmoil, and progressive deliberate erosion of their European culture and languages. They wanted to be fully assimilated Americans. How sorry am I today that I missed the opportunity to learn more of my ancestry and languages.

My parents had two sons, each of us born in years marked by an American crisis. My older brother, Marvin, was born in April 1929, at the beginning of the Depression, and I was born in May 1941, the year the United States entered World War II. Our twelve-year age gap and the instability of those decades made Marvin's and my childhood experiences very different. But our parents instilled the same core values into both of us, always sacrificing to ensure our success. They were able to spend time with my brother's family, his wife and three teenage daughters, and watched Marvin's business succeed. However, they only lived long enough to enjoy the early childhood years of our two sons and the first few years of my medical practice and role at the Columbia-Presbyterian Medical Center. They never knew how blessed we were to have earned a lifestyle that would be a fantasy beyond their dreams and imagination. The six-year-old grandson they knew, our son, Daniel, attended Tufts University, married, and lives with his wife and two sons in California and Utah. The three-year-old grandson, Peter, attended Brown University, married, and lives with his wife and three daughters in Westchester.

Time to turn to the details.

My father, Herman, born in May 1907 in Minsk, Russia, was brought here as an infant by his parents, accompanied by his grandmother. His mother, Grandma Itke, lost her firstborn baby in Russia. Dad's two sisters and brother were all born here.

The news that truly shocked me was that my dad lived his life as an unregistered immigrant. He never became a naturalized American citizen. I knew nothing about this until years after he passed away.

Thinking back to my childhood, there were clues to his undocumented immigrant status, including a trip to Niagara Falls in 1949, when he refused to cross over the border to see the sights from the Canadian side. Nevertheless, he was always immersed in reading the news about American politics, supporting his heroes, Roosevelt and Truman, but he never voted. His excuse? It was always the same—work prevented him from getting to the polls before they closed. He lived openly as an American, paid taxes, and didn't share the worries of undocumented immigrants today. But he was limited and embarrassed by his situation, so it was hidden as a family secret.

In the 1930s my dad owned a drugstore with a soda fountain in the Knickerbocker Hotel in the New York City theater district. The soda fountain was a gathering place for Broadway actors who never paid their bills. He lost the business during the Depression. It involved an ugly and vicious beating by creditors, leaving a lifelong facial scar. Yes, another secret kept from me. He became a salesman, working for a wholesale supplier to community drugstores in New Jersey. He supplemented his income with a weekend job in one of the stores he serviced.

But his commitment was to ensure the well-being of his family, in particular the education of his two sons. My brother went to Bronx High School of Science and then to Columbia University pharmacy school. The successful and innovative pharmacy business Marvin established, one of the first in the country to use computers, made my father proud.

One of my dad's happiest moments was during my high school summer tour checking out colleges. While walking around the Tufts campus on a very hot July afternoon, we bumped into Professor Robert Nichols, the chairman of the Geology Department and an early Antarctica explorer. Nichols, the quintessential picture of a rugged New England professor and a Tufts legend, led us on a tour of the campus followed by a meeting in his office, interviewing me and convincing us to elevate Tufts as my first choice. The special attention focused on my dad (who didn't go to college) was a cherished memory for him. Dad also savored every moment of my school days, from Teaneck High School to Tufts to Cornell University Medical College. He wanted to hear about the details of my classes, see my schoolwork, and always asked dozens of questions. I behaved like a typical teenager and student, impatient and annoyed. In retrospect, I didn't appreciate how proud he was and how supportive. When he passed away in 1975, I had just begun my career at Columbia. Sadly, he never witnessed the success he wished for me.

My mom's family story is very different.

Vivian Windschauer, my mother, was the seventh child of Chani Rubler and Uscher Wolf Windschauer. She was born around 1904 (Mom always lied about her birthday), in Kolomyia in Galicia, which at that time was part of Austria but is now part of the Ukraine. I recall lengthy family discussions regarding where in the region you were born, Galicia, Latvia, etc. Social status differed for each region. After the death of her mother, Mom moved to Vienna. So despite the shifting borders of the region, she always considered herself an Austrian. Later, her very American brother-in-law labeled her the "Viennese princess," perhaps disparagingly, but my mother considered it flattering. She had a strong sense of pride.

The hero and most important sibling of the Windschauer family was her brother Max, the second oldest and a maverick who was not destined to inherit the family business, since by tradition it went to the firstborn son. He fled Europe in the early 1900s for America, working as a merchant seaman. There are many stories, possibly exaggerated, of Max's wild days traveling around the United States, making and losing money while enjoying a "fast lifestyle." He finally settled down in New York, married Sadie, opened a restaurant, and launched a successful plumbing business. Because of concerns about his youngest sister's well-being in 1920, he returned to Vienna and escorted my mom on the SS *Rotterdam* to live with them on the Lower East Side. She worked as a milliner, met my dad, and they were married on September 27, 1927, in the Bronx—I'm not quite certain why they always celebrated their wedding anniversary on January 15.

All seemed to be going well for them until the mid-1930s, when the Depression struck. My parents, with my brother, Marvin, moved in to live with Max and Sadie in the Pelham Parkway area of the Bronx. Uncle Max was a volatile redhead, chain-smoking Lucky Strike cigarettes, an arm resting on the open windowsill of his Pontiac, driving recklessly fast and furiously, cursing everything in his way.

He was my favorite uncle and I was his sidekick. In 1946 he bought a small farm with a chicken coop, horse barn, icehouse, and a garage with an apartment above. Although Max and Sadie never had children, the main house was always full of visiting relatives, plus me. I stayed with Sadie and Max every summer from age five to thirteen, as well as holidays and many weekends during the years. He played pinochle with the male guests late into the night—more cursing.

Then, life changed when Max recognized the dangers coming from Hitler and the Nazis. He moved quickly to get his other brothers and sisters, nephews and nieces out of Europe. His oldest brother, David, a successful Viennese doctor, refused to leave and ultimately was lost in the Theresienstadt concentration camp. David's son Ernest, a teenager, was rescued by Max. David's daughter, Anne, fled and hid with a French family during World War II. Max, despite his fiery, combustible temper, was the family guardian, getting them jobs, providing housing when necessary, and always being benevolent.

Soon after my birth, my parents moved to Parkchester, a huge new "middle-income" apartment complex in the Bronx.

When World War II ended, my parents abandoned many Eastern European customs, making an effort to be more American. Yiddish and German were spoken less frequently in our home, except when Mom and Dad didn't want us to know what they were discussing. Living in Parkchester—white, middle-class, predominantly Christian, populated by the families of teachers, policemen, and firemen—was very different than the Jewish neighborhoods of the Bronx. We went from having Goldbergs as neighbors on Pelham Parkway to Gregorys and Dunns in Parkchester.

Although I attended Hebrew school and celebrated Hanukkah, I also had a miniature Christmas tree in my room, a gift from the next-door neighbors the Gregorys. My mother, a fabulous cook, changed the family menu from brisket to standing rib roast, from homemade gefilte fish to creamed shrimp, from freshly slaughtered chickens with "eggies" for chicken soup to chicken breast from the supermarket and roast chicken. We went from potato kugel to baked potato and *krautfleckerl* to spaghetti and meat sauce. But the stuffed cabbage remained and helped me in my courtship of Ellen Jacobson, whom I married. Okay, it was also my mom's lemon meringue pie with a few lemon pits to show it was homemade.

Jewish entertainment was replaced by television including *Father Knows Best, I Remember Mama, Playhouse 90,* and the *Kraft Television Theater.* Music was also important, so I started violin lessons in grammar school. My parents loved going to the Metropolitan Opera. The move to Teaneck in 1951 accelerated the alienation of my mother from her brothers and sister, who continued to live an Eastern European life in New York. Although their customs changed, my parents were always focused on being Jewish and on a better life for their sons.

There was no Apgar score to measure the baby's well-being when I was born, but my mother had her own assessment: "Will he become a doctor?" When I was a baby, she whispered in my ear the virtues of being a doctor and continued to encourage me while growing up. I'm so glad she did.

My parents were generous, made personal sacrifices, instilled the importance of responsibility and helping others, and were honest to a fault. They did well, although we literally lived on the wrong side of the tracks in a very small garden apartment. They always wanted to do better. They never got to know how well they actually did raising their successful sons, with daughters-in-law, grandchildren, and even great-grandchildren.

Erick Meza

Erick Meza is an undergraduate at Harvard University majoring in applied mathematics.

These days, when I meet someone for the first time, the Erick whose acquaintance they make studies at Harvard and grew up in central Florida. While this is true, the story I would like to share has roots in Mexico and a handful of other states. No matter how many times I attempt to convey my family's story, I never find the right words to express my awe and admiration for the power available to those seeking opportunity, especially in the United States.

Both of my parents are from small villages in the Mexican state of Hidalgo. They grew up in poor households. The huts had dirt floors and a sheet of aluminum for a roof. Like other households in the area, their main source of income was from agriculture. Whether it was picking peppers or shelling pecans, some would be kept and the rest taken to market. My mother tells me how it used to be a treat when she ate something like an egg along with her beans and rice. I can remember a time in my life when we could afford beans and rice and nothing else.

My mother had ten siblings and my father had eleven. They were so many because more bodies meant more harvest. It was a battle for my grandfather to let my father attend school. My grandfather saw it as a waste of time, especially when my father could be helping him do real work. When my parents attended school, they tell me, their clothes were mended more than the other kids' and they covered holes in the soles of their shoes with cardboard to make them last longer.

Meanwhile, rumor had it there was opportunity in the United States. A man could make many times what he would in Mexico and send it

Erick Meza

home to the family. So, at the age of thirteen, my father left his family in Mexico and went alone to Washington State. In all reality, he was only a child, but he tells me how he came to outwork every man picking apples or whatever crop was in season at the time. After many years, my father went back to Mexico for my mother and brought her to Washington, where my older sister was born.

Fast-forward a few more years, and I was born in Florida after my parents decided to move there because a family member promised the orange industry showed potential. Thanks to immigration reform in 1986, my parents gained legal status, which allowed my father to start his own business contracting crews of men to pick oranges. This is the backdrop against which I grew up. We were a poor migrant farmworker family. From October to June, orange season, we lived in Florida, then we moved to a farm in Michigan for the summer to pick apples and cherries. I remember making friends in first grade and then saying goodbye when I transferred schools back to Florida. I transferred schools like this every year through fifth grade.

We couldn't afford babysitters, so often my sister and I would accompany our parents to the fields and spend our time playing under the trees. Of course, that all changed when I was six or seven years old and my mother had me fill buckets with oranges that I picked up off the ground. I was too small to carry the bucket, but I still needed to make myself useful. Eventually I was strong enough to carry the bucket myself, and I did. Every long weekend, Thanksgiving, winter, and summer break, I would find myself going to work with my parents.

Middle school came to be a defining chapter of my life because I got into a magnet school that would only let you enroll if you could commit to being there the entire school year. My father made the decision that he would bring the family back to Florida early so my sister and I could attend, and then he would return to Michigan alone to keep working until the season was over. By now, I had two more younger brothers, and with my father gone I found myself shouldering additional responsibilities around the house. I've always really enjoyed learning and school, so in comparison to the other things I was going through, doing well academically almost felt like no problem at all.

Prior to middle school, we had started migrating to North Carolina instead of Michigan to work on a tobacco farm. The summer between sixth and seventh grades opened my eyes the most to the struggles of being an immigrant farmworker in the United States. I was no longer "helping" my dad; I was working sixty- to seventy-hour weeks, spending full days in the heat walking back and forth through rows of tobacco plants, earning a paycheck. I was twelve years old.

My dad always told me to work hard if that wasn't the life I wanted for myself. I worked harder than I thought I was capable of working. I ended up attending a great high school and graduating as valedictorian, but balancing those demands over the summer was not easy. I remember getting home from a long day in the fields, gathering my materials, and working on summer assignments in the middle of the night. On Sundays my dad would drive me in to town to McDonald's so I could connect to the Wi-Fi and submit my homework.

Long story short, my life path took me to Harvard, where I have been growing as a person for the past few years. I would have been perfectly fine going to any college, period. Neither of my parents were even given the opportunity to enroll in high school. My father has told me on many occasions his biggest regret in life is not being able to continue his education. From his accounts, he was the brightest student growing up, and perhaps today he would be a professional instead of a man who has spent almost forty years working in agriculture. It is too late for my father to change careers, but I guarantee his sacrifices were rewarded with opportunity and our family has a place in the States.

So, what have I learned? When life gets tough, often the hardest thing to do is believe in yourself. *I don't have an education. I don't speak the language. I am poor. My family is in another country. People think I'm only good for picking their produce.* What my father did is stand and say, "I do believe. I must believe." There is no one I respect more than him for teaching me that lesson. I also believe. Some things are truly impossible, but working toward a better tomorrow is not one of those things. My father found opportunity in the United States, as have I, and I am proud to say this is my home.

Juliana Pérez-Calle

Juliana Pérez-Calle is a graduate of the American University Washington College of Law.

I arrived in New York City at the tender age of five with my mom, two suitcases, very little if any money, and all the hopes and dreams that the United States of America had to offer. I did not know it yet, but we were leaving behind the vibrant Andean land I'd learned to walk in: Medellín, Colombia, the city of eternal spring. We left behind beautiful colors but also great chaos. My mother dreamed of raising her daughter with the freedom to pursue her own happiness.

On the taxi ride through the night into Queens from JFK airport, I noticed more bright lights than I'd ever seen in my entire life. The New York City skyline, streetlights, and storefronts all sparkled. On that taxi ride, I set my first life goal—to learn to read every single shiny word hanging above all the stores in New York City.

My mother's first job was working the night shift at a Colombian restaurant while I slept. When she got back home, she would wake me up, make me breakfast, and take me to school. On the walk to school, I'd hop along and she'd tell me to say good morning to the sun and flowers and keep me cheery. This memory has been etched into my psyche, and whenever I feel that I have too much work to do, I remember how hard my mother has worked and what a positive attitude she's maintained through great adversity.

I began the first grade on my first day of school in the United States. I absolutely loved school and was consumed with becoming a real American girl. By fourth grade I had transitioned out of my English as a second language classes into regular classes. It was a big deal for me at that time. I still remember the first essay I wrote in fourth grade. I'd been assigned to research the Navajo Nation for Native American heritage month and decided to write about the Navajo genocide, because it appeared to be the most critical topic. My teacher was horrified I'd uncovered research about the genocide and said my topic was outside the scope of Native American history. Despite being a teacher's pet and eager to please, I felt so proud that my hard work had uncovered some type of inconvenient truth that could shake an institution (aka my teacher). Reading words mesmerized me, and it was then and there that I became consumed by the importance of critical thinking and writing. I should have known then that I was born to be a lawyer, but it wouldn't be until I was an adult that I met my first lawyer and realized the profession was within my reach. I graduated as elementary school valedictorian, and my future goal of attending college seemed almost inevitable.

By the time I reached high school, I had gone through great adversity but managed to keep my grades up and my goal to attend college firm. Sophomore year came, and it was time for me to take the PSAT and bubble in my nine-digit Social Security number. I had no idea what to fill in. Since middle school I'd known that I didn't have "papers," but I never knew up until that point what you could or could not do without a Social Security number. My tower of dreams came crashing down on me as I realized that I was undocumented and could not attend college, travel the world, learn to drive, or work legally. I took a deep emotional fall and lost all sense of control. I battled through depression and several panic attacks as a result of thinking I could not continue my education or travel as I had dreamed. Guidance counselors would tell me I couldn't go to college and that I should stay silent about my immigration status. People who I thought were friends told me to "go back home" because I was a criminal and didn't belong in the United States.

I found solace by reading about the civil rights movements that had come before me and the ones that I could contribute to. I repeated

Langston Hughes's poem "Dreams" like a mantra until I began to believe in the sacredness of my dreams again. I resolved that if perhaps I proved myself to the board of education I could make it into college, despite my immigration status. I did volunteer work, joined several clubs, ran for student government president and won, got excellent grades, and worked at a Colombian bakery, where I earned my first paycheck. With time I learned through my own research that New York was then one of twelve states that allowed undocumented students to attend college. I was thrilled and tried my luck at applications.

I got into college, but two weeks before starting classes, I still did not have all the money to pay for my tuition. As an undocumented student, I was not eligible for financial aid or grants. As if from heaven itself, I got a phone call from a wealthy woman from my church who heard my story and felt it would be a waste if I didn't make it to college. She sent me a check for the remaining part of my tuition and pledged to help me pay for college for all four years. I was ecstatic that my lifelong dream of going to college would become a reality.

While in college, I uncovered the power of my voice through activism. I still struggled with the uncertainty of being undocumented, but the courage I gained in speaking up about undocumented immigrant rights lifted me higher. There is a power that is born when you step into your truth for the greater good of others. My activism in college threw me into my first lessons in the world of political decision making. As in high school, I graduated college with honors for leadership and respect from my community and the school faculty.

However, as undocumented life goes, upon graduation my college bubble burst, and I found myself unemployed and without a legal means of working. Again, I fell into a deep depression, and again I picked myself up by continuing to do volunteer work for others in more dire circumstances. I've learned from my mother that there is no better way to lift yourself out of a finite universe than by doing good for others. What you give with your heart multiplies, expands, and continues to bless your life.

A month after graduation, it was as if the heavens intervened on my behalf again. President Obama announced his executive action called Deferred Action for Childhood Arrivals (DACA), for which I qualified. DACA would allow me three things: to cease being a deportation priority, to have a Social Security number, and to have legal work authorization. As soon as the program became available, I applied for it with a free attorney I was assigned at a legal nonprofit. Little did I know then that this attorney would not only change my family's life but also become my friend and colleague.

As soon as I was approved for DACA and received my corresponding Social Security number, I applied for a New York state ID, driving lessons, and a credit card, and within three weeks I found work as a paralegal. By doing thorough research, my immigration attorney also uncovered that fifteen years earlier, my citizen uncle had petitioned for my mom and me to become permanent residents and that the visa was almost available for application. My mom and I had no idea that an application from so long ago was valid. Immigration law is incredibly complicated, but simply put, had I not been paired with that attorney, I would not have applied for permanent residency in time and would have missed out on the opportunity to be granted a visa. A year after receiving DACA, my mother and I finally applied for permanent residency. My attorney warned us that nothing was guaranteed.

Regardless, I carried on with my goals, and during that waiting period I decided to apply to law school. I was accepted, but a few months before starting classes, I wasn't sure if I would be able to attend because I still wasn't eligible for financial aid as an undocumented student. DACA did not provide legal status, but only work authorization, and under the law I was still undocumented. Just as I was considering deferring my law school entry, I learned the life-changing news that my mother's and my application for permanent residency had been approved. I was not only able to apply for financial aid to make law school a reality, but most importantly, I was finally on my way to citizenship, eighteen industrious years after arriving in the United States.

As a permanent resident, I am able to live my life the way I always dreamed as a child. I live on my own in a new city, travel the world, and continue to advocate for social justice, but this time while sitting at the table of decision-making among national and world institutions. I still have great obstacles to overcome, but my ambitions are no longer limited by my immigration status. I've never felt freer. I do not take what my eyes have seen or where I've been for granted. My entire life has only been possible because of the great efforts of those around me, particularly the sacrifices of my mother. I am most grateful that I stand on the shoulders of a great woman who envisioned an amazing life for her daughter and generations to come.

Helen Polychronopoulos

Helen Polychronopoulos was an undocumented woman living in the United States for most of her adult life. She worked in the garment district.

As told by her niece, Mary Skafidas

I grew up in Sunset Park, Brooklyn, in the '70s and '80s, the two-decade span that is usually referred to as the neighborhood's dark period. During that time, Sunset Park's streets were littered with about a dozen or so gang headquarters, gangs with names like the Assassins or the Crazy Homicides. The gangs would often fight each other for block supremacy, so much so that I wouldn't even flinch as I got off my school bus on any given afternoon and watched men attack each other with bats, chains, or knives. Never with guns, however, which might have been my saving grace as I hugged the storefronts, taking careful, measured steps for the block and a half until I reached home and could escape into the front hallway of my apartment building. It was what it was—it was our way of life.

It was the life of my family, who had emigrated from Greece to New York in the late '60s. My family included my aunt, uncle, and cousin, who lived on the top floor of the apartment building in a two-room apartment that mirrored the one I shared with my parents one floor directly below them. My grandparents and my aunt lived across the hall from me in a studio. The building had six apartments in all, and aside from one other family—a single mom and her teenage daughter—the rest changed frequently.

My family was here legally—my cousin and I were lucky enough to be born in the US—save for my aunt, Helen Polychronopoulos, also known as Poly Chroniades, an alias she used while living in fear of deportation for sixteen years before she was able to raise her hand and be counted because of the Immigration Reform and Control Act of 1986 brought about by President Reagan. She came to the United States in June 1971 on a plane leaving from Athens, Greece. She was visiting her sisters, who had been living in the US for the last year. She came for two weeks and stayed, never going back.

She was known by many names—Helen, Paula, Lela, and Poly—changing her name every time she felt that someone had gotten too close and that she was in jeopardy of being deported.

To me and my cousin, however, she was just Aunt Lella.

Lella followed her parents here in the early '70s. "Jobs grow on trees in Ameriki, the way olives grow back in Greece," her mother had told her. She booked a flight, came to visit, and never went back. My mom and other aunt got her a job in the garment district. They all worked in a Lord West factory, where my aunt was paid about five cents for every collar she matched to a jacket. She worked like a demon, producing six hundred to seven hundred jackets a day. Often abused because of her undocumented status, her work never acknowledged or rewarded, after eight years she was fed up and quit. It took a week for the company to beg her to come back, with a ten-cent increase for each collar. They had hired three people to replace her, and they still couldn't keep up with her single output.

Every so often an "inspector" would show up at the factory. This inspector would stop first at the manager's office. The manager's secretary would run through the factory floor, alerting everyone of his presence. I remember being at the factory with my mother one day, my aunt working a few feet away from her. My aunt saw the secretary running around the factory and dropped the collar she was working on. She raced to the bathroom with several others. My mother reached over and grabbed her neighbor's basket of jackets and transferred them to her own. Her neighbor quickly got up and filled in my aunt's spot at the collar station. The inspector walked around the factory floor with the manager, asking for identification and inquiring about open stations.

"Keep your mouth closed," my mother hissed as he passed us.

"You're here visiting your mother?" the inspector asked me. I smiled broadly and nodded vigorously. "That's good. Work hard and do well in school" were his parting words to me, my response the same, never once opening my mouth.

Lella was incredibly thin, with hunched shoulders from hours spent bent over jacket collars. She wore the same few pairs of pants, dresses, and shirts for years. She never spent money; she saved almost everything she earned. At the end of her life, dying from ovarian cancer, a cancer that would have been detected if she had deemed checkups important enough to spend money on, she had amassed $300,000—a fortune for her as well as for us.

Helen Polychronopoulos

My aunt died with a green card. Having never learned English, she could never pass the test for citizenship. Yet I believe her to be an American hero, embodying what all Americans hold dear—hard work, sacrifice, and the desire to see the next generation in your family achieve more than you could.

Her fortune helped my cousin and me graduate from college debt-free, paid for private schools while we were growing up, and allowed my family to move out of Sunset Park and into Bay Ridge. The neighborhoods were only about twenty blocks away from each other, but at that time they were worlds apart.

Nasser Yaghoobzadeh

Nasser Yaghoobzadeh is a civil engineer experienced in building hydroelectric dams. He is now a real estate developer and grandfather to four wonderful grandchildren.

As told by his son, Hooman Yaghoobzadeh, MD

It was time to spray for roaches. I opened the two windows in the Classon Avenue studio in Brooklyn that belonged to my brother-in-law Suleiman. My sons, seven and five years old, were sleeping on blankets on the floor of the fifth-floor walk-up. My wife, Mehri, twenty-seven, and I—Nasser—thirty-eight, had arrived that day from Copenhagen with our two sons, Hooman and Hootan. Outside, you could hear sporadic rattling of empty alcohol bottles in the street. Now and then the orange flicker of a fire in the corner trash can would illuminate the ceiling. That's when we would see them: hundreds of roaches crawling on the ceiling. While the kids were sleeping next to their mom, Suleiman and I covered them with yesterday's *New York Post*. Then we sprayed the ceiling. The night's din of whiskey bottles and too frequent yet distant police sirens was interrupted randomly by roaches dropping from the ceiling and crackling on the newspaper. It was August 28, 1979.

Only two months prior, on a warm night, Mehri, Hooman, Hootan, and I had been sleeping underneath the stars in our backyard, a regular summer ritual in Shiraz. The babble of water in the blue-tiled fountain and the ever-present smell of orange blossoms in the perfect crisp air framed the quintessential Persian night at the foot of the Zagros Mountains. As a civil engineer at an American company building irrigation systems and dams, my family and I enjoyed the good life in Iran, complete with maid and chauffeur, in a modern and very chic marble-paneled home. Probably related to the Persian Jews of Purim in Esther's megillah, we could trace back our ancestors in Iran for many generations. Unfortunately, the faint crack of insecurity among Jews in Iran during the shah's regime was becoming a widening fault line in the midst of the Islamic Revolution. Demonstrations and civil resistance, both secular and religious, against the shah in late 1977 created a very alarming and tense atmosphere. Within a short time, strikes and demonstrations paralyzed the country. Iran was not the same place it had been, nor was it safe any longer. Others ridiculed our decision to leave our birthplace with young kids in tow. They reminded me of Mosaddeq's "revolution" of two years ending in 1953, when the CIA and British MI-6 overthrew the democratically elected leader in a staged coup, and assured me that this too would pass.

I felt this time was different. Within one month of deciding to leave, we had sold everything and quietly said goodbye to family and friends. The last couple of weeks we would all sleep fully dressed in case we had to escape the ever-present Khomeini-sanctioned mobs. By this time the American Embassy had stopped issuing visas to Iranians. The Italian and Turkish Embassies had wait lists more than two months long. We knew that some were going to Copenhagen as tourists to await visas to the US. The day before our flight, the kind Muslim man who bought our house gave us an English translation of the deed. "Keep this. You will need it were you are going," he said.

The plan was to stay in Copenhagen as tourists until we could get a visa to the US. Though they did not turn us back, the Danish had other plans. Winds of revolution in Iran had started to swirl, and we were ordered to leave the country within twenty-four hours or we would be arrested. The next morning at the American Embassy in Copenhagen, we endured hours of questioning. You see, we were asking for a tourist visa. I was finally asked if I could offer proof that we were not planning to immigrate permanently to the United States. I presented the deed to our home as proof that we were returning to Iran, which they surprisingly accepted. The emigration officer obviously knew what was going on, he just needed some evidence to allow us to visit the US. We were on the SAS flight to JFK that same day.

As the roaches hit the newspaper, it was hard not to think that we had made a life-changing error. That nauseating feeling would get worse. We watched as Iran was drowning in loud demonstrations broadcasting "Death to shah, death to America, death to Israel." The loneliness of knowing there was nothing to go back to was profound. Our oldest son, Hooman, had night terrors for weeks. Covered in sweat, he would suddenly sit up in bed with eyes wide-open and see swarms of the "enemy" running down the hallway to kill his grandparents still in Shiraz. The biting cold of our first winter in New York was unexpectedly harsh (Shiraz was known for its year-round spring weather). Our youngest, Hootan, was incessantly getting sick.

Slowly, though, some things started to get better. We moved to a safer neighborhood at the corner of Church Avenue and Ocean Parkway in Brooklyn so our kids could walk to the Bialik Hebrew Academy. The principal there was an angel and lit the way when all else seemed dark. Mehri started selling Avon products, babysitting, working as a teacher's aide, and selling World Book encyclopedias door to door. I remember our sons beaming with pride when one day she walked in with a deluxe set that she had earned. Twenty-two volumes of maroon pleather-bound bliss signifying better days to come.

Unemployment was a brutal kind of torture for me. After months of searching, traveling to Los Angeles, Seattle, and Philadelphia looking for a job, it seemed hopeless. Then one day, the super at our Brooklyn apartment told my wife about a consulting firm on Staten Island that might need an inspector. The next morning, multiple trains and a ferry ride later, I showed up at their door with my (overqualified) résumé. The man asked when I could start and what salary I would require. I replied that as long as they would help me get a work permit and green card, I would be happy working for free. I was hired as a sewer inspector in Staten Island that day. Even in the midst of all that uncertainty, I remember it as the happiest day of my life.

Rough times seemed lurking around every corner, though. On November 4, 1979, the same day Iranian students suddenly overtook the American Embassy in Tehran, my wife was flying back to Iran to sell our second house. We spent two months in agony awaiting her return. With the hostage crisis, we felt the stinging prejudice of national identity politics. We took our names off the mailbox. There were those who made it more difficult, like the driving evaluator who denied me a license four consecutive times, despite perfect scores and road tests.

However, hard work, perseverance, and the occasional kindness of others were a perfect recipe. Soon, my employer helped me to become a general contractor, and I started building residential homes in Staten Island. We watched every dollar and eventually were able to invest in larger projects, including designing and building our own home in Eltingville. Our sons graduated from public high school with honor degrees and were accepted to Ivy League universities. Hooman went on to graduate from the University of Pennsylvania School of Medicine, and Hootan earned an MBA from Harvard. They are now married with children close to the ages they were when we emigrated.

There were so many forks along the road that could have lead to a different ending. At some of these points, kind human beings led us down a better path. When my wife, Mehri, and I landed in JFK from Copenhagen, each holding a young child's hand, we made our way to customs. The customs agent had no intention of being fooled by the house deed. It seemed like our journey was over before it had begun. But then he looked again at our passports. He pronounced our last name "Yaghoob-zadeh." He asked for our marriage license. He glanced at the Hebrew letters a couple of minutes extra. "I know why you are here, Mr. Jacob-son," he said. He stamped our passports and gave us his name and badge number. "Let me know if anyone gives you a problem," he said. In that terribly anxious state, I did not make it a point to write his name down. I wish I had. We are now ten Yaghoobzadehs in total who owe that customs agent a life's debt of gratitude.

The Institutions

/////

American Ballet Theatre

Monticello

The New-York Historical Society

UJA-Federation / Catholic Charities

Can one preach at home inequality of races and nations and advocate abroad goodwill towards men?

— Dorothy Thompson

Many immigrants arrived in the US without any foundation or support. However, there were a number of institutions in place that provided the helping hand or guidance necessary to build new lives. Today similar institutions work tirelessly to offer new immigrants the counsel, direction, and sense of community that's imperative for their prosperity.

American Ballet Theatre

The mission of American Ballet Theatre is to create, to present, to preserve, and to extend the great repertoire of classical dancing, through exciting performances and educational programming of the highest quality, presented to the widest possible audience.

In 2006, American Ballet Theatre (ABT) was officially designated "America's National Ballet Company." While most leading national ballet companies around the world feature dancers who grew up in those countries and trained in the same school, ABT's roster features a dynamic mix of backgrounds and training styles. This blend of eclecticism, energy, and excellence is uniquely American.

For the 2017–2018 season, American Ballet Theatre will be represented on stage by dancers from sixteen different countries. Acclaimed ABT principal dancer Herman Cornejo was seventeen years old when he left Argentina in 1998 to join ABT Studio Company, and he was invited to join the main company one year later. A rising star in Buenos Aires and around the world, he chose New York because ABT was "vibrant, joyful, inspirational, and had a delicate balance between tradition and innovation." Cornejo became a US citizen in July 2013. Like other goal-oriented, high-achieving young people who have sought opportunity in America for two centuries, talented dancers like Cornejo have flocked to ABT since its founding in 1940 in pursuit of individual freedom, innovation, and inclusion.

ABT celebrates individuality. Within the framework and rules of classical ballet, ABT artistic director Kevin McKenzie invites dancers to interpret roles and choreography in ways that feel authentic and true. The spectrum of this interpretation is multiplied exponentially with such a diverse cast as ABT's. The iconic roles of Juliet, Giselle, and Odette/Odile (the White/Black Swan) are performed differently by the ballerina inhabiting the part and the prince cast opposite her on any given night. When multiple dancers portray well-known characters, ABT's audiences relish in the suspense and discovery that unfolds as the individual performers infuse famous storylines with their own styles and strengths. Cornejo says, "I believe that the uniqueness of each dancer is what makes ABT great." In June 2016, the *New York Times* chief dance critic Alistair Macaulay wrote about Cornejo, "We do and we don't know him; he dissolves his immense energy and skill differently into each role."

Even in the corps de ballet, a level of the company that requires numerous dancers to perform in unison as one collective body, ABT's swans, flowers, and princesses are unique individuals. Cornejo reflects, "I always felt that ABT not only had strong personalities in the soloists and principal ranks, but also within the corps de ballet, which is something very unusual. Even when they maintain uniformity when dancing together, this is a group of very special individuals, each one with special skills, which is very exciting to witness." These individuals in the corps de ballet are from over a dozen US states, as well as countries including Japan, Korea, Spain, Russia, Australia, Finland, and China.

Zhong-Jing Fang, a native of Shanghai, China, and an ABT corps de ballet dancer since 2004, likens the company to a "kaleidoscope," in which varied training, skills, and approaches are woven together. ABT dancers past and present credit McKenzie, who has led the company artistically since 1992, with identifying and cultivating the individual spark in each dancer. On her personal experience of dancing for ABT under McKenzie's direction, Fang says, "I have the freedom to be a strong woman. I think you can be who you are in America and in this company."

An investment in the individual freedom of artists fosters an environment that is ripe for innovation. At its founding in 1940 and in its early history, the company—then known as Ballet Theatre—provided a platform for innovative, emerging choreographers. During and immediately after World War II, Ballet Theatre's marketing campaigns emphasized the Russian-ness of its dancers and their training, as Russia dominated the history of great ballet dancers and choreographers. However, immigrant choreographers such as Antony Tudor and George Balanchine, as well as American and British choreographers working with the company, developed groundbreaking new movement vocabularies based in the classical tradition.

These early innovators, as well as the choreographers McKenzie collaborates with today, have propelled the company to extend the repertoire of classical ballet. Dancers who thrive at ABT master a wide range of influences on the art form and develop versatility by embracing eclectic styles of choreography. Alongside standards like *Swan Lake* and *Romeo & Juliet*, ABT regularly commissions new pieces. Cornejo says of his decision to join ABT, "ABT was known around the world not only for the excellence in its rendition of the classics, but also because it was always a step forward, making the next big breakthrough with new works of the great choreographers of each historic period. This is a company that could unite all dance forms and senses of artistic movement in one repertoire."

Given the individual freedom and innovation encouraged at ABT, it should be no surprise that the organization finds strength in inclusion. As ABT's artistic staff travels the world to identify talent, they offer the most promising dancers invitations to attend ABT summer intensive programs, to train at the company's flagship Jacqueline Kennedy Onassis School, or to join the ABT Studio Company. Dancers from foreign countries or small rural towns learn from company mentors and peers about the ins and outs of living in New York City, how to keep their bodies in peak performance shape, how to manage sharing dorms or small apartments, and how to navigate the subway. This shared experience of talent, tenacity, and teamwork at a young age fosters the strong sense of community that is a hallmark of ABT.

Each dancer's trajectory is different, but each is an inspiring story of resilience and singular focus. Dancers may arrive from Argentina at seventeen, like Cornejo, who moved from Buenos Aires together with his older sister. They may upend their entire lives at age eighteen to move to New York from Shanghai, having no friends or family in the entire western world, like Zhong-Jing Fang. ABT attracts dancers from every corner of the world who strive to advance their training and pursue their dreams in New York City. Reflecting on her fourteen years with the company, Fang says, "ABT is a warmhearted and open company. In a competitive world, arriving at ABT I felt safe. Welcomed. Encouraged. Here, we are allowed to grow together as artists."

ABT's mission compels the company to reach the widest possible audience. Every year, in addition to performing at Lincoln Center in New York and the John F. Kennedy Center in Washington, DC, ABT travels across the United States and around the world with a robust touring schedule. Recent and upcoming engagements include Chicago, Los Angeles, Paris, and Hong Kong, as well as less expected locales such as Lincoln, Nebraska, and Muscat, Oman. In many ways, ABT dancers are ambassadors for American achievement just like Olympians on Team USA. ABT dancers perform at the highest level year-round, every season, not just once every four years. They are artists and athletes, inspiring audiences with their rare talents and remarkable success in their chosen field.

Herman Cornejo says of success, "Success, for me, doesn't mean empty fame or overnight recognition. Recognition comes as a consequence of your delivery as an artist. In a company like ABT, where there are talented people from all over the world auditioning all the time, the competition is always hard. You have to be very sure of that one true, special artist you are and want to become to differentiate yourself. And, of course, as it happens in every country and, I dare say, in every career, to be successful you need to have a goal and be ready to work hard to get there. That's the only way."

Some might question a Team USA composed of immigrants from Ukraine, Brazil, Denmark, Italy, and other faraway nations. Yet they left people and possessions behind and chased their dreams to New York like millions of daring artists and entrepreneurs before them. And together on stage, at home and abroad, they represent America.

Monticello

For more than ninety years, Monticello has been maintained and kept open to the public by the Thomas Jefferson Foundation, Inc., which owns over twenty-five hundred acres of Jefferson's five-thousand-acre plantation. As a private, nonprofit 501(c)3 corporation, the foundation receives no ongoing federal, state, or local funding in support of its dual mission of preservation and education.

"No man has greater confidence, than I have, in the spirit of our people... whatever they can, they will."
— Thomas Jefferson to James Monroe, October 16, 1814

On the Fourth of July, people gather at Thomas Jefferson's home, Monticello, for what is now the oldest US naturalization ceremony conducted outside a courtroom. Each year, thousands bear witness as new citizens take the oath of allegiance and a prominent American offers remarks on the meaning of citizenship, often sharing reflections on his or her family's own immigration journey.

On any day of the year, visitors to Monticello are drawn into the story of how America began. Ours was a bold experiment in nationhood, set in motion by a group of young upstarts with everything to lose. In the summer of 1776, they tasked a soft-spoken Virginian with drafting their Declaration of Independence—and the rest is *our* history. In that merely revolutionary document, Jefferson articulated principles of liberty, equality, and self-government that would become our national creed:

"We hold these truths to be self-evident, that all men are created equal, that they are endowed by their Creator with certain unalienable Rights, that among these are Life, Liberty and the pursuit of Happiness."

A visit to Monticello, once the heart of a five-thousand-acre plantation, also reminds us that Jefferson's promise of equality did not extend to all people—not to slaves, Native Americans, women, or men without property. Jefferson and the founders did not resolve the fundamental paradox of slavery in an age of liberty. It would take nearly two hundred years, a civil war, and the leadership of countless citizen activists to ensure that all Americans could exercise their "unalienable Rights."

From the beginning, ours has been a nation that requires the active and ongoing participation of its citizens. In our best moments, we find strength in our diversity and common purpose, a sense of shared identity in our quest to realize America's founding ideals: "Life, Liberty and the pursuit of Happiness."

July 4 at Monticello is one of those moments. Below are just a few highlights from past Independence Day speeches on the mountaintop. We invite you to come and experience this very special day firsthand— to pledge anew your commitment to this young, hopeful, visionary nation, and to join us in celebrating the nation's newest citizens.

— LESLIE GREENE BOWMAN, president,
Thomas Jefferson Foundation

"America has lived and grown under the system of government established by Jefferson and his generation. As nations go, we live in one of the oldest continuous forms of democratic government in the whole world. In this sense we are old. But the world has never had as much human ability as it needs, and a modern democracy in particular needs, above all things, the continuance of the spirit of youth. Our problems... call as greatly for the continuation of imagination and energy and capacity for responsibility as did the age of Thomas Jefferson and his fellows."

— FRANKLIN DELANO ROOSEVELT, July 4, 1936

"Remember that none of us are more than caretakers of this great country. Remember that the more freedom you give to others, the more you will have for yourself. Remember that without law there can be no liberty. And remember, as well, the rich treasures you brought from whence you came, and let us share your pride in them. This is the way we keep our independence as exciting as the day it was declared..."

— GERALD FORD, July 4, 1976

"By reaching for the stars, Jefferson gave us all the impulse. He liked to talk about the energy of an idea. 'It is wonderful how much may be done if we are always doing,' he said. And as few men or women ever have, he was always doing for his country. It is in that spirit that I welcome you, our new fellow Americans. The nation is the richer for you. I hope you will travel your new homeland from end to end, see as much of it as possible, read its history, enjoy its music, read aloud its poetry. I hope that in the spirit of Thomas Jefferson you will remain open to new ideas, prize tolerances and common sense and a love of the earth and its abundance. And I hope that as citizens, with both the freedoms and the responsibilities of that high status, you will someday in some way do something for your country."

— DAVID MCCULLOUGH, July 4, 1994

"As we are gathered here, on this historic property, amidst the bunting and the flags, I'm reminded of a day more than fifty years ago, when I first arrived in the United States, accompanied by my mother, sister, and brother… Like countless others before and since, we steamed into New York Harbor and beheld the Statue of Liberty—our eyes full of tears, our hearts full of hope. I was eleven and I remember being very excited, but also a little scared because I did not know whether I would be accepted in this new land. I did not know whether the differences in the way I spoke and acted would leave me in America but not really part of it. I did not know whether, after leaving my old home, I could truly find another. I should not have worried. At its best, America's embrace is as vast as this continent is broad. We were welcomed, given refuge, and provided the chance to make new friends and build new lives in freedom. For this priceless opportunity and all that has since come with it, I will be forever grateful. And, of course, it never occurred to me that I would be secretary of state and have Thomas Jefferson's job."

— MADELEINE ALBRIGHT, July 4, 2000

"That's where you come in. You come in from Togo; Bosnia-Herzegovina; Canada and Peru; Afghanistan, India, and Mexico; China, the Netherlands, and the United Kingdom; Croatia, El Salvador, Ghana, the Philippines, and Vietnam; Argentina, Bangladesh, Belgium, Chile, Colombia, Congo, Guatemala, Iran, Italy, Jamaica, Poland, Romania, Singapore, South Korea, Spain, Sudan, Sweden, Taiwan, Tanzania, Thailand, and Turkey—the names themselves a poem about all the migrating peoples who come here.

"The United States may seem like a fixed star, but it isn't. It is a relationship between citizens and an idea, and, like all relationships, it changes with the people in it. Its past is always up for reargument; its present is constantly unfolding, complex, a continuum of surprises; and the future is yet to be written. A country is alive, or it's history. As long as this country endures, it will always be in search of how to understand itself and where to go from here. That's where you come in. That's where we come in."

— SAM WATERSTON, July 4, 2007

"Those of you who will shortly be taking the oath of citizenship recognize that you will be receiving the most precious commodity that our country can give to anyone in this unrivaled democracy: citizenship. Citizenship in a country that Thomas Jefferson helped to conceive, citizenship in a country where you will have, to a greater extent than any other country, the freedom, protections, and opportunities that will enable you to pursue your life's dreams and ambitions, and citizenship that you can also pass along to your children. For that, you are no doubt grateful; you are obviously privileged; and you also feel honored. You should be. But it is we, the current citizens of this country, who should be grateful to you; it is we who are privileged to have you as fellow citizens; and it is we who are honored that you have chosen our country to bring your own talents, your own ambitions, your own dreams, and your own lives. We are grateful, and privileged, and honored because we know that it is immigrants who have made America the great and unique country which is the clear envy of the free world."

— DAVID RUBENSTEIN, July 4, 2014

The New-York Historical Society

The New-York Historical society is New York's first cultural institution. Louise Mirrer, PhD, is President and CEO.

On November 11, 1804, eleven prominent New Yorkers met in the office of Mayor DeWitt Clinton "to form themselves into a Society the principal design of which should be to collect and preserve whatever may relate to the natural, civil or ecclesiastical History of the United States in general and of this State [New York] in particular."

Today, more than two centuries later, the institution founded that November evening holds an honored place not only among the greatest libraries and museums of our nation, but among the richest repositories for the stories of America's diversity. With collections spanning the sixteenth through the twenty-first centuries, New-York Historical's art, artifacts, books, manuscripts, and documents range from early Native American arrowheads to "pussy hats" worn by participants in the 2017 Women's March. They include the personal papers and records of immigrants such as Alexander Hamilton, who fought in the American Revolution and who participated in the nation's founding; the earliest Chinese in America, who arrived on our shores long before the birth of America's Chinatowns; and Manuel Rionda, who immigrated to New York from Spain via Cuba and was one of the most successful sugar merchants of the nineteenth century.

The collections include, as well, materials relating to America's earliest Jewish families, such as the Hendrickses and the Levys, and its first synagogue, Shearith Israel, which dates from the seventeenth century; a

*Anthony Meucci, Pierre Toussaint (ca. 1781-1853), ca. 1825. Watercolor on
ivory. New-York Historical Society, Gift of Miss Georgina Schuyler, 1920.4.*

vast array of papers, records, and art that tell the story of Frederick
Douglass, the abolitionist and former slave, whose 1863 "Call to Arms"
directed at African American men holds pride of place in New-York
Historical's Patricia D. Klingenstein Library and whose life-size statue
welcomes visitors to our landmark building on Central Park West; and
the archive of Billie Jean King, the great American champion of social
justice and equality, in and out of sports, which resides in New-York
Historical's Center for Women's History.

New-York Historical grew up with the young republic, so it is not
surprising that its own history would reflect much of the nation's history. Never a purely local institution—despite its name—from the outset
the institution's interests embraced not only the city, state, and nation,
but the entire world, so that its collections reflect centuries of interactions between the United States and nations abroad, and the impact of

John Trumbull, Alexander Hamilton (1757-1804), after 1804. Oil on canvas. New-York Historical Society, Gift of Thomas Jefferson Bryan, 1867.305.

these interactions on American intellectual, commercial, and military history—for example, the assistance of French soldiers like the Marquis de Lafayette in the American revolutionary cause (New-York Historical's museum collection of Lafayette portraits, statues, and ephemera is among the greatest in the world); Napoleon's abandonment of his dream of a lucrative New World empire, which resulted in the sale of Louisiana to the United States (the original agreement, signed by Napoleon, between the French and the Americans is in New-York Historical's library collection); and the Chinese Exclusion Act (New-York Historical's award-winning exhibition is now on permanent view at the Chinese Historical Society in San Francisco), which barred virtually all immigration from China over more than sixty years.

Nor have New-York Historical's eyes been turned only backward. With admirable foresight, New-York Historical's founders appealed to the public, not solely for records of the past, but equally for contemporary documents and ephemera, which they realized would be indispens-

Arnold Genthe, Woman and Child, San Francisco Chinatown.
Photograph. New-York Historical Society Library.

able to future generations. This appeal to the public continues today, with new acquisitions such as menus of contemporary Mexican restaurants in New York, amplifying and contemporizing a centuries-old menu collection; an archive of moving speeches offered at naturalization ceremonies over the past thirteen years in New-York Historical's Robert H. Smith Auditorium, including remarks by New-York Historical trustees Norman Benzaquen, Richard Gilder, Roger Hertog, Agnes Hsu-Tang, Ira Lipman, Pam Schafler, Andrew Tisch, and Eric Wallach; and an open invitation to all new Americans, including those who use our collections to prepare for the US naturalization test, to deposit their stories in New-York Historical's library and their artifacts in the institution's museum.

UJA-Federation / Catholic Charities

UJA-Federation of New York and the Catholic Charities of the Archdiocese of New York bring people and organizations together to address prevalent modern-day needs.

Imagine what life was like before antibiotics or national child labor laws. A time when the life expectancy of the average man was about fifty-five, and if he didn't die of flu or pneumonia and was unlucky enough to be both poor and old, there was no government support to help him live with any dignity. Add to this picture the "war to end all wars" raging across Europe. And on New York's shores, millions of immigrants arriving with nothing but their dreams and the clothes on their backs.

Such was life in 1917.

It was in response to these staggering needs that the Federation for the Support of Jewish Philanthropic Societies (today, UJA-Federation of New York) was born one hundred years ago. Remarkably, it was also in 1917 that the equivalent entity in the Catholic community—the Catholic Charities of the Archdiocese of New York—was founded.

It's been said that coincidence is God's way of being anonymous. Whether or not that's true, it's extraordinary that the Jewish and Catholic communities—without any coordination—both adopted the same new philanthropic model, recognizing the need to amplify our respective communities' charitable impact by pooling resources and coming together. While we utilized the same model, our organizations had no relationship with each other when they were founded, operating separately toward the same goal.

Fast-forward one hundred years to 2017, when UJA-Federation and Catholic Charities were honored to share a centennial celebration hosted by Mayor de Blasio at Gracie Mansion. Far more importantly, our two organizations now work closely together every day to improve the quality of life for people of all backgrounds and beliefs.

In his remarks at the reception, the mayor lauded the immense impact our organizations have had over the last century. He also spoke about the critical partnership that exists between government and non-profits. Unlike in 1917, government funding today is critical to keeping many people afloat, with a significant assist from philanthropy.

Today, 1917 is preserved in black-and-white memories, and while some challenges have been greatly mitigated, they haven't been erased. Hunger is still hunger, and the scourge of anti-Semitism remains in some places, anti-Christian in other places, and anti-Muslim in others. We are as proud as ever to work with our nonprofit partners who are on the ground helping immigrants put down lasting roots.

Over the past fifty years, Catholic Charities' immigrant and refugee services have become a centerpiece of services and care for immigrant and refugee families, workers, and children in New York City and the lower Hudson Valley. Tens of thousands of newcomers are served by us each year in the areas of resettlement, case management, and job and language assistance, while others find expert legal help in fighting deportation and family separation. For over twenty years, Catholic Charities' New Americans hotline offers information and referrals, and is a critical part of safeguarding against fraud and exploitation throughout New York. More recently, this program has been the primary legal resource for assisting in the welcoming of over four thousand unaccompanied children each year who have fled persecution, abuse, and insecurity in Central America.

UJA-Federation has long supported the work of HIAS, which provides refugees, asylum-seekers, and other humanitarian migrants with initial resettlement and integration services. Our partners at the New York Legal Assistance Group offer legal aid to the low-income immigrant community, and the Hebrew Free Loan Society provides interest-free loans to many immigrants and children of immigrants, who use these funds to start small businesses. We support employment services for immigrant populations through our funding of the Edith and Carl Marks Jewish Community House of Bensonhurst, the Central Queens Y, the Shorefront YM-YWHA of Brighton-Manhattan Beach, and many other local nonprofits. In addition, our network of twenty-three Jewish community centers has long helped immigrants and other people in need.

We're also grateful for opportunities to lift people up in ways that could not have been imagined one hundred years ago. Employment and educational opportunities for those with disabilities; emphasizing quality of life for the elderly and helping them age in place; using technology to revolutionize how we connect people to one another and the services they need.

While so much has changed over a century, two principles have animated the work of both Catholic Charities and UJA-Federation from the start: the importance of building community and collective responsibility, and the idea that all people are created *B'Tselem Elokim*, in the image of God, and deserving of respect and dignity. With these abiding values, and with UJA-Federation standing shoulder to shoulder with friends like Catholic Charities, we're committed to working harder than ever to meet the needs of all New Yorkers, in this city we proudly call home.

Write Your Own Story

We hope you are inspired by these American journeys. While each story is unique, together they form a (hi)story of the greatness of our country. We have provided blank pages below for you and your family to add your own narrative to the mosaic of America. We also invite you to visit our website, www.journeysanamericanstory.com, where you can submit your story to share with others.

_____

_____

_____

_____

_____

_____

_____

_____

_____

_____

_____

_____

_____

_____

_____

_____

_____

_____

_____

_____

_____

_____

_____

_____

American Renewal

Excerpt from Ronald Reagan's speech at the Presidential Medal of Freedom ceremony on January 19, 1989.

"Since this is the last speech that I will give as president, I think it's fitting to leave one final thought, an observation about a country which I love. It was stated best in a letter I received not long ago. A man wrote me and said, 'You can go to live in France, but you cannot become a Frenchman. You can go to live in Germany or Turkey or Japan, but you cannot become a German, a Turk, or a Japanese. But anyone, from any corner of the Earth, can come to live in America and become an American.'

"Yes, the torch of Lady Liberty symbolizes our freedom and represents our heritage, the compact with our parents, our grandparents, and our ancestors. It is that lady who gives us our great and special place in the world. For it's the great life force of each generation of new Americans that guarantees that America's triumph shall continue unsurpassed into the next century and beyond. Other countries may seek to compete with us, but in one vital area, as a beacon of freedom and opportunity that draws the people of the world, no country on Earth comes close."

Acknowledgments

First and foremost, we are most grateful to the people who were willing to share their families' arrival stories for this collection. There were also several organizations which were instrumental in helping make this project a reality, including The New-York Historical Society and the Thomas Jefferson Foundation.

We would like to thank our editors at RosettaBooks for their wise counsel, especially Arthur Klebanoff and Brian Skulnik, as well as Lisa Linden and the publicists at LAK Public Relations for working so tirelessly to have these wonderful stories heard.

We'd like to thank our friends and colleagues who served as sounding boards, and proofreaders including Patricia Peters, Merida Marquez, Emily Reich, Jane Beilenson, and Laura Last. As well as Mamnur Rahman, our photographer.

We are also extremely thankful to our families for their support and to our ancestors and parents for their wisdom in choosing to come to America. Special thanks to our spouses, Ann and Aaron, for their advice and infinite insights as well as their patience as this labor of love consumed dinner conversations, weekends, and vacations.

And lastly, thanks to all of you for reading these stories and sharing your own family's history with others.